SURGE

SUSHILA RAVINDRANATH joined *Business India* as a staff writer in 1983. This was a time when business was still a bad word—*Business Week* called India an elephant on an oil spill. *Business India* was the country's first business magazine.

Sushila moved to Chennai a couple of years later. She ended up doing stories on many South Indian groups which were publicity-shy and had never been written about. She had the opportunity to set up *Business India* bureaus in all the main southern cities. As Bureau Chief, South, she was involved in the company's foray into television and cable distribution and other ventures.

In 2000 she was asked by R K Swamy BBDO, one of the country's largest advertising agencies, to set up an entertainment portal. After setting up the Hansazone website she moved to the *New Sunday Express* as its editor. After a brief spell as Resident Editor, *Deccan Chronicle*, she is now a Consulting Editor for *Financial Express*. She writes business and political columns for *Financial Express* and *Indian Express*. She has compiled the CII Entrepreneurs Handbook and the CII e-book on women entrepreneurs of the southern region.

'Writing history requires objectivity and fidelity to facts as well as intelligent subjectivity in interpreting them. This book fulfills both these measures. A slot in the top five industrialized states of the country has been secured by Tamil Nadu through an unique brand of entrepreneurship that is competitive yet understated, globally focused, yet modest. The book has captured this spirit beautifully.'

—R Seshasayee
Chairman, Board of Directors, Infosys

'Tamil Nadu's emergence as an industrial superpower happened in serendipity sans Tata, Birla, Ambani or Mittal. What were the enablers and who are the real heroes? Few have seen it from a vantage position as Sushila Ravindranath. She is lucid and compulsive. A must-read!'

—Pradipta K Mohapatra
Chairman, Coaching Foundation India Ltd;
former MD, Spencer & Company Ltd

SUSHILA RAVINDRANATH

SURGE

TAMIL NADU'S GROWTH STORY

WESTLAND
BUSINESS

WESTLAND
BUSINESS

First published in hardback by westland ltd in 2016

Published by Westland Business, an imprint of Westland Books, a division of Nasadiya Technologies Private Limited, in 2026

No. 269/2B, First Floor, 'Irai Arul', Vimalraj Street, Nethaji Nagar, Alapakkam Main Road, Maduravoyal, Chennai 600095

Westland, the Westland logo, Westland Business and the Westland Business logo are the trademarks of Nasadiya Technologies Private Limited, or its affiliates.

ISBN: 9789371972680

10 9 8 7 6 5 4 3 2 1

Typeset by PrePSol Enterprises Pvt. Ltd

Printed at Thomson Press India Private Limited

Contents

INTRODUCTION

The magazine in which I worked for 17 years was launched in 1978. *Business India* was the country's first modern business magazine, one of the products of the post-emergency media explosion and a market leader for many years. It was the brain child of Ashok Advani, a Mumbai based lawyer. He had very clear ideas about the content. He wanted long format critical stories on the country's major business houses and corporate reports on companies and industries.

In the next five years every Tata and Birla company was covered. The multinationals were given due importance. Till it became obvious that the old boxwallah companies (Does anyone remember Metal Box?) of Calcutta were crumbling and others like Brooke Bond and Lipton were fleeing to Bangalore; Calcutta stories were given pride of place. The magazine looked at public sector giants and discussed the irrelevance of many of them. We actually had a feature explaining why India needed colour TVs. Yet there were less than five cover stories from the South in five years. The South was not ignored by *Business India* alone. The national media was indifferent to the region as well.

The South simply was not on anybody's radar.

That many things were happening in the South which was going to have far-reaching consequences was missed by almost everybody. New Delhi, the capital, was the power centre, Bombay was the vibrant financial centre and Madras was an overgrown village. People passed through Madras (now Chennai) to go to Tirupathi.

It is difficult to imagine that Bangalore was truly a pensioner's paradise well into the '70s in spite of it being home to several big public sector units. Everybody sat up and started to notice Bangalore only in the '80s when Texas Instruments set up an establishment there. The city then went on to become India's Silicon Valley.

Andhra Pradesh before Chandrababu Naidu became the Chief Minister was an agricultural state. Its rich landlords invested in real estate. Naidu styled himself as the CEO of the state in the '90s and catapulted it into modern times.

Kerala had not yet become the most favoured tourist destination.

This book is however about Tamil Nadu, a state which is different from its neighbours and in many ways from the rest of the country. Tamil Nadu has always and continues to face perception problems for various reasons. To start with, Congress, the party at the centre lost out to the regional parties in Tamil Nadu as early as the sixties. This did not happen in Andhra, Karnataka and Kerala till much later. In any case the national parties were not decimated in the other states as they were in Tamil Nadu.

As a consequence when the Dravida Munnetra Kazhagam (DMK) came to power in 1967, Tamil Nadu slipped out of the mainstream. The Dravidian politicians had to learn the ways of the capital city and its politics. They were not proficient in English and Hindi. Their members of parliament took some years to network with the power brokers.

Both the DMK and AIADMK were definitely not growth-averse in their early years as they are accused of. Some understood the concept of industrial development better than the others. All their leaders recognised the need to combine welfare with development way earlier than other states. They were also fortunate to have an efficient and competent bureaucracy working with them.

Tamil Nadu Industrial Development Corporation (TIDCO) was set up in 1965 during the Congress rule. When the DMK came to power, TIDCO applied for and got many industrial licenses and promoted the joint sector concept successfully. It partnered with the private sector to establish industries. The better known projects are SPIC, Titan, Tamil Nadu Petroproducts and later the various IT parks. State Industries Promotion Corporation of Tamilnadu Ltd (SIPCOT) was established in 1971 to develop industrial complexes by providing basic and comprehensive infrastructure facilities for investors to build their factories. Both corporations had a committed set of technocrats working for them.

Surprisingly, very few established home grown industrialists were interested in partnering with TIDCO.

On the other hand many small businesses were promoted between the '60s and '70s. Fresh graduates set up small units in the industrial estates which had come up in the '60s. Most of them were middle class and did not want to take risks. Consequently they never thought big. They never planned on marketing their products beyond Tamil Nadu. They were satisfied with a turnover of ₹2 crore while a similar unit in Mumbai would not settle for anything less than ₹20 crore. The business media of Bombay and Delhi were not interested in these companies. Almost all of them remained anonymous.

The family groups, which were going to become large conglomerates later were setting up factories and going in for collaborations. They did not believe in drawing attention to themselves and were genuinely media shy. Very few outside their industries had even heard of them. It was very difficult for a Chennai reporter to get access to these industrial houses. It was not well known till the turn of the century that Tamil Nadu is the largest recruitment base for big IT companies. TCS was expanding quietly in Chennai in the eighties. Shiv Nadar's HCL always seen as a Delhi company has its largest development centre in Chennai.

Till I started working for the Chennai bureau of *Business India*, it was not apparent to me that Tamil Nadu in a modest way was keeping up with the developments in the rest of the country even in the eighties. For example, the city-based Standard Motors, the smallest automobile manufacturer built a range of light commercial vehicles called the *Standard 20* which were popular for a few years. When the manufacturing of cars was liberalised, Standard Motors introduced India's first luxury sedan, *Standard 2000*. Standard Motors was shut down in the nineties. It did have its place in the sun though for a few years in the eighties.

There were many pioneers from Tamil Nadu. Take the case of the TTK Group. This group started as an indenting agency and a trading company set up by TT Krishnamachari in 1928. He left the business to his sons to become a freedom fighter and later, the Finance Minister under Jawaharlal Nehru. This group introduced among other things, pressure cookers and condoms to the country.

It took me many months to persuade TT Narasimhan, the Chairman of the group and his wife Padma Narasimhan, the Vice Chairman to let me meet them and write about the group. Till I started tracking the group, I did not know that Mrs Narasimhan, a Vedic scholar, was literally running the group during its difficult days and working on its turnaround. She kept herself so much in the background that she was never honoured with awards like 'Woman Entrepreneur of the Year' and so on. Nor did she want them. The magazine called the TTK group the 'Dark Horse from the South'. This was the mid-eighties. Today, her son TT Jagannathan, the Group Chairman, has built up one of the largest kitchen appliances business in the country and does not shy away from media.

Many outside the automobile industry did not know that the TVS group was a super star. They were in trading and manufacturing. TVS made almost the entire range of auto components from its factories in Padi, a Chennai suburb. They had very few competitors. Sundaram Clayton, a group company had already come out with the country's first moped, the TVS 50. When the government allowed collaborations in two-wheelers, TVS with Suzuki of Japan launched the first 100cc motorbike. Sundaram Finance was a highly respected and trusted finance company where people rushed to place their fixed deposits.

Although I had met the managing directors of some of the individual companies in the group, they refused to come together to talk to *Business India*. After being shown the door constantly, we decided to go ahead with the feature without involving the family members. The TVS story was put together from published information, interviews with customers, distributors, former employees and bankers. Everybody had only good things to say. I remember there was a studied silence from the group after the cover story was published.

Things changed in a few years. Suresh Krishna, Chairman, Sundram Fasteners was chosen for the 'Businessman of the Year' award by the magazine in 1995 and I was able to do a cover story with full co-operation from Krishna.

This reluctance to talk about themselves was one of the reasons that the national media in those pre-internet days had written off Tamil Nadu as an arch conservative, inward looking place. The state chose to live in a cocoon. The exciting eighties when mergers and acquisitions were taking place every other day was a scary period for Tamil Nadu businessmen. Deals were being made with breakneck speed and many revered icons such as DCM and Escorts were becoming takeover targets. The Tamil Nadu businessmen were not willing to get into any of these activities. They would never dilute their holdings and lose control. They did not want outsiders to enter their territory. The paranoia about outsiders is a thing of the past. But the desire to hold on to shareholding and control of their companies is strongly present even today.

It was not just the industry, but the state government too was not willing to talk to media. The All India Anna Dravida Munnetra Kazhagam (AIADMK) which was a one-man party till MGR's death, and is a one-woman party today has always been inaccessible to reporters. I have looked at my colleagues in Bangalore and Hyderabad with wonder as they could just walk into the assembly buildings and even barge into ministers' offices with their press passes.

In 1972, MG Ramachandran, the charismatic actor turned politician, broke away from the DMK, established the AIADMK, swept the polls in 1977, and became the Chief Minister. His heart was in implementing welfare programmes for the poor. The famous noon meal scheme for school children had already been introduced during the Congress rule under Chief Minister K Kamaraj. MGR in 1981 made its scope universal and made sure that no school going child was deprived of nutritious food.

The MGR government did not go to town about it. The noon meal scheme had many critics who were forced to eat their words later. Nobody ever thought this project was going to be such a game changer. In 2001, the Supreme Court gave its famous judgement that made it mandatory for all state governments to provide cooked meals instead of 'dry rations' in schools. It described the scheme *as "a joy—a living example of what can be achieved when quality safeguards are in place"*.

There was a dramatic reduction in school dropouts in Tamil Nadu and the state's social welfare indices too started going up dramatically. It started catching up with Kerala which had been celebrated for leading the country in social indicators. At the same time the state did not let industry wither away as Kerala did. All this was going to be recorded and researched by scholars much later.

To quote from *An Uncertain Glory: India and its Contradictions* by Jean Dreze and Amartya Sen: *"Tamil Nadu much to the consternation of many economists, initiated bold social programmes such as universal midday meals in primary schools and started putting in place an extensive social infrastructure – schools, health centres, roads, public transport, water supply, electricity connections, and much more. This was not just a reflection of kind-heartedness on the part of the ruling elite, but an outcome of democratic politics, including organized public pressure."*

MGR did two more things which made education available to an entire new generation. He implemented a massive increase in the educational quota for backward communities, from 30 per cent to 69 per cent. This was a controversial move, still criticised by some but now accepted by most. Tamil Nadu has the highest percentage of reservations in the country.

Then he allowed private groups to set up engineering colleges. During 1983–84 Tamil Nadu produced only around 2000 engineering graduates. Today there are more than 2 lakh engineering seats available in the state in 652 colleges. There are private institutions such as SSN Engineering set-up by HCL's Shiv Nadar, VIT (Vellore Institute of Technology) started by G Viswanathan, a politician turned educationist, the PSG group of institutions in Coimbatore promoted by the PSG industrial family which are all top rated. Karnataka, Andhra and Maharashtra also freed up engineering education soon after Tamil Nadu did.

Tamil Nadu started attracting some national attention post-liberalisation when Ford chose to put up its factory in the state in the early nineties. Chennai was already a centre for auto component manufacturing. Many of these companies realised that in spite of the millions of restrictions imposed on them, their future was in exports. The TVS group started piling up international quality awards, such as ISO, TQM, Deming, year after year and the others like the Rane Group quickly followed. These awards were passports to foreign markets. The multinational auto manufacturers who started coming into the country in droves had no problems placing their orders with the component manufacturers of Chennai.

Tamil Nadu's businessmen, the family groups, were probably more prepared for the opening up of the economy than the rest of the country. They did not form a Bombay Club to ask for protection against the onslaught of the foreigners. Today they are fighting to safeguard their turf as many MNCs are trying to eat into their market. There is no complacency in spite of the success they have seen with the first wave of liberalisation.

Although the state was dominated by family businesses in the early years, by the turn of the century the landscape was changing rapidly. There were entrepreneurs emerging who were thinking global. In the '90s, the internet and the Y2K wave saw several companies of various sizes coming up in Chennai. The first NASDAQ listed internet company was Satyam Infoway which has many firsts to its credit, managed a market cap of $1 billion. Tamil

Nadu started taking the lead in areas such as finance and accounting BPOs, e-publishing and several other non-voice areas. Call centres did not become popular here because of the strong accents. Rapid growth in these enterprises became possible because colleges were churning out engineering graduates in large numbers.

Today, Chennai is among the top 10 most attractive outsourcing locations globally (ranked no. 5) and remains India's second-largest exporter of software, IT and related services. Tamil Nadu is the most urbanised state in the country. There are more tier II and III towns here than any other state. Industry is more diversified and more evenly distributed among the districts. Most importantly the state has been growing above the national average for many years and is the third largest in terms of GDP growth rate.

I have been writing about the South from the mid-eighties and have been fortunate to have had a ring side view to this so-called conservative state changing beyond recognition. It is now on top of the many lists which are being constantly compiled by magazines and newspapers. Chennai has been winning the *India Today* best city award for many years. Surprisingly it has even made it to the *Lonely Planet's* list of best cities to visit in India. Travel magazines till recently never looked beyond Delhi, Mumbai and Kolkata.

That the state administration continues to be proactive goes over many heads. The government in the centre has found it near impossible to pass the Land Acquisition Bill. The Lok Sabha gets paralysed each time the subject comes up. Arvind Panagariya Vice-Chairman, Niti Aayog (former Planning Commission) said in an interview to *The Hindu* on 3 September 2015: "*One way to make land acquisition less time-consuming is for the States to proceed with their own amendments to the 2013 Act under Section 254(2) of the Constitution. Tamil Nadu has already done this; its amended law has been in force since January 5, 2015. The amendment inserts a State-specific schedule, Fifth Schedule, into the 2013 Act as it applies to Tamil Nadu. State legislation listed in this schedule is exempt from the Act. Other States could follow the Tamil Nadu path ....*"

This book is not the result of an academic exercise. It is based on the many features my colleagues and I have done over the years and the hundreds of hours of conversations I have had with people who have made this book possible. It is a story of a state seen from my eyes. The state can keep surprising you.

Did you know that that all the *poppadums* served in UK pubs are made in Tamil Nadu?

WAS THE SOUTH LAGGING BEHIND?

A South Indian businessman in the '80s had a typical image.

Except for Sundays, he was at the factory he owned at 7 am every morning. A daily routine inspection was a must, when he might even wipe off a speck of dust from his machines. He took, perhaps, as much pride in this simple task as in conducting board meetings. In this man's dictionary, 'risk' and 'grow' were four-letter words. 'Slow and steady wins the race' was his time-tested credo.

This description is perhaps a mild exaggeration, but it matches the commonly perceived persona of the typical South Indian businessman—stodgy, introverted and leading a sedentary corporate existence.

This was written in 1989, two years before liberalisation. Winds of change soon began to blow in the country and the corporate scene underwent many changes. Aggressive new faces began to surge ahead. The new breed was willing to grab opportunities wherever they existed. In contrast, the established industrial houses of the South were still conservative. The South did not seem to be going after any of the opportunities which were beginning to emerge.

Till the end of the '80s, geographically, the big industrial houses of South India were all in Tamil Nadu which was one of the earliest states to industrialise. When one said 'Southern business', one was really talking about industrialists from Tamil Nadu.

Many of the southern manufacturers had been pioneers in the years after independence. Take the automobile industry. The Murugappa group manufactured the first bicycle in the country and Enfield the first motorcycle, both in Madras (now Chennai). Standard Motors from Madras was the second Indian car manufacturer. Ashok Leyland established a commercial vehicle unit here. Madras became the cluster for auto component manufacturing with groups like the TVS, Amalgamations and Rane setting up shop in the city. They became suppliers to the emerging automobile industry in the country. Madras came to be called the 'Detroit of India'.

Despite this background, the pre-liberalisation scenario was rather different. It appeared as though the region's early riders had turned into slow horses in the race for putting up and bidding for mega-projects. And worse, the complacent South had been attacked by an army of invaders. Traditional southern fortresses appeared to be cracking up rapidly and were seen as helpless against the marauders from the West and the North.

At an editorial meeting in the middle of 1989, *Business India*'s publisher Ashok Advani suggested that I do a story on why the South was lagging behind. He wanted me to find out why South Indian companies which were highly respected lacked the desire and dynamism to grow? Were they going to be swamped by the outsiders or would they be able to hold their own?

This question seemed relevant then because the Hindujas from the UK had acquired Ashok Leyland from its British owners in 1987. None of the Tamil Nadu businessmen who were leading manufacturers of automobile components (and for whom vehicle manufacturing would have been a natural fit) had showed any interest in putting in a bid. Bajaj Auto was the other contender. Manu Chhabria had grabbed Gordon Woodroffe, an old British trading company which was in shipping, stevedoring and leather and leather goods. RP Goenka had picked up the eighties' retail giant Spencer's for a song and Vijay Mallya beat the Murugappa group to get Best & Crompton, another British company, an engineering company making electrical goods among other things.

According to the Foreign Exchange Regulation Act of 1973 and as per the Industrial Policy statement of 1977, all foreign companies had to dilute their foreign equity up to 40 per cent if they were to be treated on par with Indian companies. By the late eighties, many of these companies were near collapse and were takeover targets. But it looked as though the big deals of the day were passing the South Indians by.

Dhirubhai Ambani had already emerged as somebody in a class of his own. Aditya Birla got into a joint venture with HPCL to promote Mangalore Refineries. He also setup Indo-Gulf Fertilisers in UP which was a ₹1400 crore project. The JK group was on the verge of bagging the ₹1000 crore aromatics project in Saleempur. The Thapar group was getting into man-made fibres and colour TV tubes in Punjab. The RPG group and Vijay Mallya were on a shopping spree. The Ruia brothers who were originally from Madras had moved to Bombay and were making waves.

It did look as though there were plenty of opportunities and the southerners were seen as missing the bus with their lack of drive. The well-known heavy weights in the South were TVS, Amalgamations, TI (which was renamed Murugappa), MRF and the Lakshmi group of companies (from Coimbatore). They were all financially sound with excellent reputations, good marketing and dealer networks, and proven management capabilities. *"Yet they are shirking away from realising their potential,"* rued many bankers and institutions. A ₹100 crore project would give them sleepless nights those days.

It is interesting to see the kind of investments the southern giants were thinking of in the '80s and early '90s. The TVS group with a group turnover of ₹900 crore were thinking in terms investments of ₹150 to ₹200 crore. Lucas TVS had dithered for eight years before going in for a fuel injection project. The cash rich MRF with a group turnover of ₹462 crore in 1988 had spent years thinking about an entry into petrochemicals. Amalgamations with a group turnover of ₹450 crore had spent about ₹20 crore on expansion between 1987 and 1989. The TI group which had displayed a lot of derring-do by acquiring EID Parry and the CWS estates in the early '80s had been consolidating ever since.

Why did they like to remain in the periphery and be content with conservative sums and sizes? L Lakshman of the Rane group said then, *"I don't believe that one has to launch a big project to demonstrate that one is doing a big job. We are well aware of our strength and weaknesses and believe in sticking to our knitting."* N Sankar of the Sanmar group declared that growth for growth's sake is not necessarily a good thing. Ultimately, it's the bottom line that is important. *"I would rather have a ₹50 crore turnover and a ₹5 crore profit than be large and shaky."*

Two things set the southern businessmen apart from the other big time players. They were obsessed with retaining their shareholding and did not want financial institutions playing a dominant role in their lives. The family holding in tyre giant MRF was more than 50 per cent. If the government had not put a gun to their heads in the '80s, many of them would not even have gone public. According to the policy of the time if the companies did not go public they were heavily taxed. Between January and December 1988, public issues worth ₹1528 crore were made countrywide. Of this, Madras based issues amounted to ₹18 crore, a figure smaller than that of a single medium sized issue in Bombay.

The UK magnate Swaraj Paul's takeover attempt of Delhi icons, the DCM group and Escorts in 1986 was not something the southerners ever wanted to face. The first real hostile takeover in the South did not take place till 1998 when Raasi Cements in Andhra Pradesh was taken over by India Cements. Ironically, it was done by a South Indian businessman N Srinivasan, a maverick, who was to do many unexpected things in the years to come.

The southern businessmen till the eighties were seen as reluctant to leave their safe cocoons and put up plants elsewhere. A quote from a senior manager in a financial institution in 1989: *"The industrialists in Coimbatore do not want to venture into Madras and those who are based in Madras feel that they have travelled far, when they cross the borders, to neighbouring Andhra or Karnataka."* The rest of the country did not share these inhibitions. Aditya Birla and

Rahul Bajaj had no qualms about entering the South. *"Opportunities are presenting themselves in the South and we are not going to miss them because of location,"* declared Sanjiv Goenka in 1989.

The '80s were the go-go decade for petrochemical and fertiliser projects. All the major fertiliser projects were gas based and were being set up in the northern region. The only South Indian businessman who made a spirited bid for the Indo-Gulf Fertilisers Project and the Madras Aromatics projects was AC Muthiah who at that time was seen as the most dynamic businessman to emerge from the South.

Almost everybody was predicting then that the business families from the South would soon fade into oblivion.

As it turned out everybody including the business press was myopic about the southern groups. The reason for getting it so wrong might have had something to do with the fact that the families were notoriously publicity shy. They still are. The Murugappa group, which was featured on the cover of *Business India* in August 1978, did not meet the press again for many years. When *Business India* did a cover story on the TVS group in March 1986, family members refused to give interviews.

As it happened not only did they not fall apart, they emerged much stronger after two traumatic decades. Unlike their counterparts in the North and the West they have reaped the benefits of mostly sticking to their knitting. Perhaps the only major corporate split Chennai has seen is in the Kothari family. The Kothari group in the 1960s and 1970s ran neck and neck with the Murugappa group. Brothers DC and HC Kothari managed the group. They broke up in 1982. The split groups have since never regained their lost glory. For the larger southern groups, family squabbles have taken a back seat when business interests were threatened.

The Early Days

In the '50s and '60s, Tamil Nadu was one of the rapidly industrialising states in the country. K Kamaraj who became

Chief Minister in 1954 had stalwarts like C Subramaniam and R Venkataraman in his cabinet. The country's first industrial estate in Guindy, the brainchild of industry minister R Venkatraman,was opened in 1958. There were 78 units in this Estate in 1959. The state worked on increasing power generation but it could not keep pace with industrial growth. By 1965, the power situation deteriorated in spite of the fact that from 1950 to 1965, the generating capacity of the state had increased five times which was a record in India. *"Remarkable growth in industry and 23 per cent usage by agriculture had caused the shortage and has placed a tremendous burden"*, said Madras Chamber of Commerce in a publication, *Championing Enterprise* by V Sriram to celebrate 175 years of the Madras Chamber of Commerce.

The State Government managed to get a 400 MW nuclear power plant at Kalpakkam. BHEL set up a plant in Tiruchirapalli, a steel plant came up in Salem and an oil refinery near Madras. All this was possible due to good relations with the centre, benign bureaucrats both at the centre and the State and the good governance provided by Kamaraj and his team.

This was the period when the private sector also came into its own. As previously stated, Madras famously became the Detroit of India. Cars, buses and trucks had always been big business in the Madras Presidency and the city. In 1948, Simpson of the Amalgamations Group ushered in the diesel revolution in the city. The breakthrough came when a lorry operator agreed to the conversion of his truck to a Perkins diesel engine. From then on diesel engines came to be the norm for heavy vehicles. Simpson initially began with importing engines from Perkins and then graduated to assembly of engines from CKD (completely knocked down) kits.

The Government decided that it would encourage the manufacture of cars in the years following independence. In the South, this resulted in three major developments. Addison, another company in the Amalgamations group who were the agents for Nuffields of England in Madras got into the assembly of the Morris Minor, a car from the stable of Nuffields. The car began rolling out in 1950.

Standard Motor Products of India was incorporated in 1948 by the Standard Motor Company of Coventry, UK to manufacture Standard cars in collaboration with Union Company Limited. It was also in the same year that Ashok Motors was set-up for the assembly and sale of Austin cars. The plant was to come up near Ennore, close to Madras. When all this activity was going on, the Government announced in 1951 that it would decide on who could manufacture cars and where. Ashok Motors and Standard Motors were given the licence to manufacture in Madras. The Government also stipulated that all manufacturers would have to embark on a phased indigenisation programme. This was not to the liking of Austin which pulled out of Ashok Motors. The latter then switched over to trucks, signing up with Leyland of England. The company was renamed Ashok Leyland Limited. Two-wheeler manufacture came to India for the first time with Enfield India being set-up in Madras by the entrepreneurs, Easwara Iyer and Sundaram Iyer who headed the Easun Group.

All these major vehicle manufacturers had to commit to indigenisation which meant that ancillary manufacturing had to start. Amalgamations took the lead in setting up India Pistons in 1950 itself, long before the Government was to demand indigenisation. Addisons went into the development of machine assembly and cutting tools. In 1957, Dunlop put up its plant in Madras to manufacture tyres. More and more auto-ancillaries and component manufacturers came up around Madras, right through the 1950s and 1960s to meet the government's deadline for indigenisation. The TVS group and Rane went into manufacturing in the '60s. English Electric Limited and Hackbridge, Hewetic & Easun Limited came up to assemble electrical equipment for power transmission.

In 1949, TI Cycles of India was promoted by the Murugappa family which tied up with TI of UK. The private sector in Madras had collaborations mostly with British companies. The British companies which did not shut shop after independence also set up manufacturing activities. Parry's ventured forth into fertilisers and sugar. Binny's got into engineering, setting up Binny Engineering

Works in 1949. Best & Co moved into the manufacture of pumps in 1957, in collaboration with Worthington.

By the '70s, this kind of dynamism was beginning to fade. People tend to attribute it to the DMK coming to power in 1967. The DMK was new to administration. It wanted to muscle into the labour unions. This resulted in a prolonged phase of labour unrest in Tamil Nadu. It was said that with a Congress government in Delhi and the DMK locking horns with the centre there was a steep drop in central investment in the state after the '60s. The private industry also lost its support systems and had to build new networks and relations. It was to take them some years to do so.

Between 1964 and 1967, the annual rate of capital formation in the state was 21.58 per cent. It fell to 14.57 per cent between 1974 and 1977 and even more dramatically to 8 per cent between 1977 and 1980. The popular perception among the chatterati was that the Dravidian parties were more interested in divisive politics and welfare schemes rather than industrial development. MG Ramachandran who became Chief Minister (after breaking away from the DMK and launching the AIADMK) was not seen as sympathetic to industry.

This is not quite true.

According to a well-researched book *Tamil Nadu Economy: Performance and Issues* (Oxford and IBH) brought out by the Madras Institute of Development Studies on the Tamil Nadu economy in 1988, the trend towards stagnation was part of an all India phenomenon and Tamil Nadu could hardly have been an exception to the general tendency. The period after 1965–66 saw a real and sharp decline in the rate of growth of public investment in India.

Between 1969 and 1974, the most draconian laws to curb industry were passed. Indira Gandhi nationalised banks and the MRTP (Monopolies and Restrictive Trade Practices) Act was passed which made life very difficult for big business houses. People of a certain generation remember waiting for ten years to get their allotment of a Bajaj scooter or a Premier Padmini car. Salaries were capped and income tax rates in some cases exceeded 100 per cent.

Private sector in the region did go into a shell in the early '70s. The number of licences applied for fell in the '70s. South Indians saw the '70s as the dawning of the era of fixing and bribing. They had not mastered the art of wheeling and dealing. Southerners admitted that they were inept at managing the environment. Big projects meant big pay-offs. They were not tuned in to the subtleties of this game. The elders in the older business families did not approve of offshore deals.

What the rest of the country did not realise was that the southern businessmen were not going to give up. They were quietly preparing themselves to face the future on their own terms.

The families

There are quite a few multi-billion dollar business houses in Tamil Nadu. The largest among them are the TVS, Murugappa, Amalgamations and MRF groups. Then there are groups like Ramco, Sanmar and Rane and many others in Coimbatore like the LMW, PSG, Elgi, Sakthi and the Rajshree groups.

If one considers the four big ones, it's clear that all of them have re-invented themselves in varying degrees and have survived many crises and have built their own business models.

The TVS group companies are run by family members, some of them now fourth generation. Although they all come under the TVS umbrella, they do not interfere with each other. Most of the TVS companies have won every quality award in sight and many of them are global. Yet, it is felt that they have not fully exploited their brand name. There are always questions raised about how long they will remain together.

Such questions are never asked about the Murugappa Group. The fifth generation has made its entry in this group. Seen as an arch-conservative Chettiar group once, they were the original pioneers, then lost ground, gained it back and have evolved with each generation. They are a close-knit family where the elder's word is final.

Amalgamations is run by a much smaller family. This group too has weathered many a storm. TAFE, the flagship company is run by the founder's granddaughter and the group companies are sustained by it. Although their share holding pattern keeps them together, there are always rumours about trouble in paradise.

MRF founded around the time of independence is the country's largest tyre company. It is tightly held by the Mammen Mappillai family which owns the Malayalam Manorama group in Kerala. The large family have many interests and MRF remains stable without any family problems.

There are smaller groups who have been pioneers in some of the products they introduced, which have turnovers between ₹3000 to 6000 crore and which have a long history. They have survived the vicissitudes of change and are much admired.

For instance, the Sanmar group which is closely held went into manufacture of PVC for the first time in the country. It continues to retain a niche in spite of a giant like Reliance. Sanmar Engineering started with a joint venture with Durametallic Corporation of Kalamazoo, US, to manufacture mechanical seals. It grew with many more joint ventures. There were 35 once. It still has five joint ventures. Although joint ventures are coming apart rapidly these days, Sanmar Engineering has maintained good relations with its partners and even with those who have pulled out. Its joint venture model is unique in the country.

Rane Group has a long history. It was established in 1929 as a trading company. It went to into manufacturing in 1959 and established a plant for IC Engine Valves The group companies now manufacture auto parts such as steering systems, brake linings, seat belt systems and valve train components. Rane introduced power steering for the first time in the country to the automobile industry. A few years ago it also introduced electric power steering for automobiles and the hydraulic power steering for tractors. Its growth has been slow and steady. It has a turnover of around ₹3000 crore.

Despite scarce capital and resources, PAC Ramaswamy Raja set up the first spinning mill at Rajapalayam in the interiors of

Tamil Nadu in 1938 which was the focal point of the Ramco Group. Today, the Ramco Group has expanded into a ₹6000 crore conglomerate with interests in cotton and synthetic yarn, cement, building products, software solutions, wind-energy, bio-technology and more.

These are all highly reputed business houses and have achieved international recognition for their quality products and services and have been appreciated for the ethical standards they have maintained.

When the country opened up, nobody thought that these tightly controlled seemingly conservative family groups would survive. As we shall see not only have they survived but have also done pretty well for themselves.

Old Money

How 100-year-old groups have changed with the times

THE MURUGAPPA GROUP

The Family

The Murugappa group was founded in 1900, when Dewan Bahadur AM Murugappa Chettiar established a money-lending and banking business in Burma (now Myanmar), which then spread to Malaysia, Sri Lanka, Indonesia and Vietnam. The Murugappa family acquired 20,000 acres of land in Burma over a period of time and the founder (1884–1949) became a wealthy and prominent citizen of the country. He was appointed to the Viceroy's council and accorded the title of Dewan Bahadur. But when Burma became independent in 1947, the Burmese government peremptorily nationalised all foreign land holdings "…*without paying a cent as compensation.*" said AMM Arunachalam, son of the founder.

"The factor that prevented the nationalisation calamity from turning into a disaster for us was our financial accounting system, under which all collections made by the branches were required to be remitted to our head office at Madras. Thus when the Burmese nationalisation blow fell, we had sufficient liquid resources in India to provide us with a base to rebuild." Fortuitously, the Murugappa family had also established a manufacturing enterprise—Ajax Products Ltd.—a company that specialised in the manufacture of steel security equipment and

sandpaper in 1939. Nevertheless the manufacturing base of the company was very narrow and early in 1949, the family held a council of war in Madras.

At that meeting a rather painful decision was taken to give up banking and go in for manufacturing in a big way. After looking around and doing some elementary market research, the founder, Murugappa Chettiar felt that the bicycle had a future in India and after very quick and amicable negotiations with Tube Investments Ltd., UK—then the world's largest manufacturers of bicycles—the TI Cycles of India factory was established in 1949 itself at Ambattur, near Madras. This was the beginning and the TI Group later renamed the Murugappa Group which was to grow into one of India's largest family run enterprises, was now in business in India.

When the International Institute for Management Development, Lausanne, a prestigious business school and non-profit foundation presented its *Distinguished Family Business Award 2001* to the Murugappa Group in Rome, it became not only the first Indian company to win this recognition but also the first Asian one. No one else from India has got it ever since.

The award given by the Swiss Foundation is based on several criteria. The family should have run the business for at least three generations; it should be a national leader in business as well as have international business; It should have strong links with tradition, yet move with the times and be innovative. It should demonstrate good corporate governance. It should also be a good corporate citizen. The family fulfils all these criteria and more.

In *Looking Back from 'Moulmein'*, the biography of AMM Arunachalam (the head of the family from 1965), by S Muthiah, he explains how the family stays united and works together as a team. Till a few years ago, all members of the family got together for breakfast on Sundays. But with people travelling to far corners of the world, this practice has come to an end. Arunachalam said, *"But we meet as a family whenever possible and discuss all business and family matters and when we can't, we consult everyone on a decision by contacting each one who is not present. Generally there's consensus, but there have been times when there have been differing views rather forcefully expressed, no matter the age of the person opposing a decision. Annoyance, irritation, resentment are all inevitable in such cases. But in the end the AMM family discipline prevails; the eldest member of the family, considered 'absolutely neutral' by all, takes the final decision and everybody thereafter supports it wholeheartedly. One thing all of us in the family have always understood is that all of us have to sacrifice something in life; we can't always have the things we want or our own way."*

"We will continue to remain together. We don't tread on each other's toes. We try to avoid one family member reporting to another," says M Alagappan, AMM's son. *"All of us cousins have played together and spent time together. That has not changed over the generations. There are ten youngsters in the next generation. Seven of them who are old enough are coming into the business. They are close, they stay connected and hopefully they will come to accept and work within the family discipline."*

Family members at entry-level work under the professionals and report to them. They may be on the fast track, but will not be pushed up unless they are good. Comparisons are not between family members, but between family members and professionals. Each one is given the kind of responsibility for which he is best suited. Each one is under pressure to prove himself. (The family does not employ its women in the Group). *"Anyway, the Group is big enough to accommodate people,"* says Alagappan.

A Vellayan is the fourth generation family member to head the company. He is the oldest in his generation. The fifth generation has just made its entry.

Vellayan's two young sons and Vice-Chairman MM Murugappan's son have joined the business. As a rule, the family members have to be qualified and must have worked in an outside company for two to three years. Arun Vellayan has a Masters in finance and worked for DBS and Karma Capital in Mumbai. Narayan Vellayan studied law and charted accountancy and joined KPMG before entering the group. Muthu Murugappan completed his Bachelor's in business management from Warwick and worked in Chennai-based FMCG major Cavinkare. *"Once they work outside, they know how to deal with employees and situations much better. They are placed in group companies according to their aptitude. There will be several rotations before they settle down into their permanent positions,"* explains Vellayan about how the family management works.

The Group

The Murugappa Group which was seen as a typical, arch-conservative, risk-averse group—in short a South Indian family business—has surprised many in the last decade. It is now one of India's leading business conglomerates with a turnover of ₹243 billion. The Murugappa family has proved wrong the much repeated claim that family groups come apart in the third generation. The family has held together making way now for the fifth generation. They have also worked with professionals giving them the necessary space.

The Group has 28 businesses including eleven listed companies. The most well-known companies of the Group include Carborundum Universal Ltd., Cholamandalam Investment and Finance Company Ltd., Cholamandalam MS General Insurance Company Ltd., Coromandel International Ltd., Coromandel Engineering Company Ltd., EID Parry (India) Ltd., Parry Agro Industries Ltd., Sabero Organics Ltd., Shanthi Gears Ltd., Tube Investments of India Ltd., and Wendt (India) Ltd.

Its product range comprises of Abrasives, Auto Components, Transmission systems, Cycles, Sugar, Farm Inputs, Fertilisers, Plantations, Bio-products and Nutraceuticals. It has strong alliances with leading international companies like Groupe Chimique Tunisien, Foskor, Mitsui Sumitomo, Morgan Crucible, Sociedad Químicay Minera de Chile (SQM), Yanmar & Co. and Compagnie Des Phosphat De Gafsa (CPG). The Group has a wide presence all over India and operates across six continents. It employs over 23,000 people. It is either a market leader or a strong number two in all the areas it operates in.

The family knew the country was going to open up and actually prepared itself for it. MV Arunachalam, grandson of the founder, was a staunch believer in liberalisation and knew that it would happen one day. By the 1980s when it became clear that the economy could be opening up, the Murugappa group started focusing on the areas it wanted to be in. Export became a thrust area. "*The decisions we took have been almost like heralding the new liberalised policies. Our way of working will hopefully realise much better rewards now than with the previous dispensation,*" Arunachalam had told *Business India* in 1992. The group's turnover topped 29 per cent annually between 1991 and 1996 vindicating Arunachalam's faith. It started its acquisition activities seriously during this period. Arunachalam approved of acquisitions as "*...they make economic sense under liberalization*".

During the licence permit raj, Murugappa like most other families from the South was not good at the game. Out of the 17 licenses it applied for, it got one. The moment the country opened up, the family shed its inhibitions. Each successive generation has not only strengthened the existing businesses but has developed new ones. It has turned around sick businesses. It has also sold and bought businesses, a remarkable transformation for a group which had qualms about takeovers in earlier years.

The TI cycle factory established in 1949 gradually led to the group expanding and setting up several component manufacturing units. In no time, the pioneer became the market leader. In the next few years, the family set up many plants to produce various cycle parts. After a decade or so, complacency set in. Government policies worked against the concern. Labour became restive. In the middle of all this, nimble competitors from the north grabbed the market right under its nose. By 1974, TI Cycles was going downhill rapidly. The company's very existence was threatened.

In many similar scenarios, companies have just gone under and have become part of history. But this story had a different ending. MV Subbiah, nephew of AMM Arunachalam was given the task of turning around TI Cycles. He had a tough job on his hands. Components manufactured in Ludhiana were much cheaper. Overheads and labour costs in TI were much higher than competition. They did not have to go for expensive high quality steel that TI's UK collaborator insisted on.

Subbiah worked on cutting costs. As a first step, the quality of steel was changed. He emerged as a tough negotiator who did not cave in even when there was a lockout which lasted many weeks. He was not averse to making unpopular decisions, and finally got labour to agree to wages linked to productivity.

Subbiah changed many practices which were dragging the company down. TI Cycles set-up a plant in Nasik where cycles were designed and assembled. The company went to the North and opened up in Noida. Slowly, cycle manufacturing was shifted from Ambattur. The company returned to profitability but not to market leadership. In the '90s it went into exports and did very well. In 1999, TI Cycles was able to celebrate its golden jubilee in a mood of optimism. By the turn of the century, it again went through a bad patch when the carefully cultivated export market to Europe collapsed. True to style, it has rebuilt itself again and has climbed up to the number two position.

Till the seventies, the Group had two engineering units—TI (Tube Investments) and Carborundum Universal (which made industrial abrasives)—and a few small plantations. The decade of the eighties changed the character of the Group totally after it acquired EID Parry and the plantation company CWC from their original British owners, and a whole lot of other smaller units.

In 1981, the ailing Parry's, the country's second oldest British company was literally on its deathbed. Parry's core businesses—sugar, fertilizers and ceramics—had remained with it through its ups and downs for more than 200 years. It was from the late sixties that Parry's started to show signs of decline. In 1976, it was Indianised. Then it went steadily downhill.

Although Parry's was in the doldrums when the issue of a takeover came up in the seventies, it had quite a few suitors. However it was MV Arunachalam, the then chief executive of the group, who the financial institutions wanted for Parry's. At that time the TI group was not really interested. It was consolidating its position. The group's New Ambadi Estates was negotiating for several plantations in south India owned by a British company (CWS) which it subsequently acquired.

The situation at Parry's continued to deteriorate through 1979 and 1980. The institutions kept pressing Arunachalam, who insisted on acquiring shares in the company. He did not think he could do much without any shareholding in Parry's. The institutions did not want to part with any of their 27 per cent. The affable and hugely popular Arunachalam stood his ground. In early 1981 Arunachalam was informed that the Commonwealth Development Finance Corporation and Pearl General Insurance, two London based organizations who between them held 11 per cent of EID shares, had offered to sell this portion to the Murugappa group.

R Venkataraman then the Finance Minister, urged Arunachalam to accept this offer. Venkataraman had had a long association with Parry's, from the days when he was a trade union leader in the forties. After a long drawn out affair and some drama, the share transfer took place. The group and its friends acquired about 17–20 per cent of the shares locally, in mid-1981. Arunachalam said then, *"The government at all levels showed so much confidence, we felt that we had to take the trouble to respond. But the purchase of the shares was the least difficult part of the whole deal. The management of the company was a more difficult proposition."*

At the end of 1981, Arunachalam was appointed Chairman of Parry's and KV Raghavan, an experienced professional who had just retired as Chairman of Engineers India Ltd., was appointed President. But, Parry's continued to do badly.

In 1984, the Murugappa family decided to ask Subbiah (Arunachalam's younger brother) who had emerged as the group's turnaround expert to head Parry's although he was at that point still needed in TI Cycles.

It did not take Subbiah long to realise that Parry's was like a rudderless ship. It had the anachronistic 'boxwallah' culture. It was vastly overmanned. Subbiah cut down on overheads, men and space, tightened up financial management, brought in more dynamic top management, shed the business lines which were not likely to produce profits, and set clear directions for the businesses with potential. It was a classic turnaround case. Everything was done according to the book. Although some of this started before

Subbiah came in, he pursued this course relentlessly and brought about the desired results. The Parry's turnaround became a case study in management institutes.

In June 1986, the company declared a 10 per cent equity dividend for the first time in nine years. As Arunachalam explained in his address to the shareholders, *"Agriculture will continue to be the country's prime base for growth. Two of our core businesses, farm inputs and sugar are agriculture based and therefore provide us an opportunity for sizeable growth."* They continue to remain Murugappa Group's core business.

Parry's went on a massive manpower reduction programme between 1983 and 1986. During this period the company retrenched or retired 2,615 persons out of a total strength of nearly 6,300 persons and paid ₹6.8 crores in compensation. This was possibly the the first time in the country when so many people were laid off at one go.

In 1992, following management guru CK Prahlad's prescription, Subbiah restructured the group (Parry's had been fully integrated with the group) based on core competence. In 1996, Subbiah took over as the Chief Executive following Arunachalam's death in 1995.

In 1999, Subbiah stepped down, brought in an external Chairman for the Group, and let the family take advisory positions. He said then, *"Hinduism has sustained itself over 1,000 years simply because of a renewal and readjustment process which goes on... Likewise we feel the need for an outsider to look at our group periodically."* McKinsey was given the mandate to develop a clear plan for improving group performance and increasing shareholder value.

NS Raghavan, a professional, was appointed as Chairman of the Murugappa Corporate Board. On his retirement in 2001, PS Pai took over as Executive Chairman. During Pai's tenure, the Group went through a period of learning and growth. *"They brought a lot of stability to the Group, playing an unbiased proactive role,"* says Alagappan (the founder's grandson) who on completion of Pai's tenure, took over as Executive Chairman in October 2006. A Vellayan, the founder's great grandson, was appointed as its Vice-Chairman and Director—Strategy. Vellayan succeeded Alagappan as the Executive Chairman in 2009.

Alagappan who had worked for 44 years with the Group had led many of the major businesses of the Group. He oversaw the Group transforming into the giant that it is today and contributed a lot to taking it forward. The financial services business close to Alagappan's heart has grown steadily over the years. Cholamandalam Investment & Finance Co. was set up in 1978. It was an NBFC offering services like hire purchase and leasing to both corporate and retail customers. It entered vehicle financing in the early 1990s. By 2005, it had a large customer base and was rated among the top Indian owned NBFCs in the country. However, given its cautious and conservative approach, Cholamandalam did not get into the personal finance business.

In January 2006, Cholamandalam tied up with the DBS group of Singapore to fill this gap. Singapore-based DBS is one of the largest financial services groups in Asia and the largest bank in Singapore. At that time, it was also the fifth largest banking group in Hong Kong as measured by assets. Following the launch of the personal loan product, the new company (Cholamandalam DBS) also introduced home equity loans. Cholamandalam was happy to acquire DBS's expertise in personal finance.

As it happened, it was the personal loan portfolio which pushed the company to the brink of disaster in 2008. Cholamandalam DBS ended up with ₹1,500 crore of delinquent debts. With 2008 turning out to be a bad year, the Murugappa side wanted to shut down the personal loan business. But there was resistance from the DBS side. Says Alagappan, *"We would have been able to correct the situation if the market had not crashed in July 2008."* When Chola DBS exited the personal finance business in September 2008, DBS lost its relevance to the joint venture.

The Group finally managed to buy out the DBS Group and dropped its title from the company's name in 2010.

Cholamandalam has been successfully turned around and has been doing well from 2011. Vellayan, son of Subbiah, and part of the fourth generation of the Murugappa Group, was given the task of running Cholamandalam in 2010. Vellayan holds a degree in civil engineering from IIT Madras and an MBA from the University of Michigan, US. His professional experience includes a six-year stint with McKinsey in the USA.

"*A lot of the gaps had been plugged by the time I came in. It was our Director — Finance, N Srinivasan, who did a tremendous job during the crunch time. His energy levels were amazing,*" says Vellayan. The family members always give credit to the professionals who work with them.

"*What we are doing now is strengthening our core business. Vehicle finance and home equity comprise 73 per cent and 23 per cent of our business, respectively. These two businesses drive the fortunes of Chola. How do we make these two a lot stronger? Chola has gone through three phases. Before DBS, it was a good, conservative, South Indian Company. Then came the DBS years. During this current third phase, we have launched several difficult initiatives. It is a four-year journey. Once we strengthen the core, we would have earned the right to do other things.*"

Chola has strong well-entrenched competitors. Is that going to make it difficult for him? "*There is enough potential for growth in vehicle finance and home loans. We have 8 per cent share in vehicle finance, which gives us space to grow. We are not stuck with an 800-pound gorilla.*"

Alagappan stepped down in 2009 after putting Cholamandalam back on track. Vellayan took over in 2009 as Executive Chairman. One of the first things he did was to change its corporate logo of many decades. The blue peacock was transformed into a sharper red one. "*Internationally and nationally, the colour red is associated with the most successful brands. We want to show that we are a vibrant group full of energy*" is his take on why that was done.

The group has been selling off companies that were closely identified with EID Parry, like Parryware and Parry's Confectionery. "*We have been shedding baggage,*" he shrugs. From the '90s onwards, there has been a flurry of acquisition activities. Apart from taking full control of its NBFC business, it also acquired Sadashiva Sugars, GMR Industries (its agricultural business) and the French company Sedis, maker of industrial and engineering chains. When the market is down, the group acquires companies and then turns them around.

Vellayan explains that the group is now broadly focused on three areas. The first is agro commodities, such as sugar, tea and fertilisers. It is not in urea anymore. Vellayan believes that one day fertilisers will be decontrolled and so will sugar. The group will be in a particularly strong position in these businesses. It has gone into agri-retail in a big way by setting up 800 shops by the name of *Mana Gromor.*

The second area of focus is engineering products, such as tubes, abrasives, ceramics chains and metal sections and the third area will focus on consumers, with products such as financial services, insurance and cycles. *"When we have a diversified portfolio, one or the other will do better. We keep growing in adjacencies,"* says Vellayan. Vellayan is also planning to enter into farm mechanisation, introducing products suitable for one acre farms. In finance, there is a little basket of adjacencies like home loans, insurance and other products.

"We have to be in the top position regionally and top or the second positions nationally. In engineering products, we are market leaders. We are the largest fertiliser and sugar manufacturer in the South. In cycles, after many years of struggle, we are now a strong number two in the country; our numbers are catching up with Hero. I strongly believe that size matters. It gives us power over purchasing, price and people" is his stated belief.

The other thing Vellayan has worked on is in making the group international in value chain management. For example, silicon carbide is sourced from Russia, brought into an SEZ for cutting into wafers and then exported to chip makers. The group owns mines in Russia, Africa and South America. *"I am in all the spots of the value, which creates an entry barrier for competitors. We spread our risks by partnering with governments,"* he says.

Vellayan agrees that the group has missed out on big ticket projects such as coal or telecom. He also says that the Murugappa Group's culture would not have made it easy for it to deal with these industries with its in-built values. *"We never make a big play and commit big mistakes. We don't do anything stupid and fancy. We take reasonable sized bets and not green field bets. We keep our cost structure under control. We will continue to expand customer base, improve competitiveness, and create entry barriers for others."* Vellayan signs off.

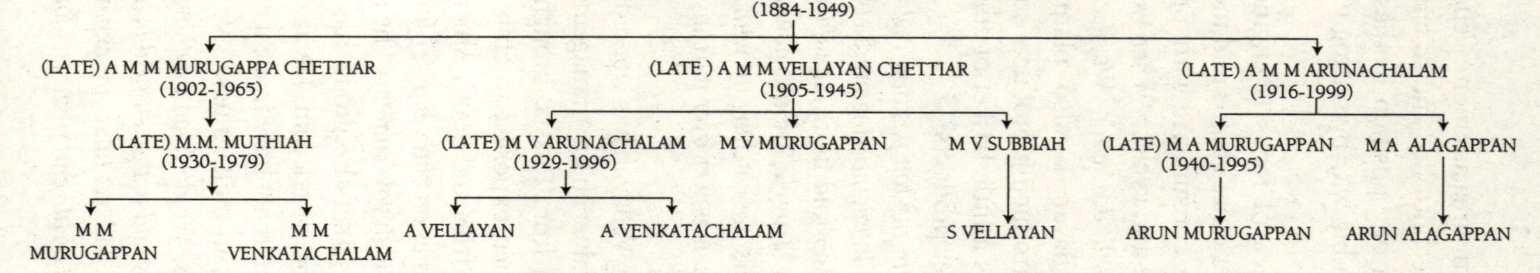
MURUGAPPA GROUP FAMILY TREE
(LATE) DEWAN BAHADUR A M MURUGAPPA CHETTIAR
(1884-1949)
(LATE) A M M MURUGAPPA CHETTIAR
(1902-1965)
(LATE) A M M VELLAYAN CHETTIAR
(1905-1945)
(LATE) A M M ARUNACHALAM
(1916-1999)
(LATE) M.M. MUTHIAH
(1930-1979)
(LATE) M V ARUNACHALAM
(1929-1996)
M V MURUGAPPAN
M V SUBBIAH
(LATE) M A MURUGAPPAN
(1940-1995)
M A ALAGAPPAN
M M
MURUGAPPAN
M M
VENKATACHALAM
A VELLAYAN
A VENKATACHALAM
S VELLAYAN
ARUN MURUGAPPAN
ARUN ALAGAPPAN

THE TVS GROUP

The TVS group turned 100 in 2011. Many will be familiar with individual group companies like Wheels India, Brakes India, Lucas TVS, Sundram Fasteners, Sundaram Brake Lining and TVS Motor Company, without realising they all belong to the same group. In spite of all its achievements, the TVS group hides its light under the bushel. The centenary year was not celebrated by the group. There was no uncorking of champagne bottles. It was business as usual at all the group companies.

Barring one or two companies, the TVS companies have been market leaders in their respective fields. It is quite likely that many automobiles manufactured globally carry one or another TVS part. Among the vehicles on India's roads, it is said thirty five per cent have TVS components. What is quite remarkable about the group is that the companies have maintained their reputation for quality and customer care over so many decades. TVS to them stands for Trust, Value and Service.

Group founder TV Sundaram Iyengar registered a company in 1911 and started South India's first passenger bus service in 1912. Although this pioneering venture was wound up a few years later, Iyengar went on to open an automobile sales and service unit in Madurai in 1919, dealing in motor tyres, auto spares and ancillaries. Over the next decade, he acquired sub-dealerships for Ford and Chevrolet cars. A few years down the line, General Motors gave him the sole dealership for all their vehicles.

In 1939, TVS ventured into transport services yet again, setting up Southern Roadways in Madurai. It soon became the country's largest goods transport fleet in the private sector. The passenger division was nationalised in 1970. Its efficiency and customer service were legendary and people are believed to have set their watches by the bus timings.

Between 1950 and 1960, TVS expanded its activities and diversified into related fields. The importance of marketing spare parts was recognised even in those early days and distribution channels were set up wherever possible. It forayed into automobile insurance. To help transport operators buy vehicles, a hire purchase company, Sundaram Finance was set up in 1954. Today, Sundaram Finance is one of the largest and most-respected non-banking finance companies in the country. The sons of Sundaram Iyengar—TS Rajam, TS Duraiswamy, TS Santhanam, TS Krishna and TS Srinivasan became the architects of the group.

Till 1960, TVS did not enter into manufacturing. The government, however, was keen on building an indigenous automobile industry. GM, which had been assembling vehicles from CKD kits, refused to manufacture vehicles in India as it did not feel the country had a proper industrial base. Years later, Sundram Fasteners, a TVS star would become a dedicated supplier of radiator caps to GM and also win the best supplier of the year award from the MNC many times over. But GM's India exit was a catalyst for change at TVS, as so many of its activities were built around the GM dealership which came to an end in the mid-50s. Premier, TELCO, Ashok Leyland and Mahindra & Mahindra were all putting up plants and the need for indigenisation was increasingly gaining momentum.

TVS with its highly profitable agency business and the transport fleet was a cash-rich group. The family did not have to rely on outside funds to enter manufacturing. Given its track record, it was not difficult for TVS to enter into viable collaborations with the world's leading component manufacturers, who at that time were all British. The manufacturing companies were set up in the vast Padi complex in North Chennai. By the seventies, the group had reached its dominant position in wheels, brakes, auto electricals, fasteners and many related components.

The group gained further momentum under the family's third generation. Some well-known names include Suresh Krishna, S Ram, S Viji, Venu Srinivasan, TK Balaji, K Mahesh and R Dinesh. Now the fourth generation is running the business. The TVS companies did not want to go public until it became necessary when unlisted companies started getting taxed more than listed ones. However, the group never got addicted to the stock market or market capitalisation. Financial institutions have been more than willing to finance their projects.

Problems emerged in the seventies. The close-knit family started coming apart. For the first time in the group's history, it faced a major strike in 1977. By the eighties, both problems were resolved. The group, in fact, has an enviable reputation for good labour relations. Sundram Fasteners has never lost a day to labour unrest. In 1980, Sundaram Clayton launched TVS 50, the country's first two-seater moped. This division metamorphosed into TVS Motor, the third-largest two-wheeler and three-wheeler manufacturer in the country, run by Venu Srinivasan. In the eighties, the group adapted itself to supply to the Japanese vehicles entering the market even though all of its partners were British.

When the economy opened up in the nineties and many foreign automobile and component manufacturers rushed in, analysts started writing off indigenous groups like TVS. They did not think this conservative family-run business could survive liberalisation. The group quietly reinvented itself and grabbed the opportunities presented by the reform era. The first thing the group companies did was to divorce their joint venture partners, some of whom had shackled TVS's export ambitions. Leaving its partners brought financial independence and the freedom to choose the technologies it wanted.

Having got rid of troublesome partners, the TVS group companies have turned global players, achieved with their fanatical commitment to quality. They have been getting the ISO certifications, Deming award (the Oscar of quality) TPM and TQM awards way ahead of others. All the awards were calling cards to the export market. Today, TVS group companies are truly international, with all of them buying companies in different countries and putting up plants. TVS Logistics, one of the newer companies in the group, has gone on a major buying spree in the last few years.

The group will have to make strategic decisions on whether to expand locally or globally in the next few years. The TVS family is also fortunate that the fourth generation has entered the business and as people who know the family say, they are all highly qualified and have earned their place in the business.

Let us look at the achievements of some of the third and fourth generations which will give an indication of how the group has evolved.

Suresh Krishna, Sundram Fasteners

Suresh Krishna, Chairman of Sundram Fasteners made the rest of the country take a serious look at the South in the 80's. As the President of the Confederation of Engineering Industry (now known as CII) in 1988 he addressed 100 meetings in 40 towns in the country in a single year, which is probably some kind of a record.

Krishna, the grandson of the founder decided in 1990 that he had to take exports seriously. Krishna's ambition when he set up Sundram Fasteners in 1962 was to make his company the market leader in the high-tensile fastener industry, which he did in less than two decades. The main customer for high-tensile fasteners (the nuts and bolts that hold a vehicle together) is the automotive industry.

Sundram Fasteners' compounded growth rate was 24 per cent in sales in the mid-eighties. The Indian market, which was growing at 6 to 7 per cent was not enough to support the company's growth. That was when Krishna decided that Sundram Fasteners had to become a leading player in the global market as well. This was way before other auto component companies started thinking about export markets.

The company was set up as a small unit of the TVS group—the only one in the group which had no foreign collaboration. The tiny turnover of ₹4 lakh with which the company started in 1966–67 in the Chennai suburb of Ambattur, reached ₹56 lakh in 1971. That year the factory was moved to the sprawling Padi complex and the company started to expand.

In its early days the company had to take on big names like Fit Tight and Guest Keen Williams (GKW) which were already established in the market. These two companies ceased to be competition in the early eighties. Fit Tight never recovered from its labour troubles in 1982 and GKW suspended the production of fasteners by 1983. These developments helped Sundram Fasteners become the market leader in the early eighties. Ever since, it has maintained the top spot.

It is the only company in the country which can offer an entire range of fasteners. The quality of its products is among the best. It has developed many products ahead of its competitors. When Japanese technology entered the automobile industry with Maruti Suzuki 800cc car, Sundram Fasteners became the first supplier to Maruti. Maruti required more than 125 items and SFL supplied them all. It was able to meet the tough Japanese design standards.

It was not easy getting to this position. Krishna recalls how difficult it was to run an industry those days. In the 1960s, fasteners were reserved for small industries. As Krishna belonged to the TVS group, which was a dominant undertaking and as fasteners came under the category of hardware and not auto components he could not get any of the concessions that small scale industries enjoyed. For any tiny expansion or purchase, he had to go to Delhi. *"I needed a licence to import some raw material, which cost ₹28,000. They permitted me to spend ₹1,400. The most productive years of my life, between 1962 and 1991, were governed primarily by running to Delhi."*

He was forced to go to a backward district in Tamil Nadu for expansion. Then, he had to offload 40 per cent of the shareholding in Sundram Fasteners at a government nominated rate of ₹14. The day after the public issue, the share was quoted at ₹28. *"The TVS group lost a lot of money because of these rules,"* says Krishna and rues the fact that the public issue restricted his capacity to raise funds. The others in the group managed as they had foreign collaborations.

In 1983, the auto industry was totally moribund. "*My company was forced to look at the outside world. We had always been dabbling with the export market. Sundram Fasteners had exported to Mercedes Benz in 1974 itself*" he says. A German buyer from Benz had come to India to look at possibilities and the company managed to get orders. "*It gave us insights into exports.*"

Krishna started taking tentative steps with exports because he sensed the change in the air in the gloomy eighties. He felt that Prime Minister Rajiv Gandhi was going to be the catalyst who would transform the country. However, there were many constraints to exports. "*The rupee was overvalued. We were overpriced everywhere. It was quite traumatic.*" Exports were not profitable in the earlier stages. The general credibility of India was low in the international market. During one of the frustrating forays into exports, Krishna's marketing manager came back from the US and said that the American automobile companies were all talking about something called the ISO 9000.

Murali Sunderarajan, the manager who stumbled upon ISO 9000 recalls, "*In June 1987, I was asked to head a new division for Exports reporting to the Marketing head. We were then selling to a few overseas customers and the annual revenue was around ₹10 lakhs. Mr Suresh Krishna said that the world was wide open and set a target of ₹30 lakhs for the financial year April '87–March '88 followed by ₹1 crore for 88–89 and then to double that every year.*

In formulating our strategy for quick growth, we decided that we should initially push standard fasteners in a developed market that largely depended on imported fasteners. In this way, we would be in a position to establish the TVS brand name in that market in a short period of time. We would simultaneously pursue the business for value added special fasteners.

Alarm bells were being raised with regard to the quality of fasteners from China, in both Britain and United States. In the British market, quality was paramount apart from price. I found one important aspect that was common amongst the suppliers of fasteners in UK. All the major manufacturers supplying fasteners in UK. had accreditation under BS 5750, for their quality systems. The distributors told me that their customers were insisting on procuring the fasteners from those manufacturers who had BS 5750 accreditation. ISO 9000 itself was based on BS 5750 of British Standards Institute. I reported this to the Chairman and he immediately called for a meeting of the Senior Management of Sundram Fasteners to draw out plans to obtain the BS 5750 accreditation in a year."

Sundram Fasteners set up a Management Committee that worked with an external Consulting firm and got the certification. It was the first Company in India to receive the ISO 9000 (BS 5750) accreditation in 1990. Fastener Quality Act also became law in USA at the same time. Having got the ISO 9000 certification, Sundram Fasteners gave a strong push to the exports of fasteners not only to UK but also to the rest of Europe and USA. Krishna saw a credible visiting card for India in the ISO 9000 quality accreditation. *"We were always committed to quality even when it was not considered necessary. But we had no way of establishing it in the minds of foreign buyers before we got the ISO 9000 accreditation"*, says Krishna.

A major opportunity came its way when a team from Opel, auto major General Motors' German subsidiary, was paying a courtesy call on the company in 1992. They casually asked whether Sundram Fasteners would like to bid for the supply of radiator caps to GM. *"We were not quite sure what radiator caps were. We were not making the product. But we enthusiastically agreed to bid"*, Krishna recalls.

A year later Sundram Fasteners became the first and only Indian company to become a dedicated supplier of this part to GM. It was a hard won global tender in which eight countries participated. Says Krishna, *"I realised that this achievement would give us enormous visibility in the world market."* The company bought GM's radiator caps plant from UK, dismantled it, transported it to Chennai, set it up and started manufacturing the product. Since 1993, Sundram Fasteners has been supplying 100 per cent of GM's radiator caps requirements.

That is not all. For five years running, the company got GM's prestigious *Supplier of the Year* award. This is an honour accorded to those who have achieved world-class levels of quality, service, technology and price in support of GM. Krishna's conviction that the association with GM would give Sundram Fasteners enormous exposure to the world out there was proved right. *"Although the radiator caps account for less than 5 per cent of our turnover, they gave us great visibility in India and abroad."* The Opel team had approached other Indian auto ancillary companies as well. Only Krishna saw the potential in the project. *"The entire project cost us ₹3 crore then,"* smiles Krishna. *"In 2012 we made a profit of ₹5 crore from this division,"* once the country opened up, Sundram Fasteners took off. *"We felt unshackled."* It was as though an avalanche had hit Indian industry. But many did not know how to face this change. Sundram Fasteners was prepared.

The quest for quality has been a continuous process. The company has over the years won every conceivable award in quality and productivity. Krishna says all these achievements are meaningless if the company does not grow. *"I do not want awards if they are going to make us complacent. Every time you cross a milestone you feel you have arrived. In reality you have to run hard to stay in the same place,"* he says. *"When all the excitement of the awards dies down, maintaining quality and productivity is backbreaking, heart breaking work. You have to change 1,000 to 1,500 people and 15 people are the chosen ones to bring about the change. You have to be strong minded to persist with this constant process,"* he adds.

Between 1990 and 2000 the automobile industry in the country went through massive changes. Global brands came in and the number of trucks, cars and two-wheelers produced in the country just zoomed up to more than 3 million in 2012. Sundram Fasteners not only kept pace with this growth, but also moved beyond the borders. In 2003, it acquired Cramglinton Forge, a UK-based forgings company which makes bevel gears. It was a sick company which was turned around. In spite of the slowdown in the major economies this company continues to do well.

Between 2006 and 2007 Sundram Fasteners spread its global network further. It went into a joint venture with a German company Bleistahl Produktions GmbH. The idea was for the joint venture to dismantle about 60 per cent of Bleistahl's production facilities in Germany and put it up in Hosur. It also acquired 100 per cent stake in Peiner Umformtechnik GmbH from Textron Deutshland.

Krishna decided to set up a plant in China in 2006, the first TVS company to do so. Going to China was somewhat similar to companies coming to India 50–60 years ago, when India was not an investment destination. *"We did not want to miss out on the China growth story and regret 25 years from now that we did not go to China."* Many warned him against the foolhardy step he was taking. Krishna chose to go beyond Shanghai where everybody was heading that time. Here again he was thinking out of the box. Sundram Fasteners set up a green field plant in Zhejiang Province. The Chinese unit has started making fairly handsome profits in the last two years.

Krishna has spent more than fifty years in business. He has not only built up Sundram Fasteners as the market leader but has also transformed it into a global player. Its turnover today is around ₹2,200 crore. About 40 per cent of it comes from exports. From the day it was founded in 1962, it has not lost a single day to strikes.

He no longer looks after day to day operations. His daughter Aarthi Krishna runs the company. He is still actively involved in the company's growth. *"I am now receiving 'Lifetime Achievement' awards,"* he laughs.

Venu Srinivasan, TVS Motors

In 1980 the TVS Group did something out of character. Group company Sundaram Clayton introduced TVS 50, a two-seater two-wheeler. This was the group's first venture in the consumer durables market. It was conceived by TS Srinivasan (son of the founder) in 1976 and he had a tough job convincing the family to take up this project. The government did its bit by slapping a substantial export obligation on the company and imposing all kinds of stringent conditions because Sundaram Clayton was an MRTP (Monopolies and Restrictive Practices)* house. In spite of all odds Srinivasan's sense of timing proved perfect. The country was ready for a fuel-efficient and a light-weight two-wheeler. It is said that the TVS moped played its bit in emancipating women of that era as they realised that they had access to affordable, easy to use transport. The moped was something they could handle. In spite of the government imposed problems, the TVS 50 was a runaway success. Sundaram Clayton became the country's largest manufacturer of mopeds.

Srinivasan passed away in 1979, and his young son Venu became the Managing Director of the company. Venu was in his twenties. He had an engineering degree from Madras University and had just got his MBA from Purdue in the US. He of course was not to know what lay ahead. A company in the TVS group was venturing into a fiercely competitive area for the first time. Venu was going to take the company places, face many ups and downs, was going to be written off several times, but always manage to stage spectacular comebacks. He put money and effort into R&D, and dared to take on market leaders at their own game. He pioneered the Total Quality Movement (TQM) in his company much ahead of most other Indian companies. His companies got the Deming prize in 2002, a global quality benchmark.

In the early '80s the government finally opened up the two-wheeler market to foreign players. Venu was young, was

* The MRTP Act of 1969 covered two kinds of undertakings. They were either single large companies or groups of interconnected companies which had assets of at least ₹100 crore undertakings. Prior to 1985 this limit was ₹20 crore. The companies which controlled at least one-fourth of production or market of a product and had assets of at least ₹3 crore (earlier this limit was ₹1 crore) were also dominant undertakings.

These dominant undertakings had to get prior approval from the central government for establishing new enterprises, expansions, mergers, amalgamations, takeovers and appointment of directors. Every export requirement was examined minutely and approval would take many months.

The MRTP Act was scrapped in 1991.

influenced a great deal by his stint in the US and had that hunger and passion to do something different. He was ready to go into the manufacture of light motor cycles. Sundaram Clayton tied up with Suzuki Motors of Japan. TVS Suzuki, a new company was set up to launch the country's first two-stroke 100cc motor bike Ind Suzuki. The two-wheeler revolution began in the country with this bike. About 40 companies received licences to manufacture fuel efficient two-wheelers and many were to fall by the wayside.

In 1984, Hero Honda was incorporated as a joint venture between Munjal's Hero Group and Honda Motor Company. Hero Honda launched CD-100 in 1985 which was going to be the most popular four-stroke 100 cc bike for years to come. In the next decade, Bajaj Auto tied up with Kawasaki, and Escorts with Yamaha. Everybody was jumping into the fray to fulfill a huge pent-up demand.

Although Ind Suzuki took the market by storm when it was first introduced, it could not sustain its lead when it had to face stiff competition from both Hero Honda and the old war horse Bajaj Auto. Hero Honda's advertisement campaign, which had the tag line 'Fill it, shut it, forget it' caught the country's imagination. Hero Honda's Splendour ruled the roost for the next two decades.

In the early '90s the country went through a recessionary phase and it was not a good time for two wheelers as well. Prices went up because of the increase in excise duty. TVS Suzuki was hit quite badly. To add to his problems Venu faced labour unrest which resulted in a lock-out which lasted from February to June 1990. It was also becoming evident he was having problems with his collaborator. TVS Suzuki could not get any help from Suzuki either in the form of finance or technology. Suzuki insisted that the bikes had to be adapted to Indian condition and the changes had to be tested on the road for around three months. *"Otherwise the Japanese would say we hadn't done our homework"*, Suzuki would then take between five and six months to validate the changes. The market wasn't prepared to wait for Suzuki's validation. Although the country fell in love with the four-stroke technology, Suzuki was not going to provide it.

TVS Suzuki was forced to formulate a turnaround strategy by itself. It went into serious cost cutting by reducing manpower and implementing inventory controls. With the help of production engineering, R&D skills and innovation, it introduced variations of its 100cc models. In 1994, the industry started to revive. The company launched a scooterette TVS Scooty which again was a big hit and it generated volumes for the company. In 1995, TVS Suzuki declared its maiden dividend and become the second largest two-wheeler company (behind Hero Honda) in the country.

Government's ruling on emission norms in 1996 made two-stroke bikes unviable. By this time TVS Suzuki had started working on four-stroke technology on its own. It launched a scooter 'Spectra' with a four-stroke engine in 1999 which did not set the market on fire. By 2001, the company's fortunes took a nosedive again. The same year Yamaha bought out Escorts' stake in Yamaha Escorts. Bajaj came back with a whole lot of new launches.

The collaboration with the troublesome partner came to an end in 2001. *"We knew that we had to get rid of them"*, said Venu, then. TVS bought back Suzuki holding of 25.97 per cent at ₹15 a share; a total outgo of ₹9 crore. TVS Suzuki became TVS Motor Company. The same year Venu staged a spectacular come back yet again by launching the fully indigenously developed 110cc motorbike 'Victor'. TVS's market share went up from 15.5 per cent in 2001–02 to 19 per cent the next year. There was a 45 day waiting period for the bike.

It has been a roller coaster ride ever since for the company with market shares going up and down depending on the popularity of its rivals' vehicles. For almost a decade the company maintained its position as number three behind the unbeatable Hero Honda and a rejuvenated Bajaj Auto. In 2012, it slid to the fourth position following Honda and Hero parting ways. Honda's fully owned subsidiary HMSI became the second largest two-wheeler maker in the country by volumes overtaking Bajaj Auto. Bajaj Auto itself started losing volumes as it stopped producing scooters and started focusing on motor cycles. The country had started to prefer stylish state-of-the-art scooters.

Once again people were beginning to write off TVS Motors. And once again Venu proved that he was no pushover. He got into a technology tie-up with BMW to manufacture and enter the high quality premium bikes (over 200cc) market. To improve its market position the company upped the ante in 2014 with new launches. The company said it would invest ₹250 crore in 2015. *"We are in the fourth position today and we target to be in the top three players in India, with the stream of product launches every quarter or four months for the next three years, which will significantly strengthen our position,"* said Venu to the media.

The company started focusing on scooters as opposed to motorcycles and that has started to pay off. On the back of strong scooter sales, TVS replaced Bajaj at the third spot once again in 2014. However the company cannot afford to relax for even a moment. Two-wheelers have been the fastest growing segment (25 per cent starting 2009) in the automobile industry. All the manufacturers are gearing up with new improved product launches. Venu is not given to flamboyant statements. He is quite clear. He will be number two someday soon.

Wheels India under the fourth generation

Wheels India, which was established in 1962, is one of the largest steel wheel manufacturers in the world. It makes an entire range of wheels for cars/ utility vehicles, commercial vehicles and tractors. Its product portfolio includes single piece wheels and construction and earth mover wheels. The company also manufactures air suspension kits for trucks and buses. With over 15 per cent of its turnover coming from exports, particularly from the construction and earth mover equipment segment, it is truly a global player in the auto components industry. In 1982, the company moved out of Tamil Nadu for the first time by setting up its second facility in Rampur for tractor wheels.

The 2000s represented a decade of growth for Wheels India when it set up several manufacturing facilities all over India. Wheels India is a partner to many global MNCs like Ford,

Hyundai, Tata, Caterpillar, John Deere, Komatsu, Hyundai Heavy Industries and Case New Holland, Leyland, TAFE and Suzuki. Srivats Ram, Managing Director of the company believes that the company's future lies in partnering OEMs (original equipment manufacturers) in their growth and providing service to match.

In true TVS style, Wheels India has won every quality award possible such as CAT SQEP Silver Certification 2010, TPM Award & Certification, Toyota Supplier Award for Quality & Cost '09 and Regional Contribution Award from Toyota in the 2013 Global Suppliers Convention.

Srivats joined Wheels India in 1994. He is a fourth generation member of the family. His father S Ram, the Chairman, built up the company from scratch. Till the mid-nineties its customers were mostly Indian companies. Maruti was the only exception. By 1995, MNCs like Ford entered the picture. Says Srivats, *"I remember people from Ford walking through the factory and doing the costing. If we wanted their business we had to be cost competitive to global players. That was the beginning of our journey to go global. Till the early '90s our focus was on internal market and competition. In 2000, real price competition came to India."*

A significant amount of change was taking place in cost expectations and demand. Quality improvements became absolutely necessary in all segments. In the mid-nineties cars and trucks accounted for 75 per cent of Wheels India's market. Now it is slightly over 50 per cent. Till 2010 the major changes were made around only automobiles. After that MNCs entered the commercial vehicle industry as well. There has been a change in the product mix. The tractor industry has done very well. The mining industry is another growth area.

Says Srivats, *"The world has come to India and said, we are interested in you only if you are global. The challenge for companies like ours was that they had been only catering to the mass market in India. There was a big gap between what the company manufactured and the highest end products in the world. However, in the Indian context, there were not that many high end applications required for the existing industry. So we have had to resolve these issues and look at our market as a global one."*

The company seriously started building on areas where it could be a global leader. *"We are one of the largest wheel manufacturers in terms of volumes for tractors, mining and construction equipment in the world. We are seen as efficient and quality focused. But we are also seen as low cost. We must be seen as cost effective volume supplier. That is the challenge."* Srivats says that in this market to become a technology leader is also a challenge.

Wheels India has been supplying to Japan, Korea and Brazil for the last 15 years. The first five years were difficult. Over the years strong relationships have been built up with Korea and Japan. With Brazil, it has always been a struggle, with their high duties and local content rules. It is difficult to compete with the Chinese on costs. *"We have to learn to provide service. We are identified with the Asia Pacific region. We have to break the shackles of being seen as an Asia Pacific supplier although we export to many countries in the world."*

Srivats says his aspirations have been forced by circumstances. *"There are challenges in a legacy company which has a history. Sometimes inheritance is more of a burden than a positive."* He is constantly trying to figure out how to remain entrepreneurial. How he can get his people to grow the business. He says he has learnt to imbibe it from people who work for him. *"We give enough room for them to have ideas. It is an employee who suggested that we make components for the wind energy sector. This has worked out well. Another has been exploring putting up a unit in China. We have to experiment."*

In the meanwhile there are new challenges. MNC presence in the auto component industry has increased. For the first time Wheels India is facing internal competition from MNCs like Mexion and AMW. Pricing is not an issue for them till they capture the market.

Srivats says Wheels India's domain knowledge, field experience, and the ability to offer products which provide value to customers will help the company stay ahead. He knows he has to rely more and more on R&D. All the buyers want to commoditise components. *"We have to learn to differentiate. Technology can solve this issue. So far we have managed."*

TVS Logistics

Dinesh Ramachandran, Joint Managing Director, TVS & Sons, Managing Director, TVS Logistics Services Limited, great grandson of the founder, is a true example of how much the TVS group has changed. He comes from the Madurai side of the family considered more conservative than those who migrated to Chennai. TVS & Sons, the holding company of the group, is still based in Madurai and runs the group's dealership and spare parts distribution businesses.

Till 1997, Dinesh had been working with the businesses directly controlled by the family such as real estate, dealership, and distribution. He was in his early thirties and was ready to look beyond Madurai. S Ravichandran, who had been the regional manager of Mahindra & Mahindra (M&M) came back from Nigeria that year. Dinesh knew Ravichandran very well as TVS had the dealership of M&M products. Dinesh with Ravichandran (who was roped in to work on new projects) decided to look at logistics as a business seriously. He had already been exposed to concepts like warehousing and aftermarket due to dealing with various UK companies in those fields.

Dinesh and Ravichandran examined various models and decided to start with third party logistics. TVS Logistics was launched in Faridabad. *"The big breakthrough came when Ford gave us their entire supply chain to handle. At that point we didn't know whether we had the capability to take this on. We had had no exposure to some of the elements of work offered to us. Ford too was not sure whether we could on our own offer them a solution. We decided to go through the joint venture route. Ford helped us form an alliance with three other service providers with whom they had worked in Brazil. These were US/UK based companies. Soon we found that there was no ongoing or real value being provided by these companies and we acquired their stake in the JV."*

In 2003, Suresh Krishna, the Chairman of the company and Dinesh's uncle, told him that if he had to go global, he needed to develop a global model and stay focused on the auto sector.. As a first step, Dinesh went for a joint venture in Thailand. *"We took 60 per cent and they retained 40. It was a warehousing company. Around this time Indian companies started going global. We got a small share of Ford's American business."*

In 2004, a UK company came up for sale and Dinesh wanted to bid for that. That's when it was decided to spin Logistics off as a separate company. Till then it was a subsidiary of TVS & Sons. This was the first game changer for Dinesh. *"I now had the freedom to grow and expand. We bought that UK company. We were learning how to run a big business. We were developing entrepreneur strategies, acquiring financial focus, separating ownership from management. We were the first TVS company to give shares to employees. We were also growing at 30 to 40 per cent, but were still a ₹120 crore company."*

In early 2007 Dinesh knew that the time had come to go truly global. *"We decided to go in for PE funding. We spent a few months learning what PE is all about. The representative from Goldman Sachs explained what is good for us. TVS Logistics was the first group company to attract private equity."*

TVS Logistics already had two small units in UK and a company in Thailand. *"I realised that we can learn a lot from UK which can be applied here in India as well. We had to make an acquisition in UK. The investors wanted to know who I had in mind. I had done my due diligence. I said we need a company like Multiparts. Three weeks later I got a call saying they are up for sale. We got $25 million from Goldman Sachs. This was the next big change."*

It was the largest overseas acquisition by an Indian company in end to end supply chain management services. Multipart Holding is among the top three aftermarket logistics companies in UK. For decades, Multipart was engaged in the distribution of vehicle parts for Leyland, UK. In 1993, it became a separate company and grew to provide aftermarket logistics services to its automotive clients and UK's defence sector besides tapping the emerging utility sector.

TVS Logistics invested in excess of ₹125 crore in Multipart to expand operations in UK and rest of Europe. *"We had to address a lot of issues. The biggest learning was how to be a multinational. Acquisitions won't teach you to run your business. We said we will learn from them. We will use that knowledge."*

It turned out to be a successful acquisition. Indian customers were growing global and global companies were bringing something to India. From Multipart, TVS Logistics learnt non-auto business as the UK company was dealing in defence parts. *"The acquisition route helps you learn people management. I don't mind being humble. I believe in feedback sessions to assess what we did right and wrong. We listen to everybody, employees, JV partners and customers."*

TVS Logistics made its first buy in the US when it acquired Manufacturers Equipment and Supply Company (MESCO) in 2011. Then it got itself a second company in the US, Missouri-headquartered Wainwright Industries, an end-to-end supply chain provider. Wainwright is a 65-year-old company, and has a sales turnover of $20 million. It has two plants in the US, and employs around 300 people, has around 13 major clients, including General Motors. TVS Logistics decided to retain the existing management in this instance as well.

Dinesh felt it was time to look at a few companies in India. He was wondering whether to opt for the IPO route or go for PE funding. *"Then we got our second round of funding with KKR coming in. We have proper alignment with private equity. They have always been supportive. Working with them has given me a new perspective."* The money raised through the second round of PE funding will largely go to continue its expansion both through acquisitions and organic growth.

TVS Logistics was started from scratch in 1999. It has become a multinational on the way. Now it has to face a multiplicity of issues. They are in a low margin business. The costs must be right. Dinesh has to figure out how to grow it profitably. There are three tiers in the supply chain before you reach out to a producer. The processes have to be just right. However in India surprises keep getting thrown up as proper processes are lacking.

Dinesh is not fazed by all this. Today 55 per cent of TVS Logistics' income comes from overseas. If the company hadn't acquired companies overseas, profits would have been lower. *"That was our biggest game changer"*, he says. His focus is 20 per cent growth and 20 per cent Return on Equity year on year. Ultimately income has to come 50 per cent from auto business and 50 per cent from the non-auto business.

"We are on track", he says.

Sundaram Finance

Sundaram Finance Ltd., is one of the oldest and largest non-banking companies in the country. It literally set the norms for finance companies. When it celebrated its 60th anniversary in 2015, one of its long standing customers placed a ₹60 lakh fixed deposit with the company as a birthday gift. The activities of the group span savings products like deposits and mutual funds, car and commercial vehicle finance, insurance, home loans, software solutions, BPO, tyre finance, fleet cards, tractor finance and mutual funds. Sundaram Finance has a nation-wide presence with 586 branches, with the farthest branch in the North just fifty kilometres from the Wagah border.

The company's disbursements during the year 2013-14 were lower by 3% at ₹9719 crore, reflecting the sharp and prolonged downturn in the automotive sector. Sale of Medium and Heavy Commercial Vehicles which is the backbone of the company's business registered a steep fall of 25% compared to the previous year, while light commercial vehicle sales declined by 18%.

However, Sundaram Finance was able to retain its market share in its key asset segments. The gross receivables managed by the Company, grew by 3% and stood at ₹18158 crore on March 2014. The company's asset quality remains one of the best in the industry, in spite of the challenging macro environment. Gross and net NPAs as at was 1.23% and 0.45%, respectively, based on the stringent 120 day NPA classification norm adopted by the company, as against the regulatory norm of 180 days. The net profit from operations was ₹442.51 crore as against ₹410.11 crore in the previous year, registering a growth of 8%. The net accretion to public deposits during the year 2013-14, was ₹188.58 crores, the second highest ever in any financial year, taking the deposits outstanding at the year end to ₹1665.57crore. The company's asset portfolio has consistently been the best in the industry.

When the company's legendary founder TS Santhanam (son of the founder TV Sundaram Iyengar) decided to set up Sundaram Finance in Chennai, it was an answer to a felt need. Santhanam said he was pressurised by truck and bus operators to get into this business. He wanted to help small and medium operators who formed the bulk of road transport industry. Bank finance was not available to them. The TVS Group was then a dealer of vehicles and components. He had taken the group into insurance in 1948 itself by starting Madras Motor Insurance which after nationalisation became part of United India Insurance. Sundaram Finance came into existence in 1954 as a subsidiary of the insurance company. The first few years saw Sundaram Finance set standards for hire purchase industry. Those were really the pioneering years – bringing uniformity of practices, documentation and transparency in this business.

The company welcomed deposits in the early years and gained the reputation of always protecting the depositors' interests. So much so that nothing has ever shaken investor confidence in it. There has never been a whiff of scandal about Sundaram Finance. Deposits alone were not sufficient to run a growing finance company. Santhanam felt that the company needed to have financing from the State Bank of India. The RBI rules forbade the SBI from lending to hire purchase companies. Finally the Hire Purchase Act was changed to give loans to these companies based on receivables. Sundaram Finance was the only company which enjoyed this facility with the SBI for years. Graduallly the way SFL functioned became standard operating procedure for others. Says R Thyagarajan, Founder, Shriram Group, *"I have followed quite a few of their practices. They have shown a remarkable quantum of trust in their customers."*

Almost the entire road transport industry was and continues to be governed by the Motor Vehicles Act of 1938. According to Santhanam, this piece of legislation was meant to curtail road transport to prevent it from competing with railways. It was due to his determined effort that many changes were made to this act and road transport started getting its due.

The company which was started with a paid-up capital of ₹2.00 Lakhs went public (its first and only public issue) in 1972 raising ₹28 lakhs. The TVS group decided to exit from the finance business as Santhanam's brothers were not comfortable with it. The TVS Group and Sundaram Finance have continued to support each other but the management remained wholly under Santhanam. The company expanded its operations to the four southern states in this decade.

In the 80's, Sundaram Finance entered leasing in collaboration with International Financial Corporation. At one point almost one-third of Sundaram Finance's income came from its leasing activities. True to its principles, it never used this activity as a tax shelter as many did. Its rigid stand used to irritate many in the industry. In a span of two years, fourteen companies jumped into leasing and raised funds through IPOs. They differed from Sundaram Finance in their methods of funding, calculating depreciation, and tax planning. They did not think Sundaram Finance's approach would work in the leasing industry. As it happened many of these leasing companies were to fall by the wayside with all kinds of malpractices creeping in and the government and the RBI coming down heavily on them.

Sticking to its principles was to bring a lot of recognition to the company. In 1988, its fixed deposit programme was given the highest rating of FAAA by CRISIL. It was the first NBFC to get this award. Two years later, it was again the first NBFC in India to issue Commercial Paper to the value of ₹10 crore. CRISIL gave it the highest rating of P1+.

In the 80's the company came out of its southern shell and started spreading its wings all over India. In the next decade, after India opened up Sundaram Finance went into various diversifications. *"These diversifications were also a response to a felt need. "When we did an extensive market survey in 1997, our customers wanted us to enter areas like housing finance, insurance,auto finance and so on. Diversifications and joint ventures happened during this period."* says TT Srinivasa

Raghavan, Managing Director, Sundaram Finance. "*With global giants entering India we also had to take these steps.*" explains S Viji, Chairman. It was always assumed that Sundaram Finance with its solid reputation and strengths will apply for a banking licence. But it did not do so. "*We have done many studies and have realised that banking is not going to work for us. There are no compelling reasons for us to enter banking.*" says Viji.

If one hears a criticism at all about Sundaram Finance, it is about its glacial pace of growth.

'After liberalisation, it should have really taken off. For a company of its stature, ₹16000 assets under management is too low', is the view of many in the financial industry. "*We didn't celebrate when we were the largest NBFC in the country. Nor do we grieve if we are not the number one.*" says Srinivasa Raghavan. "*We have not strayed from what we know best. We do not want to be all things to all people. Most important is our commitment to values. We follow the Sundaram way. It hasn't always been easy. In this business, being conservative is not a weakness. We work hard to enhance value for customers, employees, and shareholders consistently over a long period of time.*"

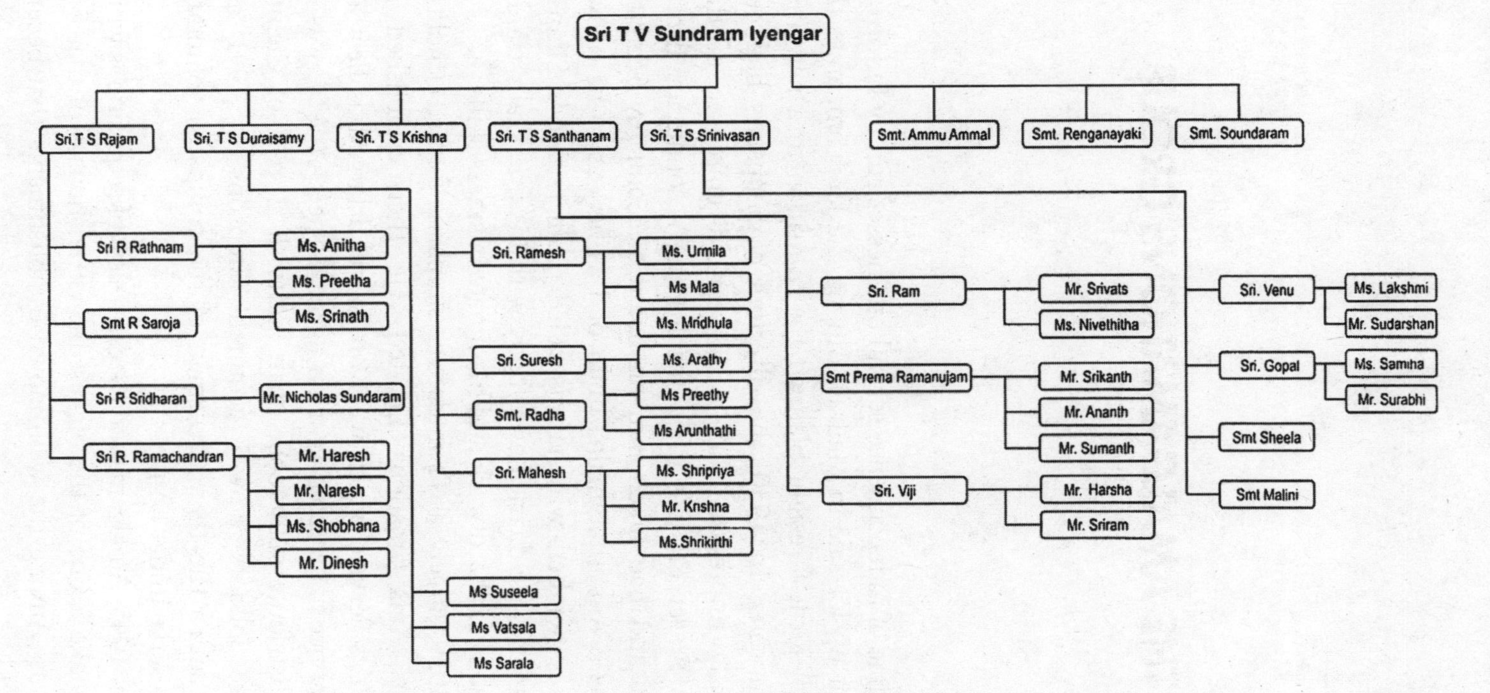

Sri T V Sundram Iyengar
Sri.T S Rajam
Sri. T S Duraisamy
Sri. T S Krishna
Sri. T S Santhanam
Sri. T S Srinivasan
Smt. Ammu Ammal
Smt. Renganayaki
Smt. Soundaram
Sri R Rathnam
Ms. Anitha
Ms. Preetha
Ms. Srinath
Smt R Saroja
Sri R Sridharan
Mr. Nicholas Sundaram
Sri R. Ramachandran
Mr. Haresh
Mr. Naresh
Ms. Shobhana
Mr. Dinesh
Ms Suseela
Ms Vatsala
Ms Sarala
Sri. Ramesh
Ms. Urmila
Ms Mala
Ms. Mridhula
Sri. Suresh
Ms. Arathy
Ms Preethy
Ms Arunthathi
Smt. Radha
Sri. Mahesh
Ms. Shripriya
Mr. Knshna
Ms.Shrikirthi
Sri. Ram
Mr. Srivats
Ms. Nivethitha
Smt Prema Ramanujam
Mr. Srikanth
Mr. Ananth
Mr. Sumanth
Sri. Viji
Mr. Harsha
Mr. Sriram
Sri. Venu
Ms. Lakshmi
Mr. Sudarshan
Sri. Gopal
Ms. Samina
Mr. Surabhi
Smt Sheela
Smt Malini

THE AMALGAMATIONS GROUP

At the time of independence several businesses run by Europeans were put up for sale in Madras. Among the few companies that had with great foresight planned the transition to a new India was Simpsons. In 1930, the directors of Simpsons had been sufficiently impressed with a 30-year-old employee of their auditors Fraser & Ross (then the leading accountancy firm of Madras), and had taken him on board as Company Secretary. This was S Anantharamakrishnan or J as he was to be known. Nobody remembers why he was called J, but J's rise in Simpson was meteoric. He dazzled everybody with his financial wizardry, his capacity for hard work and his innate business skills.

In 1939, largely at J's initiative, Simpsons formed a holding company, Amalgamations Limited. He then established Sri Rama Vilas Service which went on to run a large bus fleet and cargo service. The same year an agency, Speed-A-Way, was set up to distribute automobile spare parts. It is part of Chennai corporate folklore how J acquired Simpsons in 1941 and W W Ladden the then Chairman of the company, voluntarily opted to serve under him.

From 1945, Amalgamations began a slew of acquisitions which would make it one of the biggest industrial houses of that time in Madras. Among the well-known establishments that became part of Amalgamations at this time were Addison, George Oakes, Higginbothams, Associated Printers and *The Madras Mail*. J was a true visionary who realised that after independence, it would be necessary to go into manufacturing. He started units to make paints, pistons, batteries and tractors among other things. In 1961, he acquired interests in several plantations.

J passed away in 1964. He left a highly diversified business house which featured among the top twenty in the country. He would not have dreamt that his death would put his children and business in deep trouble. When J died without leaving a will, a duty of ₹2.5 crore was slapped on the estate which took five years to clear. With this kind of liability it was not possible for the group to raise finance for new projects.

As a result, it has always been seen as an arch conservative inward looking, unadventurous South Indian group. No one seems to remember that circumstances forced it to be so. Circumstances also enabled it to emerge a financially strong group eventually. It has held together in spite of the several crises it has been confronted with.

As soon as it settled the estate duty, Amalgamations had to face industrial unrest which turned ugly and violent in the '70s. This brought the group to a standstill for two years. Then there was a disastrous diversification into truck manufacture in the late seventies in collaboration with Ford. The group was on the lookout for an end product for the diesel engines Simpsons was making. It was also a time when both Telco (Tata Motors) and Ashok Leyland trucks were selling at very high premiums. The company started assembling 7.5 tonne load vehicles. The founder's older son, A Sivasailam, who took over as Chairman said in an interview to Business India, *"We were planning for a 60 per cent overload, but the Indian truck drivers were carrying 22 tonnes and 25 tonnes."* The losses were around ₹18 to 20 crore which was a huge amount then.

Sivasailam explained that only by retaining control and imposing strict financial discipline did the group emerge from the Ford fiasco. *"We absorbed the loss incurred by Simpsons without hampering the growth of individual companies. Each company was allowed to retain profits and use it for its growth. TAFE's growth helped Simpson's diesel division grow. Simpsons gained from increased dividends from the subsidiaries"*, he says.

Today, the Amalgamations Group is one of India's larger light engineering groups, comprising of 41 companies, with a turnover exceeding $2 billion. TAFE is the flagship company and is the star of the show. The other well-known names are Simpsons, India Pistons, I P Rings, Bimetal Bearings, Amco, Addison and The United Nilgiri Tea Estates Company Ltd. Apart from the fact that India Pistons has been losing market share steadily, many of the others are solid performers but they don't particularly sparkle. Amalgamations remains a solid business group which is yet to realise its true potential.

It is among the largest privately held business houses in the country. Some companies are listed because the group had no option but to do so. Bimetal Bearings went public in 1978 because it had to bring down its foreign shareholding. The holding company Amalgamations Pvt. Ltd. was run by the founder's sons Sivasailam and Krishnamurthy. They were the Chairman and Vice Chairman of the group. After Sivasailam passed away his brother-in-law N Venkatramani became a board member and Vice Chairman with Krishnamurthy taking over as Chairman. The shares of the holding company are divided equally among Anantharamakrishnan's four children, his two sons and two daughters. Krishnamurthy, the Chairman, is involved in Simpsons, Bimetal Bearings and Shardlow.

Each company in the group is managed by its own board. One of Anantharamakrishnan's sons-in-law KS Sundaram ran Addisons Paints & Chemicals and the associated companies. The other son-in-law Venkatramani heads the India Pistons group of companies. Sundaram and his son Shankar Sundaram feel that the Group did not support them with enough working capital to take on growing competition (Asian Paints) and implement changing trends. Addisons has closed shutters and this side of the family is isolated from the others.

In comparison to many other business families, the Amalgamations group is very small. The third generation consists of Mallika Srinivasan (married to Venu Srinivasan of the TVS group) who runs TAFE and the highly successful plantation companies. Her younger sister Jayashree Venkatramani passed away in 2012. Venkatramani's two sons are working with India Pistons and associated companies. Both Mallika's children work with their father Venu Srinivasan in his companies.

Daughter Lakshmi Venu started early at Sundaram-Clayton and has worked in group companies taking on various roles. She has done stints in business strategy, design, corporate affairs, and sales and marketing at TVS Motors. She is a graduate from Yale University and a PhD in engineering management from University of Warwick. She joined the group in 2010. Lakshmi was inducted as Director—Strategy and wholetime Director of Sundaram-Clayton. In May 2011, she was also made Vice-President in charge of global business strategy at Sundaram-Clayton.

Mallika's son Sudarshan Venu is Joint Managing Director of TVS Motor Company. He works under his father, Chairman and Managing Director of TVS Motors, Venu Srinivasan. Sudarshan, who graduated with Honors after pursuing the Jerome Fisher Programme in Management and Technology at the University of Pennsylvania, also has a Bachelor of Science degree in Mechanical Engineering and a Bachelor's degree in Science and Economics from the Wharton School. He completed his Master's in International Technology Management from the Warwick Manufacturing Group, at the University of Warwick, UK.

TAFE—The Success Story

The Amalgamations Group made its entry into the Forbes India Rich List, at No. 47 recently. The closely held group does not publish its results. Says Forbes "*Its entry was based on the performance of TAFE, now India's second-largest tractor company. Rising demand for mechanisation as a result of the falling availability of labour has given TAFE a good year (Tractor sales increased by 22 per cent in 2013–14). Also, backed by its US partner, AGCO Corp (which has a 24 per cent stake), TAFE has been able to grow exports faster than its rivals. The company, now India's largest small tractor exporter, has opened a new manufacturing facility in China which will serve as its global base."*

TAFE was founded in 1960. Simpsons in the group was already making Perkins Diesel Engines. Anantharamakrishnan had the vision to see opportunities in agriculture opening up with the green revolution in the making. He decided to make tractors when the opportunity presented itself.

Standard Motors had been assembling Massey Ferguson tractors in India for Massey Ferguson India, which was Bangalore based. Massey Ferguson was looking for a company that would, in a phased manner, manufacture its tractors in India which led to the Amalgamations Group taking over the Bangalore operations of Standard Motors and moving it to Chennai. The new company was called Tractors and Farm Equipment Limited (TAFE).

In 1960, the estimated demand for tractors in India was 12000 tractors per year and TAFE was allocated a capacity of 7000 tractors a year. Initially 50 per cent of the tractor was built with indigenous content but within two years this rose to 85 per cent. From these early beginnings TAFE has risen to a turnover of US $1.6 billion and a sale of over 180,000 tractors (domestic and international) apart from the distinction of being India's largest exporter of tractors.

TAFE is the third largest tractor manufacturer in the world and the second largest in India by volumes, with a 25 per cent market share in the country. It has had a partnership with AGCO Corporation and the Massey Ferguson brand for 52 years. The company has three tractor brands—Massey Ferguson, TAFE and Eicher. It exports tractors in partnership with AGCO and independently to over 82 countries including countries in Europe and the Americas.

With its acquisition of Eicher's tractor business and engines plant in 2005, TAFE has four tractor plants in India, an engines plant and two engineering plastics units besides other facilities, employing over 2500 engineers apart from a number of specialists in other disciplines. TAFE's R&D facilities are centres of excellence, recognised by the Centre of Scientific & Industrial Research, Ministry of Science and Technology.

TAFE's first overseas plant in Turkey went onstream in 2010 and it manufactures a range of tractors for distribution in Turkey through AGCO's dealer network.

The company in true South Indian style keeps winning quality awards. TAFE has also received the commendation for '*Significant Achievement on the journey towards Business Excellence*' by the CII-EXIM Bank Business Excellence Award jury in 2012.

Mallika Srinivasan took over as the Chairman of TAFE, when her father Sivasailam passed away in 2011. TAFE had a turnover of ₹85 crore when Mallika joined the family business in 1986. Today, it is the second-largest farm equipment manufacturer in the country, the market leader being Mahindra & Mahindra. The gap between the number one and number two narrowed considerably when TAFE acquired Eicher Tractors in 2005. Then it widened again when M&M took over Punjab Tractors Limited in 2007.

Does Mallika aim to be number one? For her it has been an interesting journey getting where she and TAFE have reached. She would rather talk about the fact that the company is number one in terms of exports. *"We have market leadership in key markets in Southeast Asia. We are world number two when you take small tractors (below 100 HP). In terms of profitability, we are number one."*

How do they pull off this performance with exports when they face strong competition from international players everywhere? *"We have different strategies for different parts of the world. In Asia, we service our markets directly. We also leverage our partnership with AGCO, a leading global manufacturer of a full line of agricultural equipment. In Turkey, we take care of production, product development, stock management and R&D. AGCO handles the sales. Ours is a very equal long-standing partnership. My father focused on long term relationships."* Mallika has been quietly buying shares in AGCO and has invested half a billion dollars in that company. She is on their boards.

The Eicher acquisition has worked very well for TAFE, giving it the range of products it needed and the all-important geographical spread. After the takeover, TAFE put in a lot of effort to build the Eicher brand. Wrestler Sushil Kumar was made the brand ambassador in 2012. Both the Massey Ferguson and Eicher brands are more than 50 years old. "*We believe in the pull of new products. In spite of the cyclical nature of the industry, we continue to invest in products, processes and people. We have also made substantial investments in IT and manufacturing,*" Mallika says. The company has repeatedly won awards for innovation.

Mallika herself has been given every award possible for women in business. She became the President of the Tractor Manufacturers Association when she was not yet thirty. She says that the older members were welcoming and she learnt a lot from them. "*There was a collegiate atmosphere.*" She also says that there was no pressure on either her or her sister to enter the family business. Her parents made sure that they received a good education. Mallika is an MBA from Wharton which gave her a different perspective of how to do business. Her children also have solid degrees from prestigious universities in the US and UK.

"*Once I joined TAFE, all my father said was that I should make a success of whatever I did and that I must grow. When I entered the business some senior people taught me the ropes. There was a senior executive who didn't quite trust me. When I was able to push through his favourite idea, he opened up. My parents and husband were a great support. The elements of success are the same whether you are a man or a woman, whether you are in automobiles, engineering or retail. Manufacturing and selling cosmetics must be just as difficult as producing and selling tractors. You should enjoy what you are doing.*"

Mallika has worked hard for this success. She might have inherited a business, but she did it at a time when running a business in India was not easy. In the mid-eighties there were elements of price control for the tractor industry. Liberalisation was still a few years away and in its wake multinational tractor giants were to enter the country. When the country opened up TAFE had to recast itself and change its approach. "*You have to have a clear vision and goal. You have to constantly moderate your approach. You have to understand how to make a difference.*"

TAFE had good products, good partnerships, and was known for its quality standards. Mallika says that the strategy evolved with the realisation that India was a land of small farms which had to be mechanised. International players were used to vast acreages. They had all pulled out of developing countries as they did not have the technology for smaller acreage. "*We knew we had to offer appropriate products and processes. We were developing a new set of skills which opened up new markets.*"

TAFE had to build its own business model. A tight-knit family group, it cannot go public. It does not borrow. It is conservative and risk averse. "*We learnt to build competency, scale, and invest in technology and people within these constraints. Our capex is low, we sweat our assets. The value system my father believed in helped. We follow prudent financial management. We strictly adhere to ethical behavior. We sacrificed growth in the early years to build a sustainable model. Our foundation is strong. We learnt to be patient and build the organization brick by brick.*" By 2000, some scale and size had been built up. The company started winning quality and productivity awards. However, between 2000 and 2004, the tractor market crashed. TAFE's numbers dropped from 48000 tractors to 24000. "*But we didn't make a loss. We emerged leaner and meaner and were ready for aggressive growth.*" When Delhi-based Eicher Tractors came up for sale, TAFE made a successful bid for it. "*It was a good fit. There was no cannibalization of market share. In 2005, Eicher made a profit of ₹15 crore. In 2012–13 it was ₹287 crore. We paid ₹350 crore for it.*"

Mallika is a great admirer of the NREGA programme. India is growing. Consumers want more fruits and vegetables and high-end food products. Health and nutrition are becoming more important in people's lives. This iconic scheme is going to boost mechanisation in agriculture, consumption and productivity, she believes. "*In farm mechanisation we will follow the latest trends. We will be introducing new products every three months. Today's profits are essential for tomorrow's prosperity. This is my responsibility.*"

The Other Companies

TAFE is the star and the stardust rubs off on all the others. Simpsons and TAFE have a symbiotic relationship. Simpsons, a pioneer in diesel engine manufacturing, supplies to TAFE. Coimbatore-based Bimetal Bearings apart from TAFE has a large customer base in the automotive sector. This company has a turnover of around ₹900 crore and is very profitable. India Pistons, IP Rings and some smaller companies in this category have a collective turnover of around ₹800 crore. This lot has been struggling because of the slowdown in the industry. AMCO Batteries is the other laggard. Addisons which is making cutting tools is another little gem. The trading companies and the plantations are all doing very well. Whether the manufacturing companies will expand and become global, time alone can tell.

AMALGAMATIONS GROUP

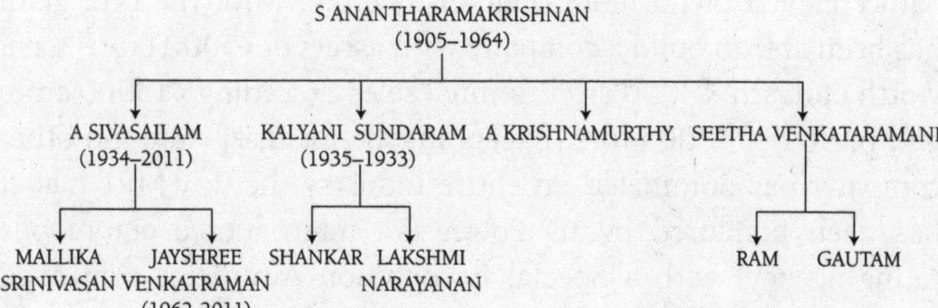

MRF

MRF is the 15th largest tyre company in the world. With an equity capital of no more than ₹4.24 crore, MRF the tyre giant has been able to build a company with assets of ₹5000 crore, a net worth of nearly ₹3000 crore, annual sales exceeding ₹13000 crore and profits of ₹800 crore. Except maybe for Bajaj Auto, no other company has dominated an entire industry the way MRF has. It has been honoured by JD Power (an international automobile rating agency) with a Special Recognition Award for continued outstanding performance. Its Chairman and Managing Director KM Mammen (older son of founder Mammen Mappillai) has also been honoured with a Special Recognition Award by JD Power for Customer Satisfaction. MRF has also won the Ford Excellence silver award and is the only Indian company to win this.

It has tyres rolling out of six interdependent facilities built across 450 acres, a 3000 strong dealer network and 180 different offices. MRF has also made its presence known globally across 65 different countries. MRF is recognised for its drive towards continuous quality improvement and customer satisfaction and has won the JD Power award not once but 10 times. It has also won the TNS and CAPEXIL awards for being voted as the most trusted tyre company in India.

When Mammen Mappillai, Founder Chairman of MRF finished college, he wanted to start a small industry and the simplest venture he could think of was a toy balloon factory. He came from the family which owns the Malayala Manorama group, the media giant in Kerala. He was one of six brothers. The family also invested in rubber plantations.

In 1946, when Mammen embarked on this business, toy balloons were imported and the market was flooded with cheap

Japanese balloons which did not compare in quality with the English makes. A good product could therefore sell well. The story of a balloon maker building the company's largest tyre company is now a corporate legend.

With an initial investment of ₹10,000, the balloon factory came into existence on a 12 acre plot at Tiruvottiyur, a suburb of Chennai. During the first year itself, the turnover was ₹60,000, a large amount then. From toy balloons, the firm progressed into the manufacture of latex goods, such as gloves, feeding bottle teats, rubber thread and items made out of foam rubber. In the early fifties the emphasis shifted to dry rubber goods like shoe heels. In the next stage, the firm expanded to moulded articles like rubber rings, stoppers, moulded engineering goods and rubber belting.

In 1953, Kurien Abraham of the Calicut Tyre and Retreading Company came to MRF with a proposal to manufacture retreading material. The raw material required for retreading, namely, tread rubber, was produced by multinational tyre companies like Dunlop, Goodyear, and Firestone. There were also 14 Indian rubber goods manufacturers making tread rubber. However, since the company had a ready buyer in Abraham, Mammen decided to take the plunge.

When Mammen went abroad in 1954 he realised that the multinationals were extruding the retreading compound while Indians were sheeting it out on open nets. The same process was then used at home and yielded good results. The firm invested in some testing equipment which was imported from Germany and conducted a fair amount of R&D to produce a superior quality of tread rubber. By 1955, production doubled. Very soon the firm was producing nearly 200,000 pounds of tread rubber per annum.

During this time, in order to kill competition from local industry, the multinationals slashed prices, which dipped from ₹3 and 14 annas per pound to ₹1 and 14 annas per pound within a period of six months. Most of the Indian manufacturers started to make heavy losses, quality suffered and customers began to lose confidence in their products. MRF maintained its quality in spite of being in a difficult position. In the meanwhile, the government was bombarded by the local industry about MNCs who were hurting them. An inquiry was conducted into the cost of tyres and the outcome of this was price control for the tyre industry. The result was that prices were slashed by 15 per cent.

The multinationals had no money thereafter to subsidise the killing of the Indian sector as the price of tread rubber had to be raised.

From then on, growth was substantial. By the end of the 1950s the firm became one of the largest manufacturers of tread rubber with a market share of 50 per cent. After that it was a natural progression into tyres. In 1962, the plant for manufacture of automobile tyres at Tiruvottiyur was commissioned. In 1962, it also went public. During the same year, the company entered into a financial-cum-technical collaboration agreement with the Mansfield Tyre & Rubber Company, Ohio, USA. *"One of the early partners in the MRF tyre operations, it held almost the same percentage of shares as our family,"* said Mammen in an interview to *Business India*.

The Mansfield connection had its advantages. Mansfield felt that nylon was the right material for tyre manufacture. Since no other manufacturer had used nylon at that time it gave MRF a definite advantage. Unfortunately Mansfield met with difficult times in the US and finally ceased to exist. The entire foreign equity participation was bought over and distributed among the existing shareholders on a pro rata basis, at a lower rate than the existing one, as per the government formula.

In 1980, MRF entered into a technical collaboration with BF Goodrich Company USA. BF Goodrich was taken over by Michelin in the 1980s. MRF wanted Michelin's technology and Michelin wanted a stake in MRF. Finally after much negotiation, 9.08 per cent of the equity was given to the French company in 1992 and 30 per cent was retained with the family.

The association with Michelin was an uneasy one. Michelin believed in a stake of 51 per cent wherever it had a joint venture. MRF didn't quite get this when they tied up with Michelin. In 1993, in what was seen as a takeover bid, Michelin started picking up MRF shares through local parties and FIs. MRF warded off the attempt with the help of FIs who had a 22 per cent holding in the company. The Mammens also got the Finance Ministry's approval to raise their stake in the company to a much more comfortable 40 per cent through a preferential allotment.

After aborting the takeover bid, Michelin eventually sold their 9 per cent stake to the MRF Employees Trust. MRF's tiny share capital of ₹4.24 crore is among the lowest in the country for a large company. And it has remained almost the same size for many years because the family is worried that any expansion of the capital will mean a dilution of their controlling stake. *"Unlike other promoter families, the Mammens have not taken money out of the company as a result of which they don't have much money outside the company, the kind that is necessary to subscribe to their portion of a rights issue if MRF had one,"* says an analyst.

After its collaboration with the French tyre giant Michelin came unstuck in 1994, it took a firm decision to go it alone. Mammen felt that at a time when one could get technology off the shelf it was pointless tying MRF up with a collaborator.

In spite of its troubles with Michelin by the '90s, MRF raced ahead of others with a turnover of ₹1,540 crore, for the year ending September 1995, the up 35 per cent from the previous year. For two years in a row MRF was polled by the readers of *Far Eastern Economic Review*, as one of Asia's 200 most promising companies and among India's top 10, the only south-based company to make the list. Almost all the new automobile units which were entering the country started knocking at MRF's doors first. MRF tyres were the first tyres selected for Maruti Suzuki 800 when it was launched.

Although MRF was the market leader in the car tyres market, there was a perception that it was lagging behind in the fast growing radial tyres segment. JK Industries was the market leader with a 30 per cent share in the mid-nineties. MRF which had a 19 per cent share, put up a new radial tyre factory at its Pondicherry facilities and caught up fast. Of the 38 lakh passenger car tyres produced in 1996–97, radial tyres accounted for about 45 per cent. This segment was dominated by MRF. By the end of the decade with the arrival of the international models, the usage of radial tyres took a quantum jump. Except for Mercedes, all other car manufacturers, including GM and Ford, have been buying MRF Radial tyres. Mitsubishi Lancer and Honda City also opted for MRF.

MRF has built up tremendous distributor loyalty over the years. An early move into nylon tyres combined with this vast dealer distribution network helped it consolidate its shares in commercial vehicle segment, supplying mainly to the replacement market has helped it survive the ups and downs of the commercial vehicle cycle. Pricing power in replacement market is quite high because sales are to end users rather than OEMs. As much as 76 per cent of the company's top line comes from the replacement market, which is likely to see a steady rate of growth due to a sustained rise in the absolute number of vehicles on the road.

Apart from replacement demand, MRF has also been helped by a wide product range that caters to medium and heavy commercial vehicles, passenger cars, motorcycles and light commercial vehicles. After consolidating its presence in the automobile industry, MRF is now rolling out tyres for Indian Air Force Sukhoi-30 range of aircraft.

With raw material costs accounting for 70 per cent of sales, access to natural rubber supplies are critical to tyre manufacturers. MRF has been able to capitalise fully on its access to cheap sources of natural rubber, thanks to its rubber plantations in Kerala.

MRF is known to be notoriously publicity shy. Its Chairman rarely gives an interview. But it has cleverly built up its brand by associating itself with cricket and motorsports, which gives it enormous visibility on TV. The MRF Pace Foundation has trained bowlers such as Irfan Pathan, Munaf Patel, RP Singh, Brett Lee, Shoaib Akhtar, Glenn McGrath and many more. Dennis Lillee was the Director of the Foundation when it was set up in 1987. When he stepped down, Glenn McGrath took over.

MRF is involved in racing, karting, rallying and various other motorsport events. Its rallying team has won the prestigious FIA Asia Pacific Rally Championship twice and even in international championships, MRF karting tyres are the preferred choice of the the body that controls motor racing—FIA (Fédération Internationale de l'Automobile).

MRF is looking at entering global markets in both inorganic as well as organic ways. It is seriously considering putting up a green field plant abroad. However, there are a number of small to big capacity tyre plants available for acquisition across the globe. If it finds a plant with the right size at the right price without any debt and labour problems, MRF will certainly look at the option for inorganic growth. In the meanwhile it is setting up three new plants in Telangana, Tamil Nadu and Gujarat.

However, its competition isn't sitting quiet either. French tyre giant Michelin Group is spending ₹4,000 crore in setting up a manufacturing facility near Chennai. Japan's Bridgestone is pumping in ₹2,600 crore in a truck and bus radials (TBR) plant near Pune. Yokohama is constructing a ₹300-crore passenger car tyre facility at Bahadurgarh near Gurgaon. Germany's Continental AG bought the manufacturing plants of tyre unit of Modi Rubber for ₹117 crore and is investing another ₹330 crore to start production of radial tires for passenger cars and commercial vehicles.

MRF would have had a much tougher time reaching the top if the Modi family had not started squabbling with each other or the RPG family was not draining Ceat for its various takeovers, or the Chhabrias and the RPG group had not fallen out over Dunlop. Once, when one thought of tyres, Dunlop would come to one's mind. Today, most would think of MRF. The Mammen family is close knit. The third generation of Mammens have now entered the business. People jokingly refer to MRF as the Mammen Rubber factory.

Will this luck last? Most foreign manufacturers are mildly critical of MRF's quality and technology as compared to a Bridgestone or Michelin, off the record. But then MRF is a battle scarred veteran. It is certainly going to face interesting years ahead.

MRF FAMILY TREE

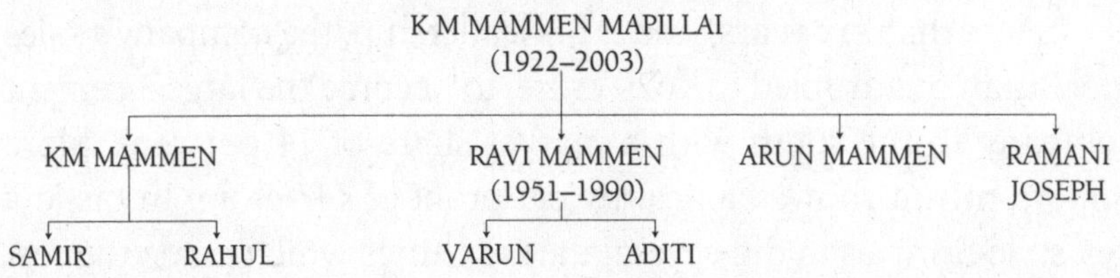

INDIA CEMENTS

India Cements, the cement industry leader in the South, has seven integrated plants in Tamil Nadu and Andhra Pradesh, one in Rajasthan and two grinding units, one each in Tamil Nadu and Maharashtra. It has a capacity of 15.5 million tonnes. It has coal mines in Indonesia, ships to carry them, and captive power plants in Tamil Nadu and Andhra. Its turnover in 2013 was ₹5310 crore.

When N Srinivasan became the Managing Director of India Cements in 1989, its balance sheet was in the red. Labour indiscipline was rampant. The organisation lacked vision, direction and leadership. Input costs were spiralling while cement prices were under pressure in a glut market situation. For most entrepreneurs, this would have been a nightmare. But for Srinivasan, it was a dream come true. He was confident of turning around a company which had once been co-promoted by his father. India Cements was one of the first cement plants to come up in the country in Tirunelveli district in Tamil Nadu in 1946. It was also the first company in India to have a public issue.

In less than six years, under his leadership, the company's sales more than quadrupled to ₹629 crore, to become the largest cement company in the south with a market share of 14 per cent. More importantly, it showed a healthy net profit of ₹47 crore. In his low key style Srinivasan did several daring things which made the rest of the country sit up and take notice. He aggressively bid for the million tonne Chilamkur cement plant of Coromandel Fertilisers Ltd. in 1990, a year after he took over the management of India Cements. The company had made an operational loss. The market was in the dumps.

Srinivasan offered ₹125 crore for a plant of 1983 vintage, which was widely believed to be suffering from structural and design defects. Given the circumstances, this was considered a rash move. *"I was prepared to pay the price to emerge as the largest cement manufacturer in the south. With it, we gained a tremendous edge in marketing and entered the big league,"* says Srinivasan.

For the kind of balance sheet the company had at that time, it required a lot of persuasion from its side to get loans from financial institutions. For the company it was a great bargain, since it neither had the funds to build a new million tonne plant, nor the time to wait through the gestation period. *"It was a calculated move, not a gamble. A lot of thought had gone into it. Our conclusions were backed by in-depth technical studies. All this is beside the point. Where I scored over others was in my grasp of the projected outlook for cement, which, thank God, proved accurate."* he maintains.

Srinivasan is the son of TS Narayanaswamy who co-promoted the company with SNN Sankaralinga Iyer, grandfather of the Chairman of the Sanmar Group, N Sankar. The company was run in the 1970s by Narayanaswamy and KS Narayanan, Sankar's father. On the untimely death of Narayanaswamy, Srinivasan, then barely out of college, was made Joint Managing Director. Subsequently, a rift resulted in the removal of Srinivasan in 1979. Though evicted, Srinivasan wouldn't give up. He went to court against his ouster and the company's annual general meetings became noisy affairs. As the battle raged, FIs which held substantial equity, took control of the company. They appointed their nominees to run India Cements.

Srinivasan was determined to get back to the company. He knew he had to get close to the powers that were in Delhi. He won friends and influenced people in Delhi. This was the time when the DMK leader Murasoli Maran became a close friend. Srinivasan has never denied his close association with Maran." *My single-minded objective was to get India Cements back,"* he has always said.

In the '80s when everybody was diversifying wildly, ITC, which was not yet a big name in hotels and other businesses decided to bid for India Cements. Cement seemed a good business to invest in for many wanting to diversify. The industry had been partially decontrolled. The institutional nominees running India Cements were all for it and ITC bought the equity holdings of LIC and UTI. *"I had to approach the courts and the Company Law Board and get this deal nullified,"* says Srinivasan. ITC finally gave back the shares to the institutions.

A decade later, the Srinivasan and Narayanan families buried their differences. Sankar was made Chairman and Srinivasan the Managing Director. Srinivasan had pulled out all stops, and finally got what he wanted. We will know how he did it when he chooses to write his story. He showed the kind of tenacity which would become the hallmark of all his activities, be it business or sports. Eventually he bought out his brother Ramachandran's and Sankar's shares to become the largest shareholder (28 per cent) in the company.

Srinivasan's comeback at ICL coincided with the time when the cement industry was waking up to total decontrol. *"I realised that we needed enormous marketing skills to face the new challenges. Plant location and nurturing of strong brands in home markets became crucial,"* he says. In the era of controls, a cement company had to merely produce cement. Equalised freight rates allowed movement across the country. But, after decontrol, cement became a freight sensitive commodity. Srinivasan and his marketing team seized the opportunity to reinforce the company's brand leadership in the south where ICL fortunately had a good distribution network.

Srinivasan showed a lot of aggression in his acquisition strategies but he kept his accounting and investment policies conservative. In October 1994, ICL raised about $49.5 million through a GDR issue. Despite difficult market conditions at that time, it was oversubscribed. It was one of the few Indian GDRs issued in 1994 to be trading above the issue price. The proceeds were spent on upgradation of Chilamkur and other units, setting up of another plant and the retiring of debts. After the Euro issue the company had enough equity to handle its debt requirements.

Srinivasan set up a shipping division in the early 1990s. That did not surprise anyone who knew him. Srinivasan's father, TS Narayanaswamy, was a pioneer of Tamil Nadu's shipping industry. He was a co-promoter of the South India Shipping Corporation (SISCO), which was in the dry bulk cargo trade. When SISCO was put up for sale in 1990, Srinivasan did not bid for it. He was committed to acquiring the Chilamkur plant from Coromandel, which was more important from ICL's core competency point of view. Eventually, the Ruias of Essar bought the stakes of the co-promoter Tarapore and the Tamil Nadu government to acquire the highly successful SISCO.

He did not rush into a diversification binge as many groups in this period did. *"We do not believe in diversification for the sake of diversification. We are also wary of entering fields unfamiliar to us. We step in only when we are sure of success."* His executives with one voice credited ICL's turnaround to the leadership and vision of Srinivasan. As Srinivasan himself put it, *"I think I have succeeded in motivating my team to perform to the best of its ability. I did it mostly by setting an example and also by involving them. The emphasis has been on application, commitment and a conservative approach."*

By 1996 ICL's turnover had gone up to ₹832-crore. It was building size. A number of acquisitions had been completed. These included its ₹198-crore bid for the public sector Cement Corporation of India's 0.4 million tonne plant at Yarraguntla in Andhra Pradesh and Visakha Cements, another Andhra-based company. Visakha was then setting up a 0.9 million tonne plant and India Cements bought out its entire equity at a cost of ₹60 crore. In addition, it had taken over Aruna Sugars Finance and Aruna Sugar's license to put up a 2,500 MT per day sugar plant in Karnataka.

The hostile takeover of Raasi Cement by India Cements that started with a bang finally ended with a whimper. Ever since Srinivasan announced his intentions to bid for Raasi Cement, its Executive Chairman, BV Raju, made noises about coming up with a counter-offer. He was all the while negotiating with Srinivasan to sell his 32 per cent shares in the company. Raju got over ₹150 crore from the sale of his shares. For Srinivasan this was a great victory. He won despite stiff opposition from the institutions.

Srinivasan's boldness in digging his heels in the face of opposition from the FIs set a new precedent for many other companies to follow. It was widely acknowledged that there was no political pressure brought upon by Srinivasan either at the centre or at the state level. Financial industry sources were delighted that these kind of M&A activities shored up the stockmarkets. Raasi, which was never a star performer on the bourses, saw its price shooting up to ₹260 from ₹60 in end-1997.

This was a time when FIs disapproved of deals which did not receive their blessings. IDBI Chairman SH Khan apparently was not keen on this takeover. He went on record saying that IDBI would not fund hostile takeovers. Many in the industry said that institutions like IDBI were so used to playing God that they found it difficult to come to terms with market realities. IDBI apparently faced a lot of pressure from Gujarat Ambuja, L&T and the Aditya Birla group to prevent the Raasi takeover by India Cements as they all wanted a larger share of the southern market.

Eventually Raasi got delisted and merged with India Cements so that the company could get the benefits of the combined operations as early as possible. As it happened India Cements also ended up acquiring the one million tonne Vishnu Cements in which Raasi had a 40 per cent stake. This was originally not a part of the deal. However, when India Cements came up with its open offer for Raasi Cement, it was discovered that the latter's entire stake in Vishnu had been sold to some of the promoter's group companies.

By August 1997, India Cements had made big investments in Raasi and its interest in the company was out in the open. At this point Raasi hurriedly convened a couple of board meetings and its shares in Vishnu were divested at ₹10 each, allegedly to Raju's friends and relations. After the takeover was completed, India Cements examined Raasi's books and found that it had violated the Sebi takeover guidelines which prohibit the target management from disposing of any asset during the open offer period. Then India Cements staked a claim to the control of Vishnu Cements complaining to SEBI that a valuable asset was stripped from the company to the detriment of Raasi's shareholders. Vishnu Cements was part of Raasi and had been sold below par. A million-tonne cement plant had been acquired for barely ₹9 crore. Srinivasan had his way. India Cements ended up acquiring Vishnu Cements as well.

In less than two years, India Cements' capacity had grown to nine million tonnes. The acquisitions cost was ₹1,600 crore and was predominantly funded by debt. What was not anticipated was that every other cement company worth its name would charge to the southern region to set up capacities before the government withdrew all sales tax-related incentives. Without these incentives no cement plant was viable at the cement prices prevailing then. Too much capacity was added which sent prices crashing. At one point a truckload of sand cost more than a truckload of cement in parts of AP. India Cements began to incur losses and its ability to service debt suffered.

By the turn of the century the company had defaulted on some of its loans. Production had to be curtailed as there was no working capital. Srinivasan sold Vishnu Cements to keep the company going. This could not resolve the crisis. He said in an interview to *Business Today*, *"We realised we were in a hole and opted for a corporate debt restructuring (CDR) scheme, which came into effect from January 2003. The CDR bought us time to focus on operations. We shed manpower (about 1,000 employees), cut production costs, sold our ships and some land."*

In September 2005, India Cements came out with a Global Depository Receipts issue while still in the CDR scheme. *"Many warned us that it was an unwise thing to do. Investors would not even look at a company that had defaulted on its debt obligations. But we went ahead and raised ₹477 crore, which was used to pay off some debt. That was the turning point."* said Srinivasan. Soon cement prices began to improve and this accelerated the company's revival. In the following years, he raised more funds from the market to finance the company's growth plans. From 2010, the cement industry has been facing problems once again. The economic slowdown had hit the company hard. According to the company's annual report, "*With the huge supply overhang in the South, the industry had to face the brunt of severe competition in the market resulting in lowering of the prices particularly in Andhra Pradesh during the second half of this fiscal. The cost of production has been impacted with the increase in the price of input materials, fly ash, gypsum, power and fuel and higher transport charges.*"

The cement industry twenty-five years ago was in a different place as most industries had been set up in the pre-liberalisation area. It was dominated by Indian giants based in the West such as ACC promoted by the Tatas. By 2004, the scene changed totally. The management control of ACC was taken over by Swiss cement major Holcim in 2004. Gujarat Ambuja which was the most celebrated cement company in the country which had tied up with L&T also sold out to Holcim. Today, the largest Indian cement company is Birla Ultratech, which is part of the Grasim Group. It took over L&T Cement.

Holcim itself has announced its merger with the French cement maker Lafarge. If the merger takes place it would dwarf every other player in the world. The industry is dominated by a lot of international players who have been picking up Indian cement companies all over the country. About 60 per cent of cement industry is controlled by four or five large players and the rest are fractured small units here and there.

In this situation can Srinivasan hold on to his company and make it profitable once again? Can he retire his company's debt? Srinivasan remains his unflappable self. He says, "*One cannot borrow all the time to grow. One cannot try and increase market share in a fractured industry with debt. In the last few years capacity has shot up from 170 million tonnes to 320 million. Maybe there will be a resurgence. Then I see a lot of M&A activity happening. It always takes much longer to set up a new plant. Let's look at the positive side. There are only eight states with limestone reserves. Tamil Nadu is one of them. Per capita cement consumption compared to the rest of the developed world is very low in India. I have a sugar company which provides 4000 tonnes of co-generation capacity. I have 25000 acres of land bank. We have invested in coal and power and shipping. In a licence free atmosphere, there are no short cuts to success."*

Is he paying as much attention to cement as he did to cricket? People who know him say he will never sell out India Cements.

THE NEW

Starting from scratch in the '80s, they have become market leaders

THE SHRIRAM GROUP

Shriram Group's focus is on financial services that reach out to a large number of common people—providing them opportunities to improve their prosperity. With its philosophy of *'Customers Are Really Everything'* (C.A.R.E.), Shriram Group has taken financial services to the doorsteps of the common man. This focus on the common man has proven to be a profitable business strategy.

Shriram Capital Limited (SCL) is the holding arm of all the financial services entities of the group. Financial Services constitutes the core business of the Group. The Group's presence in financial services covers many diverse businesses from Commercial Vehicle Financing, Retail Financing, Enterprise Financing, Mortgage Financing, Equipment Financing, Chit Funds, Life Insurance, General Insurance, Retail Stock Broking, Distribution of Financial Products, Wealth Advisory Services and Asset Management.

Shriram Transport Finance Co. Ltd., (a listed entity) the flagship company of the Group is one of the largest Asset Financing NBFCs in the country and a leader in the commercial vehicle financing business. Under its fold is one of the leading players in the chit fund business in India. The Group has a presence all over India in retail finance through Shriram City Union Finance Ltd. (a listed entity) which is also a leading NBFC. Shriram City is a leader in the small enterprises finance segment. Shriram has entered both the life and general insurance businesses with Sanlam, a leading insurer in South Africa. It has investments in manufacturing, pharmaceuticals, information technology and property development.

The Group's consistent strong growth pattern and track record have attracted a large number of private equity funds and strong partners. Investment into the Group from private equity/strategic investor exceeds ₹7,500 crores. It has more than ₹80000 crore assets under management, has more than 2800 branches, employs over 60000 people and has a customer base of over one crore.

The Shriram Story

R Thyagarajan the Founder Chairman of the Shriram Group, which is one of South India's spectacular success stories, keeps such a low profile that many may not be aware that he founded the group in 1974 with ₹100,000—ten friends putting in ₹10,000 each. What started as a small chit fund operation has expanded into one of the largest financial services groups in the country.

Thyagarajan did his Masters in Mathematical Statistics from Indian Statistical Institute and is also an associate of The Chartered Insurance Institute, London. He worked with New India Assurance (before nationalisation) and with JB Boda—the largest reinsurance and insurance broker in Asia, before branching out on his own. Did he know when he started out in such a small way, that one day he would be creating a financial giant? *"Certainly not,"* he laughs. Is he being modest? Thyagarajan says he does not believe in false humility or false modesty. But he is truly a man of minimal needs. He drives an Alto, didn't own a house till 15 years ago and holds less than 3 per cent in his listed companies. He doesn't have a cell phone either. *"Everybody around me has a phone. I can always use theirs, yours."*

Thyagarajan has set up a trust that will offer profits and equity to employees who helped the group build its different businesses. All the executives who have participated in the growth of the group business will be beneficiaries of this trust. *"This is one way of making executives own their group."* he says. Some 33 employees are now beneficiaries of the trust. They more or less own stakes equal to the

2.5 per cent owned by Thyagarajan himself. The trust will expand by inducting more employees selected by a panel of experts. He does not see himself as first among equals but one among equals.

How did this man who is actually a left liberal born into an affluent land owning family from Thanjavur get into this business? Thyagarajan says he had to convince himself that there is a social service aspect in lending to transport operators. Then how did he achieve this phenomenal success? *"Maybe I was good at survival. I could find solutions during difficult circumstances. I don't look at environmental changes. My world revolves around my colleagues, my bankers, my customers."*

The chit fund business was no cakewalk. The margins were wafer thin. A bunch of aspiring entrepreneurs took a chance and went into it without quite knowing the business. Having got into chit funds, Thyagarajan learnt to manage it, build it further and worked on the advantages that can be derived through customers and agents. In that process, many close relationships were built. *"We then realised that there was a real need for commercial vehicle financing. Handled properly, it is also a very safe business to be in."*

The large banks lacked the infrastructure or insight to evaluate credit risk in financing truck purchases, especially of second-hand ones. Money lenders were fleecing their customers charging very high rates. In 1979, Thyagarajan set up Shriram Transport Finance Company (STFC) to get into this market. Today STFC is not just the flagship of the Shriram Group but India's largest asset-financing NBFC. It finances almost 20–25 per cent of the trucks in the country.

In the mid-nineties, his group faced a major crisis when regulators came down hard on non-banking finance companies, which were registered with RBI and mobilising public deposits. Scores of RBI registered and non-registered (those coming under the Companies Act) were all going down the tube. With the CRB Capital scam blowing the lid off many market malpractices, RBI imposed stringent norms to regulate the deposit taking NBFCs. Three entities of Shriram group came under a cloud.

When Thyagarajan and his team were seriously discussing their business plans in the board room one evening, the RBI faxed a press release to all publications stating that three companies belonging to the group were barred from accepting fresh deposits as they had no credit rating. This came as a bolt from the blue as the companies had not solicited any fresh deposits from the public but had only carried a statutory advertisement in a local paper for renewal of deposits. This had caught the attention of regulators.

Senior business journalist V Balasubramaniam recalls that when he had called Thyagrajan to get his reaction, the Chairman was not aware of the RBI press release. This was potentially an explosive situation which could have led to a run on the companies. Thyagarajan salvaged the situation by converting a large portion of deposits into debt instruments. He was able to restore investor confidence without any harm to the companies. Shriram never defaulted on a payment and did not lose its deposit base either.

Shriram City Union Finance was set up in 1986 and started operations in truck financing. In 2002, the company discontinued the truck financing business as that business was consolidated into STFL. It now finances consumer durables, two-wheelers, three-wheelers, personal loans and small and tiny businesses. *"It is really like a medium-sized private bank. The biggest loan amounts to ₹10 lakh. We don't want to get into competition with the banks."* Thyagarajan insists that a business should look at what value it is adding to the community. *"Large and attractive customers are not our target market. Shriram City Union borrowers are the same borrowers as those of the chit fund. We don't want to make money through smart deals."*

It is interesting to know why Thyagarajan thought Shriram group should enter insurance. When the insurance industry opened up, Shriram found itself losing agents and staff to this business. The executive running the chit fund business in Andhra suggested that the group should get into insurance. Akhila Srinivasan, Managing Director of Shriram Life Insurance who has had 18 years of helping build businesses for the group had also played a role in striking global alliances for group companies. When a cold call came from a consultant about the Sanlam group from South Africa looking for partners to enter the insurance business in India, Akhila met them and found that there was a meeting of minds. She visited the group in South Africa, which resulted in Shriram Life Insurance, a joint venture with Sanlam. A few months later, Shriram went into general insurance too.

The company sold its first policy in January 2006. It has since sold over 9 lakh policies. The total number of lives covered is over 48 lakh. "*We have provided close to 10 lakh life covers to the poorer sections of the population. There is so little awareness about what happens when a primary earning member dies in a poor family. This is something we have to address.*" says Akhila. In an industry where almost all players have recorded accumulated losses till recently, Shriram Life has accumulated a profit of ₹163 crore, which is almost equal to its share capital of ₹175 crore.

Akhila is among the most influential persons in the finance industry in the South. She is one of the Directors of the Group and part of the Shriram Ownership Trust which holds the parent company, Shriram Capital Limited. She has made it to the power lists of women in magazines and has had many awards and honours bestowed upon her. She, however, true to the group's profile remains low key and never flaunts her achievements. People in Chennai recognise her more for her CSR activities. Akhila is an example of Thyagarajan's ability to spot talent in the young and nurture them.

Akhila joined Shriram in 1986 and says she knew that she would never look elsewhere for another job. "*I was doing my MPhil in Economics from the Madras University, having completed my post-graduation from Trichy. I was quite sure I wanted to work. An advertisement in a newspaper for executive trainees from the Shriram Group caught my attention. I decided to apply.*" Several aspiring candidates were interviewed by PB Sreenivasan, who had just retired as Chairman, Indian Overseas Bank. It was not necessary to have an MBA degree as qualification. What was required was somebody who had excelled in academics and extra-curricular activities. Akhila, a university rank holder, fitted the bill, having won debates and quizzes for her college. Of the 12 candidates selected, three were women and Akhila was one of them. They were the first batch of executive trainees.

By the middle of the 2000s, Shriram started attracting PE (Private Equity) investors. By 2012, twenty-three PE investors had invested over $750 million in the group since 2005 according to Venture Intelligence, a research firm that tracks PE investments in India. Some of the early investors have done very well for themselves. In 2005, ChrysCapital (the first to come in) invested ₹100–120 crore in STFC and exited in 2009 for ₹1400 crore, about twelve times what they put in. Citi Financial which put ₹11 crore in the group exited with ₹200 crore.

Ajay Piramal, head of the Piramal Group from Mumbai made his entry into Shriram by acquiring TPG's 9.9 per cent stake for $304 million (₹1,652 crore). In April 2014, Piramal Enterprises also acquired 20 per cent equity stake in Shriram Capital Ltd for ₹2,014 crore ($334 million). It bought 9.9 per cent of consumer lending finance company Shriram City Union Finance in June for ₹790 crore as well. Ajay Piramal has taken over as Chairman, Shriram Capital Limited in 2015.

Insurance partner Sanlam Ltd in 2015 is buying 26 per cent in Shriram Capital. The estimated investment is ₹2,000 crore. This would not only help SCL expand the insurance business but also help to buy out shares from some of the private equity (PE) investors in the Group. Thyagarajan has said that the aim is all the three groups (Shriram Ownership Trust, Piramal and Sanlam) should have equal shareholding in the company, eventually.

The next big project is banking, if RBI grants it a licence. Thyagarajan has very clear ideas about the kind of bank he would like to set up. *"We will take the responsibility of fulfilling our social objectives seriously. We will be dealing with that class of customer to whom credit is not available in mainstream banking. We can do it."*

Another little known fact about Thyagarajan is his role as an angel investor. He has been quietly helping people who come to him with good ideas including employees seeking to set up businesses. Whenever he has spotted a technocrat with a vision, he has backed him unconditionally. He does not see the need to publicise such ventures. He just says that one should not fear failure.

APOLLO HOSPITALS

Dr Pratap C Reddy, Founder Chairman of the Apollo Hospital group turned seventy-five in February 2008. His pioneering effort, Apollo Hospitals completed 25 years the same year. There were various functions to mark all these events and the Reddy children and grandchildren kept joking with him to relax and not talk about Apollo. Now that he is over eighty, they are still telling him to relax. It is just not possible for the man who is a pioneer, a trailblazer and an icon in the healthcare industry.

Apollo began as a 150-bed hospital, Apollo Main Hospital, in Chennai.

It was India's first corporate hospital. As Asia's foremost integrated healthcare group, Apollo Hospitals has treated over 37 million patients who have come from 120 countries. Each year over 50,000 patients come to Apollo Hospitals from all around the world. The Group has over 51 tertiary and quaternary care hospitals across the nation, 13 hospitals are under construction mostly in tier II and III cities in India. Its annual revenues have soared from ₹2,605 crore in 2010 to ₹5179 crores at the end of 2014–2015.

Today, it may be very difficult to find somebody who hasn't heard of Apollo Hospitals. But it was Dr Reddy's tenacity against all kinds of roadblocks and rigid mindsets which made it happen.

"When I came back from the US to set-up practice in India, I found there were no adequate services when people needed it. As a cardiologist I was forced to send them to the US when patients needed advanced medical attention. The last straw was when I lost a young man who could not afford ₹40,000 for a surgery."

Reddy knew Indian doctors were highly skilled and they were performing extraordinarily well abroad. *"We had everything going for us, but our systems and laws were muddled."* He was determined to do something about healthcare facilities in India. Initially, he toyed with the idea of setting up a heart care unit. That thought expanded into a vision of a multi-disciplinary hospital. He had thought of setting up a charitable trust (*"I was not rich, but was networked enough to make it happen"*), but on second thoughts he realised that once the original promoter passed away, the others never had the passion needed to run a hospital.

To Reddy, it became clear that the time had come to infuse professionalism into healthcare. He felt it was necessary to set up a corporate hospital in the country. It may be difficult to recall today, but hospitals were then run only by charitable trusts or governments. The thought of a hospital run for profit was anathema to many. *"I had no land, no funding for my dream,"* recalls Reddy. *"I had to make many pilgrimages to see Dr Manmohan Singh who was then the Governor of the RBI, and the then Finance Minister, Pranab Mukherjee. I had to make 12 applications to 20 babus. I had to spend two days every week in Delhi."* All this was necessary because Reddy had to make an initial public offering and get institutional finance to raise the funding for putting up the hospital. Nobody believed him when he said he wanted the money to build a hospital. They said he was going to turn it into a hotel!

However, one man thought differently and had faith in the concept and Dr Reddy. That was Rajiv Gandhi. He understood that a hospital should be funded by financial institutions. Health insurance is an absolute must and health benefit should be treated as income. In spite of the support of Gandhi, it took three years for Apollo to be given recognition as a healthcare institution. Incidentally, the concept of health insurance was non-existent till the 1980s.

Apollo was to be a multi-crore super speciality hospital in Chennai offering a comprehensive range of services. Four years were spent in collecting information about the cash flows in existing first-class charitable trust hospitals, and in preparing a feasibility report. The results clearly showed that hospitals were essentially sound commercial propositions. Eventually, convinced by the feasibility reports, the Indian Overseas Bank (IOB) came forward with its offer of a term loan for the hospital project.

When Reddy had to import a CT scan costing ₹1.5 crore for the hospital, he had to cool his heels at the Department of Electronics which had to give him a no objection certificate! Although the then Finance Minister and later the President of India, R Venkataraman was ready to release funds from the IDBI for the hospital, he could not do so because of obscure and outdated legal tangles. Reddy always jokes, *"If it took a million bricks to build Apollo, I also faced a million problems."*

Finally, the first hospital of the group came up in Chennai in 1983. Like any business of those times, the early days were slow and full of uncertainties. Conventional wisdom has always held that large, well-equipped hospitals, whether publicly or privately owned, cannot be run as commercial propositions on a profit making basis—if we also expect them to charge 'reasonable' prices. Therefore the Apollo venture was of considerable significance and was about to mark a turning point in medical care in India.

After initial losses, Reddy was able to show a profit and declare a first dividend of 10 per cent to its shareholders at the end of 1987. *"We learnt from our mistakes and started developing good systems for hospital management. The second hospital was a little easier."* The government, bureaucrats and the public were still coming to terms with accepting a hospital and a healthcare facility being run for profit. Although he faced any number of hurdles at every stage, Reddy kept moving forward constantly.

He has always believed that hi-tech equipment may be more expensive, but it allows faster and more effective testing. Diagnosis is also faster. Apollo acquired the first multi-organ CT scan in the country, the first MRI equipment, treadmill, colour doppler… the list is endless. The group also has the most modern equipment in their Oncology departments outside of Tata Memorial Hospital in Mumbai. In its very first year, Apollo had a success rate of 97 per cent in heart operations. The next year, 700 surgeries were performed and the success rate was 97.7 per cent. Today it is 99 per cent—the highest in the world. The number of surgeries performed has crossed 100,000. It is the top ranked group for heart surgery.

Today, his hospitals attract talent from all over the world. *"When I started I had only three doctors from the US. All the others were local doctors. I just told them to do their very best. Think of every patient as their closest friend or relative. By the time I launched in Bangalore, 50 per cent of my doctors came from the US or UK."*

Reddy's success has inspired many others to follow suit. No one any longer questions the concept of corporate hospitals. Is he feeling the heat because of increasing competition? Not one bit. He says India's deficiencies in physical infrastructure like roads, public transport, potable water and power and so on pale into insignificance in comparison to those in social infrastructure. The tragic statistics are all at his fingertips.

With almost 2.5 million births per year, India needs an annual incremental addition to healthcare facilities equivalent to almost half of what a UK or a France or an Italy may need for their entire population. While India has made remarkable achievements in improving its health indices since independence, we still lag behind other emerging economies like Brazil, Russia and China. We always compare ourselves with China. But China has 2.2 beds per thousand population and Russia as many as 9.7, while we are way behind at 0.7 compared to the global average of 2.6. We need to put up at least 100,000 beds a year. And investment for that is a huge amount.

Reddy's four daughters have been working with him from the time Apollo was a vision in his head and when he was working on top of a garage next to a nursing home (H M Hospital) he was running then. *"They have all been emotionally involved with Apollo even when they were studying,"* he says. Preetha Reddy, his eldest daughter, remembers her father having to make constant trips to Delhi and other places, struggling to raise funding.

Before they knew it, his daughters got caught up in his plans. Consequently, Preetha's introduction to hospital life began early. Every evening after school, she and her three younger sisters would visit the hospital where her father worked. "*We helped out and silently watched how healthcare delivery was done,*" she remembers. They used to potter around in the nursing home, carry files and run errands. At the time when he was building the first hospital, there were no hospital architects. "*I gave the room next to mine to the architect so that I could work with him. My daughter Shobhana interviewed hundreds of doctors to get their inputs before we built the ICU unit.*"

He recently brought his daughters closer to taking over the enterprise when he steps down by announcing a major re-organisation in 2014. Preetha was named Executive Vice Chairman (she was Managing Director till then). He has said in an interview: "*I chose Preetha to head the hospital because I saw she could make split-second decisions and still have compassion. On hindsight, not allowing her to do medicine wasn't so bad a decision. If she were a doctor, she would have cured a certain number of patients. But now, there are more than a million patients grateful for her presence.*" Preetha got married at nineteen and was not encouraged to take up medical studies.

Suneeta Reddy was promoted as Managing Director (from Joint Managing Director), Shobana Kamineni was made Executive Vice-Chairperson and Sangita Reddy moved to the post of Joint Managing Director. Their roles have been more clearly defined than before. Preetha Reddy will lead the organisation's thrust on continuous quality improvement processes to achieve the highest standards of patient satisfaction and drive Apollo's aspiration of becoming a global healthcare destination.

Suneeta Reddy has concentrated on the financial management of Apollo for many years. Now she will lead the corporate strategy, corporate finance, funding and investments and will leverage mergers and acquisitions to achieve the accelerated pace of growth and optimise profitability. She will also handle branding and marketing. Holding the third position in Apollo's pecking order is

Shobana Kamineni. Though her designation is the same as Preetha, she is clearly the junior partner, with responsibilities for the Apollo Pharmacy chain—a portfolio that she has managed for quite some time in the past. Shobana continues to be a whole time director on the board of Apollo Munich Health insurance, the company she founded. The youngest sister Sangita Reddy will assume greater responsibilities as Joint MD, which will include creating an IT-enabled patient-centric operation across the Apollo footprint.

The daughters will have their hands full. Though the company as a whole has performed well financially, its reach has not widened as quickly as planned. The total bed strength of 8,600–8,700 in 2014 has more or less remained the same over the past three years. In contrast to the hospitals, Apollo Pharmacy has been a sluggish performer. The group has been looking for a 'strategic partner', who might agree to pick up a sizeable stake in the pharmacy business. Then there is fledgling Apollo Munich, the group's health insurance business, which handles the issues affecting the health insurance sector as a whole. This too has to expand and grow.

Reddy is convinced that India will become the global healthcare destination and that Apollo will have a great future. Apollo has 16 beds for hip replacement. Six of them are occupied by Americans and Canadians. A surgery that used to cost $2,500 about 27 years ago can still be performed here for less than $3,000. *"I can cross-subsidise my general ward patients from what we earn from international ones."* He says that we have to decide now whether we will be the leading healthcare provider to the world in the next five years or fifty years.

SOME FAILURES

Not for lack of trying

PETROCHEMICAL PROJECTS IN TAMIL NADU

Why did Tamil Nadu miss out on the petrochemical boom of the eighties in spite of being one of the first movers in this area? It had early pioneers in Chemplast (now Chemplast Sanmar) which set up the country's first PVC plant in 1967. There was DCW (which was known as Dhrangadhra Chemicals) which had put up a plant to manufacture caustic soda in Tamil Nadu and Gujarat even earlier. And yet it fell by the wayside.

The first fertilizer factory in Madras was built by EID Parry, the second oldest British company in the country. SPIC (Southern Petrochemicals Industries Corporation) was incorporated in 1969, the first joint sector company to be established in the state. Tamil Nadu Industrial Development Corporation (TIDCO) and industrialist MA Chidambaram were the joint venture partners. SPIC then was the largest fertilizer unit to come up in the South. Earlier, Madras Fertilizers Limited (MFL) was incorporated in December 1966 as a Joint Venture between the Government of India (GOI) and AMOCO Incorporated of USA (AMOCO) with the GOI holding 51 per cent of the equity share capital. In 1972, National Iranian Oil Company acquired 50 per cent of AMOCO's share and the shareholding pattern became 51 per cent GOI and 24.5 per cent each of AMOCO and NIOC.

There was no further movement in the '70s in the petrochemical industry in the state. Tamil Nadu in the eighties desperately tried to get its petrochemical act together. It was not unaware of what was happening around it. It had to fight for downstream chemical industries which could be set up by using the raw materials produced by Madras Refineries Limited (MRL). In 1987, a couple of projects were commissioned and several private sector companies were making efforts to get into manufacturing petrochemicals.

MRL set up a plant in 1984 to produce paraffin wax of different types with a capacity of 20,000 tonnes. The second was Tamil Nadu Petroproducts Ltd (TPL), a joint venture between TIDCO and SPIC, for the manufacture of linear alkyl benzene. TPL was one of the star projects for the state for a few years. In addition, RPG Enterprises was also setting up a plant to manufacture MEK (methyl ethyl ketone).

There were two new projects which came up simultaneously to manufacture propylene-based chemicals in the '80s. One of the projects was promoted by SPIC and the other by TIDCO and Vijay Mallya's United Breweries. They were racing with each other to get to the market first with the products.

In 1981, Kothari Industrial Corporation (KICL) and TIDCO had applied for licences for the manufacture of these chemicals. The propylene was to be manufactured by MRL. KICL was given a licence for propylene oxide (12,000 tonnes), propylene glycol (6,250 tonnes) and 6,000 tonnes of polypols in 1982. TIDCO obtained letters of intent for the manufacture of 6,000 tonnes of polyols and 10,000 tonnes of propylene oxide.

Both these projects did not take off for various reasons. TIDCO did not proceed beyond the licence stage. KICL tied up with Technip of France for technology. The chlorine produced by KICL's caustic soda plant was an important raw material for making propylene-based chemicals. In spite of these advantages, KICL could not implement this project as it ran into financial problems. So KICL registered a new company, Manali Petrochemicals, and transferred this licence and sold its chemical interests to SPIC.

In 1985, another company, Kamar Chemicals (Syed Yusuf Group), secured a letter of intent for the manufacture of 6,000 tonnes of polyols. As it was not viable to put up a polyol project in isolation, Kamar and TIDCO joined hands and promoted Kamar Petrochemicals and Plastics Limited. For a long time, this company was not able to secure any technology tie-up (very few international companies were willing to part with this technology). Around that time there were dark rumours that TIDCO was trying to prevent KICL from transferring Manali Petrochemicals to SPIC.

By 1987 the project cost had shot up to more than ₹60 crores. It was apparent that TIDCO's co-promoter, the Syed Yusuf group could not come up with such large funds. Then the UB group entered the picture. It stepped in as the co-promoter with TIDCO and Syed Yusuf retained a nominal interest with ₹20 lakhs as its share. UB was able to tie up technology after many months. Kamar Petrochemicals' collaborator was Montedison of Italy.

Kamar Petrochemicals was going to manufacture 12,000 tonnes of propylene oxide, 8,000 tonnes of polyols and 7,000 tonnes of propylene glycol. The project outlay was about ₹65 crores. The equity capital was ₹20 crores and TIDCO was taking up 26 per cent of the equity and the UB group 24 per cent. The balance was to be issued to the foreign collaborator and the public. Commercial production was expected to commence by early 1990. It never did.

Manali Petrochemicals (MPL), whose project cost was ₹63 crores, also hoped to complete its projects by 1990. MPL, through its tie-up with Technip was getting technology from ARCO of USA, one of the best known names in this filed. *"Arco Chemical Company, a subsidiary of ARCO, has a polyol application technology laboratory which is like a huge kingdom and we have a separate R&D tie-up with them,"* said MPL officials then.

These were all import substitution products. No one quite knew about the kind of demand they would have in the country. Polyol glycol is an essential raw material for flavours and some pharmaceuticals, Polyol is required for thermoplastics. In the late eighties the demand for propylene glycol was 10,000 tonnes and of polyols only 6,000 tonnes. Promoters of both the projects were confident that the demand will pick up once the products were indigenously available, as happened in the case of HDPE and LDPE.

When the economy opened up, all these projects fell apart.

On the fertiliser front, EID Parry was taken over by the Murugappa Group who focused on fertilizers as one of their core activities. It is today one of the leading fertilizer manufacturers in the country. MFL after some good years became a BIFR case and iscoming up with one revival plan after another.

Chemplast remains a much respected name in PVC but has been reduced to a pygmy after Reliance came in. It never thought in terms of scale and its innate conservative nature was no match for the giant.

SPIC which seemed unstoppable till the mid-nineties and was seen as the future Reliance of the South could never live up to its promise essentially due to bad judgements and mismanagement.

SPIC

In the 1980s and '90s, AC Muthiah's name always stood out. Muthiah, whose father MA Chidambaram promoted the joint sector fertiliser giant SPIC was willing to tread a different path. One could not have predicted even in the mid-nineties that one day the Asset Reconstruction Company of India (ARCIL) would be selling off several of SPIC's properties in an attempt to revive the company, which started losing its lustre around 2000. Its turnover has fallen from ₹2,711 crore to less than ₹500 crore in the past ten years.

Incorporated in 1969, SPIC was jointly promoted by Chidambaram and Tamil Nadu Industrial Corporation (TIDCO). TIDCO held 26 per cent equity and the private promoter 25 per cent, the rest was with financial institutions and the public. It was the state's first joint sector project. The only businessman in Tamil Nadu who was willing to go with the government then was Chidambaram, while well-known southern groups like TVS, Amalgamations, Murugappa, Chemplast and Kotharis stayed away. They were criticised for not taking up opportunities which were opening up.

It was not smooth sailing. SPIC was plagued by cost overruns, problems with feed stock availability, pricing policy and shaky management. By 1977, SPIC was tottering with losses of ₹68 crore, which was more than three times its equity capital of ₹19 crore. At this point, S Venkitaramanan, a senior IAS officer (who later retired as RBI Governor) was roped in to revive SPIC.

Venkitaramanan as the state's Industry Secretary had been keen on Tamil Nadu getting a major fertiliser unit. During his tenure, he had tried to rope in various entrepreneurs in vain. When his dream project was in trouble he had no hesitation stepping in. SPIC under Venkitaramanan performed a near miracle, becoming a well recorded turnaround story. Among many other factors, the retention price scheme for individual fertiliser companies as recommended by the Marathe Committee came at the right time for SPIC. When Venkitaramanan returned to the centre in 1983, Muthiah who had worked closely with him took over.

By the mid-eighties SPIC's turnover crossed ₹500 crore and it became a profitable company. It could invest in the LAB (bio-degradable raw material for detergents) project of TIDCO, named Tamil Nadu Petro Products. It managed to pip Hindustan Unilever to the post in getting this project. It also promoted Tamil Nadu Alkalines and Chemicals with TIDCO to manufacture soda ash. It hoped to become a major supplier to the detergent industry. SPIC Electronics was set up to manufacture computer magnetic tapes.

SPIC got into trouble yet again with the state's changing political scenario. Its growth phase, mostly during Chief Minister MG Ramachandran's (AIADMK) years, stalled when M Karunanidhi (DMK) became Chief Minister in 1989. SPIC got caught in DMK-AIADMK rivalries. The DMK government examined SPIC's shareholding in 1990 and declared that the Chidambaram family held far less than 25 per cent in the company. Although there was a dire need for SPIC to raise resources through a rights issue, TIDCO would not allow it to do so.

Meanwhile, Muthiah had also taken over Standard Motors which was in deep trouble after it launched the Standard 2000 car. The company was under lock out. He had put in his personal investment of ₹2 crore in the company. But he was not allowed to bring in funds from the joint sector companies SPIC had invested in. SPIC's fortunes were to change once again when Jayalalithaa won the elections and became chief minister. The re-opening of Standard Motors became an election issue for Jayalalithaa. Things improved overnight for Muthiah when she swept back to power in 1991. SPIC was allowed to put in ₹6 crore in Standard Motors through Tamil Nadu Petro Products. (Standard Motors was never revived). In 1992, when SPIC went in for a zero-bond issue on a rights basis for ₹42.50 crore, TIDCO renounced its rights to participate in this. This was to make SPIConce again an election issue. The SPIC disinvestment case became *cause celebre* for Karunanidhi. Jayalalithaa was accused of giving away SPIC to Muthiah virtually free.

But that was later. During the Jayalalithaa period, Muthiah pulled off what was then seen as many stunning coups adding to his reputation of being the only daring and visionary businessman in Tamil Nadu. He promoted ventures through his joint sector companies to manufacture, among other things, detergents (collaborator, Henkel of Germany), and penicillin (Spic Pharma).

The beginning of the end came with his most ambitious venture, the ₹1,500-crore Spic Petrochemicals to manufacture PTA and PFY. It was planned as a joint venture between SPIC and Chennai Petroleum Corporation, which got a stay order against the project when SPIC decided to go solo. To make matters worse SPIC was not allowed to raise finances through a public issue. Having invested ₹1,000 crore on this project, SPIC's liabilities started to mount.

Other projects also started failing one after the other. Most of them belonged to the import substitution era. For example, penicillin became unviable with cheap imported penicillin coming from China. Spic Electronics never took off.

The fertiliser industry itself changed with the scrapping of retention price. SPIC's Tuticorin plant with naphtha as feedstock cannot compete with gas-based plants. Plant and machinery have to be modernised. Its loans (nearly ₹3300 crore) have been bought and are being managed by ARCIL, which has been selling SPIC's assets and investments. The units were shut down between 2007 and 2010. There have been attempts to revive them from 2010.

Tuticorin Alkalais and Chemicals promoted by SPIC and TIDCO has now literally downed shutters as SPIC is not in a position to supply carbon dioxide, the raw material needed to produce soda ash. TPL, one of the best performers in the SPIC group is now dwindling down to a loss making unit and heading towards closure.

As part of the restructuring, SPIC has sold its phosphatic fertilizer business to Greenstar Fertilizers for ₹300 crore. The company was unable to operate its phosphatic fertilizer plant to the optimum capacity due to lack of working capital. The plant required sizeable capital infusion for modernisation.

Earlier, SPIC sold out its engineering division SPIC-SMO to a Kolkata based company for around ₹50 crore. It has also sold its joint venture Technip India and its stake in Indo Jordan Chemicals. In addition, many properties, guest houses, and godowns have all been sold off.

Muthiah's son Ashwin Muthiah, who has taken over as Chairman, has been presiding over various sales in an attempt to revive SPIC. Ashwin has said in an interview to *Business Standard* dated November 9, 2015 that SPIC is now geared up to take advantage of the stable policy regime which allows naphtha usage till natural gas is made available and that he has a clear roadmap for growth in the next three years, including expansion worth ₹ 6,000 crore. While analysts have raised doubts if banks would give loans for the proposed expansion, Ashwin insists it will not be a problem.

Pioneers of the '90s

The '90s opened up new opportunities. Several took the plunge

SIFY

Sify was launched in 1995 as Satyam Infoway Ltd. by Satyam Computers in Chennai. One may not remember today what an important role Sify played during the early spread of internet and e-commerce in India. Sify was a true pioneer. It actually kept up with the developments in the internet space in the West in spite of the outdated Indian regulations of that time. Says R Ramraj who started Sify and was the CEO till 2006, *"We worked on setting up a truly world class company which would make a global impact. From the beginning, we partnered with the internet pioneer, CompuServe. I was able to bring on board a very entrepreneurial team which could dream big. Mistakes were made but were not punished."*

Let us see what was happening in the internet world a navigating at that time.

In 1993 the Mosaic web browser was launched as a navigating system for the World Wide Web (www). Mosaic was developed by Marc Andreesen at the National Center for Supercomputing Applications (NCSA). It became the dominant navigating system for the World Wide Web, which at that time accounted for merely one per cent of all internet traffic.

By 1994 many things happened. Netscape was founded, the White House website was created and Yahoo was launched. E-commerce was also making a tentative beginning. The next year, AOL, CompuServe and Prodigy introduced dial up internet services. Amazon and eBay who were later to become internet giants were launched. Netscape made its highly successful IPO and the beginning of the gold rush for internet businesses began. In 1996, Hotmail made its appearance.

The point is that the founding employees of Sify actually managed to conceive, develop and launch internet businesses almost simultaneously with the best in their class in the world, despite Indian infrastructure and regulatory constraints. In those years, Sify was really skating on thin ice as far as legal boundaries were concerned.

Think of the kind of roadblocks an internet company faced then. The Department of Telecommunications (DOT) was the sole basic service provider till 1997. It allowed only X.25, an old, slow network protocol, which was outdated even in the '90s, to be used for building networks. TCP/IP is the underlying internet transport protocol which should have been used. Third parties could not provide data networks. VSNL was the sole provider of internet services from 1996–1998. The internet Service Providers Association of India founded in early 1998 had to fight for internet deregulation which would only happen around the turn of the century.

With all these constraints Sify managed to build India's largest private internet network, covering 220 cities and with more than 4 lakh subscribers. It was also the only Indian company with several internet based businesses under one roof. It had a presence spanning connectivity, e-commerce and e-consultancy. Sify's e-commerce/content development services were set up in partnership with Broadvision and Openmarket. Sify portal was launched with multiple 'owned' content sites—news, finance, movies, music, sports, games, a B2B market place and user generated content. In contrast, rediff.com was a pure portal play and Dishnet and VSNL only provided access.

In 1998, the same year Google search engine made its appearance, Sify came up with shopping through payment gateway services. Auctions were offered on the Sify portal. Network alliances were made with Singapore Telecom and CompuServe Business Network Services. Ipass (the first internet roaming service) was made available to customers. The UK Government's private funding arm, CDC Capital Partners, invested in Sify.

By 1999, there was a massive explosion of e-commerce sites with Yahoo acquiring Geocities for $3 billion. The same year, Sify launched the first private internet services to corporates and consumers offering dial up and leased lines. It set up cyber cafes. It also went public on Nasdaq in October 1999 (Infosys and Cognizant listed in Nasdaq in 1997 and 1998 respectively).

Sify managed to raise $74 million. And with that it paid ₹499 crore and took over the Indiaworld portal launched by Rajesh Jain. Sify till then was only an internet service provider. It created a major storm in the Indian internet world withthis very expensive acquisition. Investors obviously approved of this move. Sify was able to raise $143 million for another 1 per cent of its equity four months later. It also took a stake in Cricinfo. It was thanks to Sify that people realised that entrepreneurs could make serious money from internet.

By then doubts were being raised about if Sify was spreading itself thin by trying to be an integrated player? Of the $217 million the company raised from Nasdaq, $173 million was spent in acquisitions. Its accumulated losses, on the other hand were about $35 million (₹163 crore). Said *Business Today* in its cover story on Sify, *"For a company like Sify, every dollar that is invested in growing a currently non-revenue generating business (like Sifywebex or Learnatsatyam.com) is a loss. Some analysts blame it on Sify's integrated play. There are significant downsides in trying to do everything."*

Sify was certainly thinking ahead. It was planning on tapping synergies with parent Satyam Computers to offer infotech-enabled services such as business process outsourcing. Founder of Satyam Computers, Ramalinga Raju himself hoped that all the investment would act as an entry barrier for competitors two or three years down the line.

Things did not quite work out that way. Its revenues did not grow as anticipated. Sify was an idea before its time. It was not able to consolidate its lead in practically every sector of the internet particularly in every content and e-commerce area. Critics say that it made poor strategic choices in terms of deployment of capital raised such as the Indiaworld acquisition. This had such a large cash component that the war chest raised in Nasdaq was not conserved. Post Nasdaq there was too much wasteful spending on very high salaries, travel and advertising.

There was an upside as well. Says Padma Chandrasekaran, one of the founding members of Sify, "*Sify created many ripple effects. It broke many barriers created by the regulatory body. It helped the internet industry open up. There were many who emulated Sify. More importantly, it created a large pool of internet skilled workforce.*"

Ramalinga Raju, promoter of Satyam and Sify made known his intention to put Sify on the block soon after Sify's listing in Nasdaq. In November 2005, Satyam sold its shares in Sify to Infinity Capital Ventures, which is owned by Raju Vegesna, for US$62.62 million.

THE SIVASANKARAN SAGA

It is a forgotten fact that the telecom revolution actually started in Chennai with Sivasankaran and his Sterling Group. Sivasankaran's story is full of high drama.

On August 26, 2014, the Supreme Court of Seychelles declared Chinnakannan Sivasankaran bankrupt. An official receiver will compile a list of Siva's assets and sell them to pay back his creditors. Amongst Siva's creditors, the largest is BMIC, a Bahrain Telecom or Batelco company. In a statement issued from Manama in Bahrain, Batelco CEO Alan Whelan said that the bankruptcy will not "*...thwart our determination to recover the substantial monies that he owes us*".

In October 2013, WinWinD, his Finland-headquartered wind turbine venture, submitted a voluntary bankruptcy petition because it had "*been incurring heavy losses for the past several years*" and its debts had ballooned to around $300 million. "*The efforts of WinWinD in trying to arrange for necessary funding and approval for restructuring process has not been successful and hence this decision,*" the company said at that time.

At the turn of the century Siva had become a citizen of Seychelles. He purchased several properties in Seychelles and was reportedly developing resorts. Meanwhile he was also into the commodity business based out of Africa. He was even appointed

Ambassador-at-Large for Seychelles. However, whatever he has recently touched has turned into straw. He seems to be on a downward spiral. People who know Siva think he is in a big mess. But they do not put it past him to survive this crisis.

Siva has always had a maverick streak. Quite unknown and completely unpretentious with no background in electronics, he burst into the Indian computer scene in the '80s. He understood the cost-conscious Indian market much before the much bigger names did. He changed the face of the Indian computer industry by offering the lowest priced PC and delivering it on the same day. His overheads were low. He literally thumbed his nose at established giants like HCL, Wipro, Hinditron, and DCL. He started assembling IBM compatibles for these larger manufacturers, and then launched his own label, Siva PC. He claimed it was named after Lord Siva and not himself.

Many saw him with wonder and suspicion. There were stories doing the rounds that he brought the computer hardware in plastic bags from cheap markets like Taiwan and South Korea and assembled them to sell them at what was then rock bottom prices (less than ₹30000) when the bigger names sold their assembled PCs for prices three or four times this. They called him a fly-by-night operator. They predicted he would make a packet and get out.

Get out he did, but only from the PC market. He realised that there were going to be many Siva PC clones. So he wanted to move on. He took his chances, was not bothered by failure as his mind was already working on the next big thing. He burnt his fingers trying to sell Osborne word processors which was one of his earliest ventures. He said in the mid-eighties, that the electronics industry is one place where reputations do not matter that much. The level of obsolescence is very high and even an established manufacturer is not necessarily up-to-date. His heroes during this period were Steve Jobs and Bill Gates much before they became household names. Siva was absolutely confident that he was going to hit big time. He could see the potential in computers, electronics and telecom ahead of others. His networking skills are legendary.

There was a brief period when Siva flirted with joint ventures with the Tamil Nadu government. He wanted to get into nitro aromatics and titanium dioxide. He got the licences, but nothing came out of all this. He tried his hands at various things. He talked about a mega housing project. He bid for the Yellow Pages and got into legal trouble. But his heart was always in the hi-tech cutting edge businesses. He said in an interview during this period about his commitment to the hi-tech industry, *"I like taking quick decisions, I enjoy learning new things, and the business is full of thrills. It is entirely suited to a creative entrepreneur like me."* This was in the early '90s. He was seen then as being close to the then DMK regime. When the AIADMK came to power, he literally disappeared from the scene, before surfacing again by successfully bidding for the Delhi Telecom circle.

When the current telecom boom was just a blip in many people's minds, Siva had realized that the future was going to be big in this area. He was willing once again to take a huge risk and put in money in an unknown entity. In November 1994, Sterling Cellular entered into a license agreement with DoT. At that time Siva's company had an equity base of which 49 per cent was to have been subscribed by the little known American company Cellular Communications International Limited (CCIL). All this was done according to the then prevailing rules. By May 1995 Siva had managed to get the Essar group to take over the Delhi circle. This was not as simple as it sounds. DOT did not allow license swapping then. The deal was put through with various twists and turns in which Swiss Telecom also played a part. Interestingly it was this deal which triggered major policy changes which eventually legitimised the buying and selling of licenses.

With the money he made (which exceeded ₹200 crore from the Ruias and several million dollars from Swiss Telecom) Siva turned NRI and started operating out of Singapore and California. There were tremendous lifestyle changes as well. Siva had become seriously rich. He had armed guards accompanying him everywhere. He had an entire floor of Singapore's luxurious

Ritz Carlton and in California he moved into rap musician MC Hammer's vast estate.

The Essar group could not pay up the committed amount. They settled their account by handing over some fabulous real estate in Chennai.

The Ruias had got into a mess by buying up the majority shareholding in Tamilnadu Mercantile Bank (TMB), a bank promoted by the Nadar community. A faction of the community which held the major shareholding had sold its shares to the Ruias because of some family squabble. The rest of the community was up in arms. The RBI raised questions about the Ruias being allowed to buy the stake. Siva bought over the TMB shares from the Ruias and held on to them. For almost ten years the Nadars tried to buy the bank back from him. He said that he did not understand the fuss the Nadars were making. *"After all, my best friend is a Nadar (Shiv Nadar), I went to a Nadar school, I buy provisions from a Nadar shop. I am an honorary Nadar,"* he declared.

It is very difficult to keep track of Siva's activities. Some are public and some very private. With no publicity whatsoever he promoted his venture Fresh and Honest Company to sell coffee and other hot beverages from vending machines brought from Switzerland. He put up a factory to make soya products. Incidentally he also turned a health freak during this period. People who came to discuss his telecom plans were served soya milk and soya products. A generous offer would be made to use his well-equipped gym. Another little known activity was AIWO, possibly India's largest and most luxurious health spa which he set up for men in Chennai. There was also talk of his acquiring a stake in the ETN TV channel.

In his bidding for telecom circles, Siva had acquired the Tamil Nadu circle, barring Chennai. True to his style Siva brought down the cellular prices on par with basic rates and became the largest operator outside the metro. However, he had obviously made up his mind that he had to have the network operating in Chennai as well. Probably that motivated him to pick up a 9 per cent stake in Sunil Mittal's Bharati Telecom Ltd a year after he sold off the Delhi circle. After registering 1.5 per cent of the shares, Bharati refused to register any more shares in the name of Siva. Accusations and counter accusations flew back and forth. Siva sounded surprised at the attitude of good friend Sunil. The issue got amicably resolved and Siva probably ended up making some more money in this transaction.

A couple of years later Siva launched Dishnet Ltd as a subsidiary of his Sterling group. It was the second private internet service provider to come up in the country. Dishnet brought DSL (digital subscriber line) technology to the country. It set up cybercafés, acquired corporate and domestic subscribers and also talked about submarine cables, went into narrow band and broad band and struggled like everybody else for the last mile connectivity. Although earlier announcements promised the usual Siva kind of Kmart pricing, it was not possible this time round. The telecom circles talked about Dishnet losing money. But Siva hung in there till he found the right buyer, who was Ratan Tata. For the Tatas this was a good fit after their VSNL take over. VSNL acquired the internet businesses of Dishnet. The broadband assets had the capacity to service more than 50000 customers in key cities in the country. Dishnet's 20 dial up locations were not among VSNL's existing 30 locations of operations. Thanks to this deal, Ratan Tata became a close friend and he became the advisor to Tata group for their telecom business. Siva acquired a 3.75 per cent stake in Tata Teleservices which he sold out later.

He also acquired the entire 65 per cent stake of Turner Morrison in the coffee pub chain Barista. Barista was jointly promoted by Turner Morrison and Tata Coffee. The Tata group continued to hold its 34 per cent stake in Barista. Since then Barista has changed hands several times and has been shut down.

Siva could not stay away from telecom. He bought the licence for Tamil Nadu and then acquired the one for Chennai from RPG Cellular. From here, he decided to expand his footprint. In March 2004, Siva applied for the licence in the eight circles of Madhya Pradesh, Assam, North East, West Bengal, Bihar, Orissa, Himachal Pradesh and Jammu and Kashmir. Letters of intent were issued on April 6. The company submitted compliance to the letters of intent on April 20 for seven circles, and sought additional time for Madhya Pradesh.

The next day, the company applied for licences for Uttar Pradesh (east) and Uttar Pradesh (west) as well. On May 7, licences were issued for all the circles, except Madhya Pradesh. Then, on May 26, Dayanidhi Maran took over as the Union Telecom Minister. Nothing was ever the same again. All clearances got stuck at the Department of Telecommunications. In June, Siva entered into an agreement with Hutchison to sell his Tamil Nadu operations for ₹1,200 crore—this would have given him the funds to roll out in the rest of the country. DoT delayed approvals. On March 3, 2005, Dayanidhi Maran sent the file back saying a report on mergers and acquisitions was awaited. The same month, Siva cancelled the deal.

In December 2005, Siva sold Aircel to Maxis of Malaysia, promoted by T Ananda Krishnan, a Malaysian of Sri Lankan origin. Eventually Siva accused the Maran brothers of forcing him to sell out to Maxis which resulted in CBI filing a charge sheet on the Marans saying that the Marans received ₹742 crore for coercing Siva to sell Aircel to Maxis to get investments in group companies Sun Direct (the DTH operator) and South Asia FM.

Siva then moved on. One of the companies to get controversy-ridden licences under A Raja, the Telecom Minister, was STel. It had got six circles: Orissa, Bihar, Himachal Pradesh, Northeast, Assam and Jammu and Kashmir. Siva had acquired 51 per cent of it. Batelco bought 49 per cent in STel in 2009 for ₹1,000 crore. By then, opposition to the allotment of inexpensive spectrum had gathered momentum. Raja was removed. Several people, including Raja, were taken into custody. Finally, in February 2012, the Supreme Court cancelled all the 122 licences allotted by Raja. STel, which had about 3.6 million subscribers in five circles, had no option but to shut shop. That is when BMIC, which owned 42.7 per cent in the company, invoked the "put" option under which in an exigency like this Siva had to buy out its stake at the price at which it had been bought: $212 million. BMIC says Siva never paid up.

There has always been an element of mystery about Siva's life and deals. His deals have always been complex to unravel. People close to Siva say he will be able to meet his current challenges.

THE MARANS OF SUN TV

Kalanithi Maran, Chairman and Managing Director of Sun TV, does not believe in also-rans. He has to be the market leader or till it happens, a strong number two in whichever business he is in. He is the undisputed king of regional media. Sun TV has consistently outperformed not only the regional channels, but most of the other Indian media companies as well. His media conglomerate dominates the southern television market, with 33 channels in four languages that reach more than 95 million households. The Sun Group owns the largest chain of TV channels in India. The group's other business interests include direct-to-home broadcasting, 45 FM radio stations, two daily newspapers and six magazines.

After toying with the idea of getting into the aviation sector for almost three years, Maran took over SpiceJet (possibly the largest deal from Tamil Nadu) which in 2010 was a profit making low cost airline. He is reported to have paid ₹750 crore for the airline. It ranked second among the airlines in that category. Maran wanted a big project as he did not want the Sun TV group to stagnate. Neither launching channels in the northern markets nor starting an English newspaper, ideas he had toyed with, were seen as viable options.

In 2012, Sun TV acquired the Indian Premier League's Hyderabad cricket franchise and named it Sun Risers. Till then

Kalanithi Maran could do no wrong. He was called the 'man with the Midas touch'. He was not to know then that SpiceJet was going to knock him down from his pedestal. Nor did he know that he was going to get caught up in all kinds of legal tangles.

Maran's critics (they are legion) tend to attribute his achievements to his political ties. His granduncle M Karunanidhi has been the Chief Minister of Tamil Nadu five times and is the head of the Dravida Munnetra Kazhagam (DMK) party. His late father, Murasoli Maran, was among other things, Industries minister in New Delhi. Maran senior was a true intellectual and the party ideologue. Younger brother Dayanidhi has been union minister twice.

Maran has always pointed out that the opposition party (AIADMK and Jayalalithaa) was in power when he started Sun TV in 1993 and again when he took the company public in early 2006. Also, DMK had been in power only about half of those 16 years. It is not as though his uncle and cousins supported him all through. There was a famous family fallout in 2007. Karunanidhi's family launched *Kalaignar TV* to take him on. The family made up in 2009. He did very well even during this period.

Although he grew up in a family where *"politics was discussed over breakfast, lunch and dinner,"* Maran had no desire to enter politics. However he understands politics very well. Murasoli Maran believed in giving his children a good education more than anything else. Maran went to the US for an MBA degree at the University of Scranton in Pennsylvania. He discovered the multiple channels available on American TV. The cable revolution in India was still a few years away. What was available was staid and boring DD fare. He returned to India in 1987 and joined the family's small publishing business that included a weekly women's magazine.

This was the time when when 'video magazines' in cassette format were becoming popular. He sensed an opportunity there. In 1991, he launched *Poomalai*, a monthly news and current affairs Tamil video magazine. He had to look for overseas markets as piracy ate into his sales and profits at home. So he marketed it overseas, targeting Sri Lankan Tamils who had fled to the West because of the ongoing war in their country.

By this time the government had opened up satellite television. Zee TV, India's first Hindi channel was launched in 1992. To quote from *Forbes* magazine in which he was featured on the cover in 2006, *"At age 28, Maran started Sun by raising $86,000 through a bank loan guaranteed by his father and his own savings. He also got some money from his granduncle's family, who took a minority stake (which Maran later bought out). The original team of 25 people included a number of Maran's college buddies from Loyola College in Chennai, 20 of whom are still with him."*

At first Maran approached Zee to give him an afternoon slot on its transponder. He couldn't get an appointment with Subhash Chandra the founder of Zee TV and was directed to a junior executive who rejected his proposal, saying it wouldn't work as there wasn't a big enough audience for Tamil programmes.

It rankled. But he managed to strike a deal with ATN, a smaller channel then competing with Zee, for a three-hour slot. Not many thought he could pull it off. But given his video magazine experience he was confident that there was a vacuum of regional language fare, especially in South India where Hindi wasn't as widely spoken. Maran took a calculated risk. TV penetration was high in the South and people were ready to watch something different. The South was also more prosperous than people in the North realised. In 2006, the Hong Kong research firm Media Partners Asia named Sun TV Asia's most profitable broadcaster, ahead of its biggest rivals Zee and Star.

Sun TV rarely spends money on expensive programming. It sells airtime slots to content producers, charging them a fee. Sun channels give them a percentage of commercial airtime that producers can sell. Sun insists on an exclusivity clause and so these producers can't work with its competitors. This business model has worked out very well for Sun.

Success came with hard work. When satellite broadcasting opened up, broadcasters were not permitted to uplink directly from India. It was only in 1998 rules were liberalised and Sun TV was among the first to uplink directly. ATN then was linked to a Russian satellite that required shipping the programme tapes to Moscow 20 days in advance. The tapes were often played in the wrong order. But viewers desperate for different programming did not mind. There were many other early glitches which had to be sorted out. Maran had to help establish cable operations in the state. To Sun TV goes the credit of getting video shop owners to turn cable operators.

Maran could see that films were going to be the most popular viewing. Sun TV started buying TV rights for South Indian films, which weren't very expensive at the time. Today, Sun has a vast movie library. From one channel in Tamil, he expanded his operations to the other southern states, launched separate channels for news, movies, music and so on. He set up a film production division Sun Pictures, which within two years acquired and distributed 21 films, most of them doing well. Sun Pictures produced the block buster *Endhiran* (*Robo*t in Hindi) with Rajnikanth and Aishwarya Rai which was the most expensive film made at that time. He acquired a Tamil newspaper *Dinakaran* which was not doing well, and turned it around to run neck to neck with the market leader *Dinathanthi*. Now he has a clutch of Tamil magazines and a large newspaper in his fold.

Maran launched direct-to-home (DTH) service, as a joint venture with Malaysian billionaire Ananda Krishnan's Astro All Asia Networks. Sun Direct was the third entrant in this segment after Subhash Chandra's Dish TV and Tata Sky, a joint venture between Tata and Star. This deal later led to a CBI inquiry and a charge sheet against Maran. When C Sivasankaran came to the Central Bureau of Investigation (CBI) headquarters in Delhi and said he had been forced to sell his telecom venture, Aircel, to Maxis in 2005 by the Maran brothers, Maran's troubles began.

Maran faces investigation because Astro All Asia Networks, a company related to Maxis, had invested ₹629 crore in Sun Direct. This included a premium of ₹549 crore. During this time, Kalanithi Maran and his wife Kaveri were issued shares at par.

SpiceJet after the initial flurry of excitement turned out to be a disaster. SpiceJet registered its highest loss of ₹1,003 crore in 2013–14, and at the end of March 2014, its debt was ₹1,738 crore. Its net worth has turned a negative ₹1,019 crore as of March 31, 2014. The civil aviation ministry told Parliament in July that SpiceJet owed the Airports Authority of India ₹110 crore in unpaid airport usage fees.

Maran had to keep injecting funds into the airline to keep it afloat. In January 2015, Maran decided to cut his losses and the board of SpiceJet Ltd decided to transfer control of the airline to Ajay Singh, who used to run the airline previously. Details of the financial dealings were not revealed.

Sun TV continues to be the undisputed market leader in Tamil Nadu and a strong number two in the other South Indian states. What worries investors is whether Maran be able to sustain this position with all the problems surrounding him?

Disasters of the '90s

The early '90s was when stock market went into tail-spin. Those who thought the bull market would never end...

THE NEPC FIASCO—TOO MUCH, TOO SOON

In the conservative atmosphere of Madras of the nineties, the NEPC group was seen as a rare breed. The group had doubled its turnover consistently between 1990 and 1995. It was then the leading producer of wind power in the country; it had launched the Trupti brand of mineral water and packaged foods. NEPC Airlines was touted as a success story; the group had diversified into textiles and paper and was planning to enter cement. NEPC, which was virtually unknown in 1990 had emerged as a ₹600 crore conglomerate in 1995. It was on a frenetic diversification spree. *"Diversification is the life of business,"* said Group Chairman Ravi Prakash Khemka. *"How can you put all your eggs in one basket? We are not fly-by-night operators."* Words he possibly came to regret later. NEPC proved that Chennai based companies were not beyond financial skullduggery.

Khemka belonged to a Marwari family which had settled in Punjab many generations ago. He arrived in Madras in the early 1960s to set up a steel trading business, which eventually led to his getting into the fabrication of machinery for sugar and cement. Being a sub-contractor had its own problems. The Khemkas wanted to get into an end product. So, they decided to focus on wind turbines. Wind turbines require structural fabrication work, which the Khemkas understood. In the early 1980s they began marketing small water-pumping windmills, which were sold for ₹20,000 to ₹30,000. Later, they became an agent of Micon of Denmark, one of the leaders in wind turbine generators.

In the 1980s, the government, in an effort to boost energy, started giving considerable concessions for non-conventional energy. Companies were allowed 100 per cent depreciation in the year of installation, which served as a tax shield. The producers could use the electricity generated for captive power; it was also fed into the local electricity grid at a pre-determined price. No taxes or duties were charged on the power generated by wind turbine generators. Financial assistance for the project was available at concessional rate of interest from IREDA and other financial institutions. There was also a tax holiday for five years in respect of profits and gains from private wind farms. In addition, the state governments also offered some concessions. All these incentives led to many private sector companies setting up wind farms, especially in Tamil Nadu and Gujarat. NEPC was the major beneficiary of these developments.

In 1989, the Khemkas renamed themselves NEPC-MICON and announced that they were the *"No.1 company in the world, in manufacturing and marketing wind turbine generators"*. The company went public in 1991. Analysts called them a major success story of the 1990s. NEPC then had an 80 per cent share of the wind energy market—a market share which it would eventually find tough to hold on to. The growing interest in wind energy brought in a whole lot of new players national as well as international.

NEPC claimed that it had a major advantage over newcomers in that it had become an expert in handling total turnkey projects. There were murmurs even then that they seemed to have a special relationship with the TNEB and the state government. Some of their successes were due to this. Chairman Khemka brushed this off saying that NEPC happened to be the most experienced player in the business.

The success and the steady cash flows in the windmill business spurred the company on to diversifications into foods, airlines and textiles. In 1993, NEPC acquired tea plantations spread over 1,300 acres at a cost of ₹15 crore. Apart from bulk sales of tea, NEPC was also packaging it, to be sold through outlets. In 1992–93, NEPC Agro's turnover was ₹32.5 crore, and it made a profit of ₹4.8 crore. For the year ended 1993–94, turn over catapulted to ₹102 crore, with a profit of ₹12 crore. The company was confident of reaching ₹200 crore in 1994–95 with a profit of ₹28 crore. For 1997–98, NEPC Agro Foods was targeting a turnover beyond ₹600 crore.

After food came transportation. NEPC Airlines, a division of NEPC bought five fairly new 55-seater Fokker aircrafts. It had one executive eight-seater aircraft, which was used for charter flights. Travel industry sources said that NEPC Airlines was the most successful private airline then. The Khemkas were even seriously considering turning a plot they owned into a functional airport.

In 1993, the Khemkas acquired a textile unit in Coimbatore and incorporated it as NEPC Textiles Ltd. They also got themselves a five-year-old paper mill in Muzaffarnagar, Uttar Pradesh. NEPC Paper and Board Ltd went public in 1995. NEPC then launched a TV channel. Much of these diversifications were funded through internal accruals or the capital market. NEPC-MICON was virtually debt-free. Khemka had some very fixed notions about financing his projects. *"I don't believe in borrowing,"* he said. *"Most bankruptcies are due to FIs. Interest is such a burden. I can pay dividend and interest,"* he said.

The NEPC group went to the public 10 times. In 1991, NEPC-MICON came out with a ₹5 crore issue. The promoters brought in ₹2.5 crore and the public ₹2.5 crore. Micon had a negligible shareholding. The next in line was NEPC Agro Foods, first with a ₹2.3 crore issue, followed by one for ₹13 crore, for which a premium of ₹30 was charged. The Khemkas managed to raise ₹105 crore from a public-and-rights issue, when they went into the airlines business. In keeping with the policy of not borrowing, each plane was bought outright for ₹11 crore. The company also raised $48 million through a GDR to fund a 100 MW wind farm. There were equity analysts who worried about the Khemkas' tendency to rely so much on the capital market. But, till the crash came, shareholders were kept happy. In 1995 the share was quoting at around ₹70—around nine times the company's earnings per share for 1994–95.

With less than 5 years' experience, NEPC did not have a well-defined management structure.

Khemka was the Chairman and his sons and nephews, all in the age group of twenty-five to thirty-five were Directors in the various companies. The Khemkas became more and more ambitious. They wanted to enter telecom, solar power and whatever else they could lay their hands on. They were raring to grow big. They were over-stretching themselves by grabbing every business which excited them.

By 1997, there was a remarkable reversal of fortunes. NEPC's survival started looking increasingly doubtful. Chairman Khemka was puzzled why everyone thought he was in trouble. "*We are different. We are simple and solid. The problems are all with the others. Not with us,*" he said. Khemka's creditors begged to differ. An irate NBFC manager said, "*They (NEPC) have zero integrity, zero principles and zero morality. They live by their wits.*" Left with absolutely no cash, Khemka started offering some of his creditors windmills from NEPC's huge inventory pile up instead of cash, while to the others the group offered free air tickets till the Airline was grounded. The group's reputation nosedived so much that there were no takers for its stock even though the shares of all its companies were being quoted well below par value.

NEPC built its resources and name on the tax breaks companies got as a result of buying windmills from NEPC Micon. NEPC prospered in a way even the Khemkas could not have imagined. In 1995–96, the company had a turnover of ₹728 crore and the profits soared to ₹99 crore. Those were the heady pre-MAT days, when every company—and that included finance companies which wanted to write off profits—found windmills an ideal purchase. Khemkas thought they could do no wrong.

The good times came to an end with the 1996 budget, which introduced the minimum alternate tax (MAT) on profits. The liquidity crunch and the 1997 budget, which reduced corporate tax further, sealed the group's fate. With a 13 per cent MAT and corporate tax having come down from 46 to 35 per cent, companies lost the incentive to buy windmills. And without the tax breaks, wind farming was no longer a lucrative industry that attracted many entrepreneurs (a wind farm then cost as much to set up as a thermal power plant of equivalent capacity). Consequently, NEPC's sales crashed.

Analysts found that the figures the company had been presenting in its annual reports were highly suspect. In 1995–96, though the company showed an operating profit of ₹118 crore, its cash flow was negative, indicating that it had to borrow to survive. And it was widely known in Chennai corporate circles that the various group companies were surviving on large-scale borrowing from the market. NEPC owed money to various suppliers and faced numerous court cases. It laid off people, cut costs drastically and held back salaries. Khemka became highly litigious and took to court whoever crossed his path.

All of Khemka's growth, before the roof came crashing down, came through public issues, GDRs and a ₹70-crore loan from IFCI. If planned well, this could have been a good nest egg when NEPC Micon lost its tax advantages. So while diversification made sense for the future, the reckless manner in which Khemka went on investing in one industry after the other did him in.

NEPC Agro Foods Ltd, promoted in 1991, was the first diversification. The company grew rapidly. Others in the food industry were always sceptical about the figures. Said an owner of a large flour mill in the south then, *"It is very difficult to have the kind of margins NEPC Agro has managed to show. Very few of us can afford to incur advertising expenses. Then there are packaging costs and margins for the wholesalers and retailers. Every time the entire industry is doing badly, as in 1993, NEPC manages to show impressive profits."* NEPC Agro ended up owing its advertising agencies HTA and RK Swamy BBDO several crores.

The second major diversification was the airline business. In its first year of operation, the Khemkas claimed it had a turnover of ₹50 crore and a profit of ₹5 crore. Aviation industry sources couldn't believe these figures. *"It is not possible to make such profits out of Fokker aircraft unless the fare is much higher than what Indian Airlines is charging,"* they said. According to former senior employees of the company, the airline was a drain on the wind energy profits.

However, before the feeder airline could stabilise, the Khemkas bid and acquired from the Damania family a controlling interest in Damania Airlines, which was renamed Skyline NEPC. The subsequent public offer to the shareholders was oversubscribed by about 1.28 times. The original offer price of ₹19.60 was paid to 10,198 shareholders out of the total of 19,358. NEPC's problems started with this acquisition when SEBI hiked up the offer price to ₹35. This meant that the Khemkas had to fork out an additional ₹10 crore from the originally planned ₹11 crore. This was a company with a net loss of ₹45 crore.

The cash crunch forced the Khemkas to halt airline operations. NEPC owed Indian Oil Corporation almost ₹30 crore for fuel and the customs authorities ₹4.5 crore on account of inland air travel tax. The two impounded its planes. NEPC Television went off the air. One of the reasons the channel was off the air was due to Khemka's inability to pay its dues to Singapore Telecom, which uplinked the channel.

NEPC Paper and Boards got entangled in all kinds of problems with SEBI. Another bad investment was cement. NEPC Textiles too turned in poor performance.

With so many lemons in its basket, the group faded into oblivion.

STERLING MAXWORTH – AN IDEA BEFORE ITS TIME

Building castles in the air

R Subramanian, the Chennai-based professional turned entrepreneur, was one of the so-called success stories of the 1990s. He introduced pioneering concepts and innovative ideas. Along with two other entrepreneurs, PN Mohan and VN Pai, Subramanian promoted Sterling Resorts in 1986, and introduced the concept of time share to Indians. On his own he promoted the Maxworth Group of companies to introduce among other things corporate farming in the country. Subramanian sought to build an empire as large as the Ambanis. Before these dreams could come true, the liquidity crunch, the crashing capital market, and the slowdown in the economy of the mid-nineties gave Subramaniam a rude reality check.

Sterling Holiday Resorts was set up by the three promoters as a partnership firm in 1986. The company took five years to establish itself because time share as a concept was unknown till then. In time share, a customer buys a week's holiday in a resort for 99 years for a one-time payment. By 1991 it had created a product which was much appreciated by customers and soon, it earned itself a good reputation. The time share gained acceptance as a cost-effective way of holidaying, largely on account of Sterling. By 1996 it had more than 73,000 customers. It had a turnover of ₹128 crore, made a profit after tax of ₹24 crore and declared a dividend of 35 per cent. The company had 12 resorts in operation and had announced 11 more resorts which were in various stages of development.

Flush with success, Sterling announced various new schemes and expansion plans. Subramanian wanted to position Sterling in every segment of the tourism business. Sterling Crown was introduced to tap the upmarket segment in the time share industry. Sterling Grand was planned in Greater Noida in UP where the company was allotted 437 acres of land for the development of a sports-cum-resort complex. In February 1995, the company launched a new product, Heritage India under which the customer was entitled to stay for three days and three nights every year for 33 years in places of religious and historical importance at a one-time cost of ₹25,000. Heritage resorts were planned at 25 locations over the next five years. Sterling also planned to build 15 three-star hotels for its inbound tourism project. A grand ₹1,500 crore plan involved investing in 2 and 3 star category hotels, a floating hotel at Raichak, a luxury cruise liner touching the Far East and Australia, and golf courses in five metros. In addition, the company was awarded two contracts by the Ministry of Railways to run luxury trains in the northern and southern circuits.

All these grand plans depended upon Sterling's ability to raise finances. But Sterling, like many other companies, did not anticipate the slowdown in the economy. Unlike other products, time share is not a priority in peoples' lives and is a purchase decision many potential customers choose to postpone. The unprecedented liquidity crunch had a direct impact on the company. Its plan to raise ₹150–200 crore through a GDR or public issue never came through. Reportedly, an effort to get a Hudco-ICICI-TFCI consortium loan of ₹250 crore also failed. This meant that a lot of its projects had to be shelved.

In most cases the company had already spent some money doing the ground work. This affected the already cash-strapped company further. This mismatch in its financing requirements made Crisil downgrade its proposed NCD issue by two notches from A+ to A-. The liquidity crunch apart, Sterling's problems were brought about by the complacency engendered by nearly five years of tremendous growth. The company became overmanned. According to people in the know, verification of sales became lax. The heavily bloated marketing staff started playing with numbers to fulfill their quotas. It is said that the company showed sales of more than 5,000 units in March 1996. By the next month it crashed to 100.

The company responded to the crisis by refocusing the management. Subramanian, who was looking after the day-to-day operations of Sterling, decided to concentrate on Sterling Holiday Resorts International Limited, a fully-owned subsidiary of the company which would deal with the Heritage project and hotels for inbound tourism. Mohan, who was in charge of the projects took charge of the day-to-day operations of Sterling.

Sterling changed many hands, limped along and got taken over by travel company Thomas Cook.

Maxworth Group—The Rise and fall

Following the success of Sterling Holiday Resorts, Subramanian wanted to give shape to his other dreams and decided to launch a group of his own. He was convinced that forestry and agriculture could be a very profitable business if you did it right. Unfortunately, he did not do it right.

In 1993, Subramanian promoted Maxworth Orchards. The concept was that the company buys 200–300 acres of dry land, decides the crop pattern, develops it and sells it to customers in packages of one acre, half or quarter acre. In an interview to *Business India* in June 1994, Subramanian had claimed that to generate ₹ 50,000 each year per acre is no problem.

Maxworth Orchards was just the beginning. From 1993 onwards, Subramanian promoted a whole lot of companies. At one point the Maxworth Group consisted of, apart from Maxworth Orchards, Maxworth Green Harvest Ltd, Maxworth Country Ltd, Maxworth Dairies Ltd, Maxworth Innovisions (India) Ltd,

Maxworth Corporate Services Ltd, and Maxworth Home Ltd. Some of these companies never saw the light of day. Of these, Maxworth Orchards, Maxworth Country and Maxworth International went public and managed to raise ₹11 crore from the market.

Initial response from both customers and investors was good. Maxworth Orchards was at one point quoting at ₹88 on the Madras Stock Exchange. The other two companies also went up to around ₹30 each. Subramanian and associates held 75 per cent of the shares in these companies. The strategy was to sell 25 per cent of the shares at a premium after they were listed and raise money for new companies. This never happened.

Within a few years, Maxworth Orchards started facing credibility problems. Again like the time share business, Maxworth's success depended on its growing number of customers and its ability to acquire land. Acquiring land in India is not an easy proposition. In some areas, Maxworth sold to investors land far in excess of what it had in physical possession. In quite a few cases, it had to go back to customers and offer an alternative plot of land to what was originally offered.

Subramanian failed to put in checks and balances. A lot of land deals made in haste led to problems. Maxworth announced the sale first and then began the land purchase. Some farmers went back on their word and others hiked up their prices. In the frenzy of achieving targets, a lot of norms were flouted. When all this was happening, sales also slowed down and the company started facing a massive liquidity crunch. The mounting cancellations did not help the situation.

There were problems on the methods employed on the planting and irrigation front. Having had no experience in horticulture, Maxworth did not understand that their nurseries in India could not provide the required quantity of graft seed samplings at the right time. They were not able to get the timing of the planting of the samplingright. The company had expert advisers from reputable academic institutions. In spite they could not master water management. Whereas farmers in the rain rich Konkan region do not plant more than 40 mango trees to an acre,

Maxworth attempted to plant 180 mango trees and 350 guava trees in the same space, which turned out to be a disaster in some places. Besides, experience with drip irrigation on dry land was also not very encouraging. All of this affected investor returns.

The company's managers at the field level were academics who did not have practical experience. They were not trained to solve problems. These supervisors themselves being untrained could not train ground level workers. Subramaniam's dream of getting returns from an industry which could not be professionalised by him failed. The marketing staff was quite clueless. They did not understand what was happening at the orchards. They would make tall promises to the customers and take them to visit to the orchards, which would turn out to be a disappointment. Subramanian was known only in the south. He was virtually unknown in the north and the west. Hence, sales in these regions were poor.

Those who were dealing with Maxworth hold Subramanian personally responsible for the mess. They say that though he was a brilliant man who came up with fantastic ideas, he refused to recognise a problem until it acquired an insoluble dimension. When the problems of land and water were brought to his notice, he simply swept them away. He had the best of people but did not use them properly. His ambition was to commercialise 1 million acres of dry land by the year 2005, as against which the company could acquire only 20,000 acres.

Even without waiting for Maxworth Orchards to become a success, Subramanian set-up a string of other companies, none of which really took off. Before Subramanian became cash-strapped, he went on a recruitment spree. He was able to sell his ideas to professionals and persuade even multinational employees to come and join him. The packages were more than attractive and Chennai companies blamed him for pushing up salary levels. It is said that the Maxworth Group at one time had more general managers and vice-presidents than Reliance. Subramanian never quite understood what hit him when his dream just collapsed one day.

The Maxworth companies wound down and were not to be heard of again.

P RAJARATHINAM – THE MYSTERY MAN

Nobody knew P Rajarathinam in the beginning of 1994, yet he rose to become a star on the Indian corporate horizon by the end of that year. The man from Coimbatore sought to grow by gobbling up companies. His takeover of Tunghabadra Sugars (renamed Deve Sugars), around which his so-called acquisitions were built, was not all that publicised. But when he took over Benares State Bank, it stunned the corporate sector. This was the time when many business houses wanted to acquire a bank. Rajarathinam was then pushed into the limelight. A string of takeovers followed in quick succession—Apollo Tubes, a cluster of 16 firms belonging to Madras Motor Group, Garware Paints, Annapoorna Foods, to name a few.

He was very cagey about revealing his source of funding. Some speculated that top-ranking politicians from Tamil Nadu were backing him, others talked about offshore money. But that did not bother Rajarathinam. Today, nobody remembers how his acquisition mania extended even to the field of media. But it was news then when he bought over the loss-making *Illustrated Weekly*, the magazine which had been shut down by the owners, The *Times of India* group. *"We are looking at a five lakh circulation,"* Rajarathinam told journalists in Bombay at the press conference organised to announce the acquisition.

A year down the line, each of his acquisitions got bogged down in some problem or the other. Income-tax authorities and the RBI started encircling him. Employees of his companies started to quit. His most cherished possession, Deve Sugars was in deep trouble, with the Company Law Board initiating enquiries.

All his deals turned out to be dubious. Some examples: the IT department questioned Rajarathinam and his men on the purchase of machinery from the Madras-based Sivannayagi Engineers Enterprises Private Ltd, a company supposed to be owned by an associate of Rajarathinam. It was just that neither the supplier company nor the machinery could be traced. The authorities then revealed a reverse entry in the balance sheet. The entry pertained to fees paid by the Singapore-based Agrimari Impex Enterprise for export of 'lobster development technology', which sum was never received.

Deve Sugars acquired the soya division in Madhya Pradesh from AV Thomas & Co (India) Ltd. The deal with AVT followed his buying Rajadhiraj Industries, a soyabean extraction unit in Madhya Pradesh. This move of Rajarathinam drew derisive comments from industry watchers. For one, the mere location made Rajadhiraj Industries an unattractive proposition for any southerner (even the much experienced and respected AVT had hived off its soya division precisely because it could not manage a losing unit located far from its base in the south). For another, the acquisition was ill-timed. Rajarathinam took over Rajadhiraj Industries when the soyabean extraction industry was facing a recession. A sick company, Rajadhiraj Industries had serious labour problems as well.

In September 1994, he took over 16 companies belonging to Sivan Nair of the Madras Motor group at an agreed price of ₹2 crore. He increased his holding in each of these companies to 60 per cent. However it was subsequently revealed that what he had done was a mere book entry. No money was pumped in. He gave shares of one company to another in lieu of the money. The 16 firms he took over together owed nearly ₹22 crore to banks and institutions. There was an outstanding of nearly ₹12 crore in dividend payment by Udaya Business Financiers Ltd. to Sivan Nair's companies. Rajarathinam's game plan revolved around his ability to get Deve Sugars' shares listed on the stock exchanges. With this end in view, he sought to merge it with Udaya Business Financiers Ltd. This proposal suffered a setback with the Madras High Court granting a stay against the move.

Rajarathinam's targets were companies which were perfect BIFR cases. He was confident that he could turn these companies around. His takeover of Garware Paints turned out to be a different story. In all his takeovers, his entry was facilitated by infusion of fresh funds and creation of further equity. But it was only in Garware Paints that Rajarathinam bought into the shares of the existing promoters. He picked up a 17 per cent stake. But the going was far from smooth.

In the renamed Deve Paints, the FIs which held 42 per cent of the stake, did not allow Rajarathinam to raise capital through preferential allotment. Deve Paints' liabilities to a consortium of banks was about ₹20 crore. Besides, its exposure to market borrowing was ₹12 crore. He had in all ₹80 crore worth of liabilities at Deve Paints. When one of the creditors of Garware Paints, Bhor Industries, threatened him with legal action, he bought peace through an out-of-court settlement. This resulted in many creditors making a beeline for him. He had over 18 cases pending against him at Garware Paints. He then let Deve Paints go to BIFR. So much for rescuing BIFR companies.

Rajarathinam sought to build his empire by buying what he thought was underpriced shares. He did not give any thought to management and other related problems. His entire gameplan came unstuck when the market collapsed. He could not raise funds in the market. By 1996, SEBI was acquiring teeth and started examining Rajarathinam's deals seriously. He went underground in 1997 leaving a trail of unpaid clients, bounced cheques and ruined companies. He was rumoured to have been hibernating at Delhi for two years.

Rajarathinam had the audacity to return in 1999 in the *avatar* of a saviour of Chennai's down and out financial sector. This time, the takeovers seemed to involve no monetary exchange. The stalwarts of the financial sector were not amused. He started his second innings with the takeover of the Maxworth group. Maxworth had already accumulated losses amounting to ₹20 crore. Rajarathinam acquired every loser in sight, such as Iggi Resorts, Readymoney, Sanmac Motor Finance and Sanmac Finlease, Abco Plastics and Synergy Finance. Most of the original promoters of these companies were fleeing from their liabilities and enraged depositors/investors. The common problem of those companies was liquidity. Rajarathinam this time round dispensed with even the formality of making financial commitments. He was acquiring companies almost free. It was claimed that the buying price was ₹1 a company! The story behind this throwaway price was equally interesting. The promoters of these companies and their families apparently received threats from local thugs—some of them major underworld figures. Irate depositors were said to be behind these thugs. Added to the promoters' woes was police harassment. Rajarathinam was actually able to bail out some promoters like T Arunachalam, the core promoter of the Sanmac group. How he did it is something we will never know.

Sources in the NBFC sector squarely blamed the RBI for Rajarathinam's second coming. The RBI was trying to cleanse the sector of unincorporated companies, post-CRB scam in May 1997. The RBI regulations linking the quantum of deposits accepted by the company to the company's credit rating in January 1998, and the stipulation that required NBFCs to refund the excess deposits within a year put tremendous pressure on them. Though the norm was later relaxed to three years, the damage was done as far as investor confidence was concerned. Regular RBI ads giving the list of NBFCs rejected for registration also set off a panic reaction. Recession too made it difficult for the NBFCs to recover their loans, finally leading to defaults.

People in the financial markets did question the deals Rajarathinam was getting into. SEBI's takeover code was totally ignored. The Madras Stock Exchange on which most of the companies in question were listed was in the dark about these 'takeovers'. The depositors of the companies Rajarathinam took over bid goodbye to their money.

This time round Rajarathinam disappeared never to be heard of again. People say that he has been spotted in London!

Leading Industries

Many of these industries are much larger than people realise

TAMIL NADU'S IT STORY

The IT industry in Tamil Nadu started to grow without drawing attention to itself. It is said that every fourth household in Chennai has an IT employee. At last count, Chennai has 1683 Software Exporting units employing about 285,000 Software professionals. Every big name in the IT industry has a large campus in Chennai·. The city has the largest bandwidth in India—13.52 tbps through two submarine OFC cables linking Chennai with the rest of the world. Electronic Corporation of Tamil Nadu (ELCOT) is currently developing IT SEZs in tier II cities such as Coimbatore, Madurai, Tirunelveli, Salem, Trichy and Hosur. The IT story in Tamil Nadu started with the country's largest and the most prestigious IT giant TCS setting up operations in Madras.

TCS

India was an unlikely place to start any export activity in the '70s, especially in computing. PCs were still not invented and databases did not exit. TCS had imported a Burroughs 1728 machine and, under the rules of the times, had to export twice the value in four years. So, software services exports were critical.

One of the early orders was from the UK to build a product. S Mahalingam who joined TCS in 1970 and who retired as its CFO in 2013, travelled to the UK to get the details. Those were the days when the requirements and specifications from the UK to India could be sent only through post. International calls were difficult and expensive and there was no direct dialling. The first post was followed up with another from a different post office to ensure that even if one was lost in transit, the other would reach.

Then Mahalingam was sent to the US to run the operations there before moving back to India. FC Kohli, the legendary founder and CEO of TCS dispatched him this time to develop the Chennai centre, which had less than 30 people. (TCS Chennai has almost 60000 people working for it today). Very few remember that TCS entered Chennai in 1983 and that was the beginning of serious IT industry in the city.

Kohli, S Ramadorai (successor to Kohli) and Mahalingam started testing the waters in Chennai. In 1976, TCS had set up the computer operations for Best &Crompton. It had a contract for four years. This was the first time IT operations was outsourced in the country. The first IBM mainframe TCS acquired was installed at the company's Chennai facility in 1988, four years after Mahalingam moved to Chennai. "*We wondered how we were going to make use of it. We ran out of capacity in two years.*" says Mahalingam.

The city had infrastructure. There were educational institutions. In those days the South was preferred for safety reasons as well. It was far away from Indo-Pak conflicts. Housing was available. Compared to Bombay and Bangalore, Chennai had the capability to scale up and grow during those years. The power situation was better as compared to others. Veterans from that era joke that Chennai was the best kept secret of TCS. They also joke that TCS was known as Tamil Computer Service. The legendary Nasscom Chief Dewang Mehta used to refer to TCS as Tamil Cobol Sangam.

TCS, Chennai, started operating out of Best & Crompton. It then moved to its own office on Cathedral Road. TCS started its training programme in 1985 in Chennai which was highly valued. In the '80s India was quite computer illiterate. It was time for experimentation. Says G Kameshwar, Principal Consultant, TCS, who has led and been part of teams architecting solutions for clients in many parts of the world, "*We had been working on an ICL mainframe which was a good workhorse. Then there was transformation to mini computers, unix boxes, enterprise machines till the arrival of the personal computer (PC). The first PC landed in Chennai in 1985. We recognised ahead of others that the PC had commercial applications and started experimenting to create a market.*" A sugarcane accounting system for Thiru Arooran Sugars was designed by TCS which Kameshwar says was a fascinating project in this genre. The sugar industry is such that during season the factories work 24/7. Using innovative software architecture designs, new generation PC-XTs were used to deliver enterprise application from weighment to accounting. In addition to new generation PC applications, the old ICL workhorse continued to deliver Bureau Processing services. TNEB, TVS and other corporations leveraged this.

Corporations also started building in-house EDP departments with mini-computers. English Electric Company in Chennai contracted TCS for developing a suite of applications on their PDP-11 computer. The Income Tax department of the Government of India in Chennai, used TCS to develop systems for Summary Assessment, Scrutiny Assessment, Challan Processing etc. Companies in Tamil Nadu were alive to this new era of Information Processing and were open to experimentation. Hardware companies were introducing all kinds of new models. Sundaram Finance bought a Norsk-Data computer, a name that current generation IT professionals may not recognise (Norsk Data wound up in 1992).

Meanwhile, banks were now looking to take first steps in automation. TCS developed a single user PC based system called IBS, in Chennai, which was implemented in Bank of Madura. As a next step, TCS looked to develop a mini-computer based software product, which would cater to total branch automation. Thus was born ISBS (Integrated Standard Banking System). ISBS was also developed in TCS Chennai, and went on to power the branches of most of the nationalised banks, all over India.

Around the same time, the birth of offshore IT development was happening. This was at a time when there was no overseas network links, no email, and phone connections were expensive and limited. A lot of innovation took place around this model that made offshore services work. Solutions had to be found continuously. Everyday there were new questions. There were technological and logistical challenges. There were limited phone lines. In spite of these hurdles TCS started developing the offshore model which completely changed the game. "*This was disruptive innovation*", says Mahalingam. Teams would go overseas, do the study, do the analysis, come back to Chennai, develop in TCS machines, take the work back and implement it in the customers' machines. Another disruptive innovation by TCS was introducing maintenance services for off-shore operations.

In the period between 1985 and 1990, TCS had become pretty mature in software engineering. CASE (computer aided software engineering tools) for various machines were developed. All this enabled the company to pitch forward to the next level which was a most challenging assignment. TCS won the Swiss SegaInterSettle (SIS) project in 1989. It was implemented entirely from Chennai. This was one assignment that took not just TCS, but the whole of Indian IT industry to a different level altogether.

To quote Ramadorai from his book, *The TCS Story:*

"In 1989 TCS was presented with an opportunity that helped catapult the company into the big league. SegaInterSettle (SIS) also known as SEGA, wanted to create a real-time securities settlement system or Settlement Communication System (Secom). SEGA already had a depository which it had been using for the past twenty years, but now it wanted a second generation system. Therefore, the fixed price project involved a mixture of migration work and new software development. TCS bid for and won the SEGA project in conjunction with our Swiss partner, TKS-Teknosoft, and we won it against competition from Andersen Consulting (later renamed Accenture).

TCS had no experience in clearing settlements while Andersen Consulting had undertaken many depositories and was an established leader in this field. So how did we do it? First of all a team of young, eager and bright TCSers was dispatched to study the SEGA requirements. They spent about three months talking to the customer in order to understand what they required. We proposed that we would do the entire development in India whereas Andersen Consulting said they would do it in Manila. I think Andersen took it for granted that they would win the bid and that SEGA would never award it to a company from India. This overconfidence perhaps showed in the way they projected themselves.

In comparison, we were the underdogs. We wanted the contract badly and we saw it as a game changing opportunity. We had the passion and inclination to go the extra mile so we worked as though we were possessed. Although the bid pricing was quite similar, the major difference was in our approach and our commitment. We gave a timeline which was more realistic and produced a technical proposal that was very detailed and comprehensive."

All settlements are made in real time. Billions of dollars change hands every day. To give this to an Indian company was a brave decision. It continues to be done out of Chennai. Those who worked on this project have made it big in TCS and outside. Lakshmi Narayanan who went on to set up Cognizant Technologies was the Resident Manager of TCS at Switzerland during the course of this assignment. Baru Rao, who went on to head Cap Gemini in India led the Database Design in SEGA. S Padmanabhan, who was leading the core Clearing module in SEGA, was a member of the TCS Board of Directors, and is now the Chairman of TQMS (Tata Quality Management Services). LN Srinivasakrishnan, who headed the Banking module, later left TCS, and went on to lead the Citibank Relationship for Infosys in America. NG Subramaniam, who headed the Quality function in SEGA, is now the Chairman of Tata Elxsi. The list is long. Many of the current top leadership team in TCS earned their stripes in SEGA. Says G Kameshwar, who was in charge of Architecture Design of SEGA—"*This was like the Apollo 11 moon-landing. A new planet had been reached. There cannot be another SEGA.*"

Every time a stock is traded or settled in Switzerland, software code from Chennai is at work....

When implementation of SEGA was taking place, TCS Chennai was also working for an assignment for IBM research labs in Sweden. One of the young programmers who worked on this assignment in the early 1990s is N Chandrashekaran (Chandra), who is now the CEO of TCS and who has taken TCS to the global stage as the leader of the Indian IT industry. The IBM assignment that Chandra worked on was one that demanded the highest levels of quality. Chennai IT had come of age.

TCS soon started doing highly demanding assignments with zero defects. The world literally opened up. Jobs for British telecom, American and UK insurance companies and banks were all done out of Chennai. Then TCS opened a centre for HP in Chennai in 1995. TCS Chennai set the benchmark for Indian IT. It was the first centre of any Indian IT company to get the ISO 9000 certification. In the mid-nineties it also got CMM level 5, the highest certification in Software Maturity. All this work was also done out of Chennai.

A M Murugappa Chettiar
Founder, Murugappa Group

A Vellayan
Chairman (4th Generation)

T S Santhanam
Founder, Sundaram Finance

Suresh Krishna
Chairman, Sundram Fasteners

Venu Srinivasan
Chairman and Managing Director, TVS Motor Company
(Picture Courtesy -- TS Ramesh)

T V Sundaram Iyengar
Founder, TVS Group

Mallika Srinivasan and A Sivasailam
Chairman, TAFE
(Portrait – Founder S Anantharamakrishnan)

Mammen Mapillai
Founder, MRF
(Picture courtesy : *The Hindu*)

K M Mammen
Chairman, MRF (2nd Generation)

N Srinivasan
Vice Chairman and Managing Director, India Cements
(Picture Courtesy – *Business India*)

R Thyagarajan
Founder, Shriram Group

Dr P C Reddy
Founder and Chairman, Apollo Hospitals
(Picture courtesy : TS Ramesh)

A C Muthiah
Former Chairman, SPIC
(Picture courtesy – TS Ramesh)

C Sivasankaran
Chairman, Siva Group
(Picture courtesy : *Business India*)

Kalanithi Maran
Chairman and Managing Director, Sun TV
(Picture courtesy : TS Ramesh)

S Ramadorai
Former Chairman, TCS
(Picture courtesy: *The Hindu*)

Nalli Kuppuswamy Chetty
Chairman, Nalli Business House

Lata and Pandiarajan
Founders, Ma Foi

J Murugavel
Founder CEO, Bharat Matrimony

V Shankar
Founder, CAMS

R Srinivasan
Founder and Managing Director, Redington

Rajiv Mittal
Managing Director and CEO, VA Tech Wabag

G K Sundaram
Founder, Lakshmi Mills

Rajshree Pathy
Chairperson and Managing Director, Rajshree Group of companies
(Picture Courtesy: *The Hindu*)

Hemalatha Annamalai
Founder and CEO, Ampere Vehicles
(Picture Courtesy: *The Hindu*)

N Mahalingam
Founder, Sakthi Group

CK Ranganathan
Founder and Chairman, CavinKare

Sridhar Vembu
Founder and CEO, ZOHO
(Picture Courtesy: *The Hindu*)

Girish Mathrubhootam
Co-founder, Freshdesk

Girish Ramdas
Co-founder and CEO, Magzter

Mithun Sacheti
Co-founder and CEO, CaratLane

CK Kumaravel and Veena
Co-founders, Naturals Salon and Spa

In the mid-nineties Tamil Nadu government made its move. TCS was asked to give a presentation to the group of Secretaries of different departments of the state Government on IT. Mahalingam was part of the task force that was asked by the Government of Tamil Nadu to do a feasibility study for setting up a software park in Chennai. Thus was born the TIDEL Park.

Though that was small, it was in the right direction: the OMR, or the Old Mahabalipuram Road, which has now become the main hub of Chennai IT. In 1999, TCS created an IT campus in the Chennai suburb Sholinganallur which could accommodate 1500 people. The seed for the IT corridor in the city was sown by TCS. *"We had to build the roads. We had to buy land from government and private parties. When we had a problem with some clearance the then Chief Minister Jayalalithaa stepped in and sorted it out. We thought that the campus was too big. As it happened we needed more space,"* says Mahalingam. Ratan Tata himself came to inaugurate the Sholinganallur facility. In 2005, Infosys set up a complex here. Companies like Polaris, Pentafour and many others also built big facilities in Sholinganallur.

Then came the complex in Siruseri Special Economic Zone, which was the single largest of its kind in Asia, showcasing the technical and engineering capabilities of TCS. This facility, housing six software development blocks, accommodates over 27,000 IT professionals in a built-up area of 5 million square feet. What started in the 1980s as a small office having less than a hundred people had now grown to a giant industry with 500 buses plying everyday bringing employees to TCS campuses. The future expansion will be in the Tier II cities of Tamil Nadu.

COGNIZANT

The other Chennai based global company is Cognizant. Its Vice-Chairman Lakshmi Narayanan's project as a student of management at the Indian Institute of Science, Bangalore, was on the use of computers in corporations. This was in 1975, when computers were used so infrequently that some companies just leased machines. But his project turned out to be most appropriate as he went on to set up one of India's largest IT companies in Chennai. Lakshmi (as he is known) entered the industry when he was selected by TCS at a campus interview, the second-ever conducted by the organisation.

Lakshmi was sent to Switzerland in 1989, where he headed the famous SEGA project and also to set up the European offices for TCS. When he returned, he was posted in Delhi, but he did not enjoy living in Delhi. That was when he decided to take up an offer from Dun & Bradstreet to move to Chennai to set up Cognizant. D&B was keen on establishing a unit in India for some of its development work. It was too big an opportunity to pass up.

After various push and pulls, as he puts it, Lakshmi took the plunge in 1994. He chose Chennai to locate the start-up, despite hailing from Bangalore. It was a start-up in the real sense with a very small office. *"In the first two-three months, I kept wondering what I had got into."* Today with over 50 delivery centres worldwide and approximately 199,700 employees as of September 30, 2014, Cognizant is a member of the NASDAQ100, the S&P 500, the Forbes Global 2000 and the Fortune 500 and is ranked among the top performing and fastest growing companies in the world.

In the initial years, Cognizant did not take any outside work other than D&B. It was doing business between $1 million and $5 million. However, the employees wanted more challenges. D&B being a huge conglomerate, every year there were shake ups. People were constantly moving, which led to a lot of uncertainty. Besides, the Chennai operations could not attract good talent. By 1997, Cognizant was allowed to take-up outside work, just before it went public in 1998. The IPO was expected to raise $70 million, but it was during an investor conference in the US that the news of nuclear tests by India broke. The company ended up getting around $40 million.

This did not worry D&B, as their investment in the Chennai operations was only $1 million. However, things started moving much faster after the IPO. *"As a public company, we learnt to stand on our feet. We had to master the art of selling. So we hired sales people. Thanks to D&B, some doors were opened. We started getting tier II, III, IV kinds of customers. For instance, we handled Pacific Stock Exchange, which is like the Madras Stock Exchange,"* recalls Lakshmi.

Cognizant pursued financial services and healthcare as its focus areas. Though Cognizant is an American company listed in the US, most of its operations are run from Chennai. *"We have never thought of India, US or Europe differently. A Vice-President is a Vice-President, whichever part of the world he is working from."*

Kumar Mahadeva, Vice-President of D&B, whose responsibility was to help set up Cognizant in Chennai, came in full time when the company went public in 1998. He was the Chairman and CEO. Lakshmi was President and COO. After Mahadeva stepped down, Lakshmi took charge as the CEO in 2003. Under his leadership as CEO (2003–2006), Cognizant became the youngest IT services company to reach the $1 billion revenue milestone. The same period saw Cognizant triple its revenue and net profits and enter the NASDAQ 100 and S&P 500 index.

Today, Cognizant is the largest IT employer (including Coimbatore) in Tamil Nadu. It is the second largest US Company in the country after IBM. "*We are continuing to grow. Chennai is the hub for Cognizant's offshore operations*", says R Chandrasekaran, Executive Vice Chairman, Cognizant. Tamil Nadu accounts for 17 to 18 per cent of IT exports in the country. "*If it were 25 per cent by 2023, it will amount to $100 billion. Today, the industry size is $100 billion,*" says *he.*

There are a couple of medium-sized Chennai IT companies who have been aspiring to hit big time for a couple of decades. They are still trying. One individual came from Delhi and made Chennai his home. The other, a scion from the old economy followed his dream to set up a world class IT company from Chennai.

POLARIS

Arun Jain, a first generation entrepreneur from Delhi, chose to set up Polaris in Chennai in 1993. He graduated in electrical engineering from Delhi University in 1983. Jain comes from a large family of eight brothers and two sisters. His father was a government servant. There were no luxuries to think of. However, young Arun wanted to build something on his own and had always been a man with a *lakshya* (goal). With two other friends, Jain started scouting around for opportunities to work in the IT area. A small set-up, Nucleus Software Workshop, came into being in 1986. This unit essentially provided back-end services to Citibank global consumer banking operations.

The friends bought a scooter, which they shared. They graduated to an old Fiat the following year. The association with Citibank and the fact that this MNC was impressed with the youngsters led to more projects. Citibank's takeover of the Diner's Club card business presented further challenges, which were met. When Citibank decided to relocate its global consumer banking business to Chennai from Delhi, it was time for Jain to look at Chennai seriously and also think about launching his own organisation.

Polaris Software Lab was set up in 1993 with just ₹25,000. "*In 1994, our lakshya was to turn this ₹1.5-crore company into a ₹100-crore company in six years. We ended up doing ₹270 crore."* Polaris went public in 2000 and did something audacious the next year. Jain merged his ₹294-crore company with ₹321-crore OrbiTech Solutions, a technology subsidiary of the Citigroup. Overnight, he headed a company that had 3,800 employees with a turnover of over ₹600 crore.

From 2004 onwards Jain has been focussing on building the largest financial technology suite in the country. Many companies are only in one space in financial services. Polaris has developed 95 products in all areas like core banking, lending, cards, wealth, brokerage, securities, cash management and so on. Jain says that in financial technology, Polaris can provide most complex solutions, end to end. *"From 2001, we knew that providing just services will last only for a decade. We had to get into products."* When Polaris took over OrbiTech, the product had very rich functionality. But it was a monolith that had to be broken down into different services to provide clients whatever they wanted. Jain put 800 people on the job in Delhi, Chennai and Hyderabad. The OrbiTech consolidation was the beginning of Polaris's services to products journey.

Jain says the biggest challenge in this business is to keep reinventing oneself every 7 to 10 years. *"Course correction is a very painful process. The biggest bottleneck is old management. To start with, I have to change myself. I have to be willing to take the pain myself."* When Polaris grew rapidly in 2002, with several new subsidiaries, it earned the reputation of not being able to retain people. That was a course correction Jain had to implement. He started concentrating on building his human resources. The attrition rate among the top management is now less than 3 per cent.

When the business model had to be global, Jain decided to play the role of the chief architect himself. *"I rolled up my sleeves between 2003 and 2007 and plunged into technology architecture."* He followed it up by taking over marketing for a year. *"I read every book on marketing available. We took 1,000 TV spots on Wall Street alone for six months in 2009 to let our market know what Polaris is all about."*

Polaris finally restructured its businesses into services and products divisions for greater focus and efficiency in 2013 and announced the demerger in March 2014. When the separation was happening, the profits of Polaris remained flat. Jain has always been an optimist. He then restructured Polaris's businesses into services and products divisions for greater focus and efficiency in 2013, and separated the two businesses in March 2014.

In November 2015, he and a few other shareholders sold the 53% stake they held in the company to Massachusetts-based Virtusa Corporation for a consideration of ₹1,173 crore. His focus is now on building a great IT products company, Intelligence Design Arena. He hopes to grow his products business by twenty-five per cent in the next five years.

RAMCO SYSTEMS

Chennai-based Ramco Systems Ltd (RSL) came out with what it thought was a path breaking Enterprise Resource Planning (ERP) offering on the cloud about five years ago. It launched Ramco On Demand Analytics and Ramco On Demand Gateway products. These are India's first full-fledged ERP offerings on the cloud. Typically, ERP systems take months, sometimes years, to implement and require hundreds of consultants. Ramco says its products can cut the process really short and with minimum man power.

The low profile, low key PR Venkatrama Raja, Vice-Chairman and Managing Director of the company is a chemical engineer from Madras University and an MBA from the University of Michigan. He worked in the family business for a few years before taking the group into IT. This was just before liberalisation, when entrepreneurs were looking for businesses that did not require licensing and the rigmarole of clearances.

Raja's grandfather had founded the Ramco group, starting a textile mill at Rajapalayam in Tamil Nadu almost 80 years ago. Today, the group has interests in cement, building products, textiles and, of course, software. *"We are in business and we understand business. We wanted to develop products to do business. So ERP was a good choice,"* says Raja. In the initial years, he experimented with products similar to CorelDRAW and Adobe Photoshop. He was fascinated by the combination of art and computing. As he ruefully admits, the products were not built on Windows and the company didn't quite know how to market them.

At this point, the services market opened up. Raja decided to stick to products, that too business products, and focus on ERP. RSL which was set up as the research and development division of the group was spun off as a separate company that was incorporated in 1997. Ramco is already one of the world's largest providers of aviation maintenance and engineering (M&E) and maintenance repair and overhaul (MRO) software solutions to customers around the globe. It is the only company in India in this niche market.

In the early 2000s Raja's team created a brand new architecture and moved its entire product line to it. "*These are very powerful business applications that mature over many years. It took Oracle and SAP 15 years. It took them loads of people to create an application. We wanted to do it with far fewer people. We wanted to deliver it quickly with fewer errors and with the same results. We have worked on cutting through complexities,*" he says.

RSL's ERP applications can be launched on any digital device. You can do ERP from a car or even a mobile. Raja calls this approach an abstraction. "*It is not about the number of programmers. It is not about clever coding. It is an approach. Nobody believes that a small company can do this.*" He admits that investment in an abstraction is a very risky business. It took them five years to come to this stage. "*We could not show any results overnight. In fact, people thought we were fooling around with something and had gone to sleep. We had a team of 40 to 50 people who were passionate about this.*"

"*I wanted everything running on the internet. Luckily, cloud happened and we were ready for it. Business models are changing. IT models are changing. People are setting up cloud infrastructure and are looking for partners. We want to be there for the next generation.*" Ramco's product allows customers to build their own unique sets of extended functionalities and integrate with the core ERP on the cloud. "*It allows you to get a multi-million-dollar ERP system with no investment,*" Raja explains. "*You can stop worrying about your software—just run your business.*"

Can Raja really take on the world leaders with his radically different product and approach? *"We can offer far more complex products than what the traditional companies can do because of our architecture. There are only four or five ERP systems in the world. We are one of the new ones with a new architecture. We automate completely. For the market leaders it is going to take time and enormous investment to make the changes. Adaptability and stability are two opposites. We have managed to marry them. Now larger customers have started looking at us,"* he says. Raja says that even if RSL manages to get 8–9 per cent of the international market share that will be a good achievement. *"I want RSL to be a company that India can be proud of."*

However, after many years of struggles and ups and downs, adopting new technologies ahead of others and also being admired by the industry, Ramco Systems never really made profits. That seems to be changing now. Ramco appointed a new CEO, Virendar Aggarwal, who is from HCL Technologies in 2012. He has turned the company into a profitable one. He has also transformed it into a hundred per cent software product company. Industry is now keenly watching Ramco Systems to see whether it will finally succeed in its current avatar.

Chennai has been the first city that shaped India's IT punch. But many feel that it has not received enough appreciation for that role.

THE AUTO INDUSTRY IN TAMIL NADU

Several times a year, there are performances by artists from South Korea in Chennai's up market Sir Mutha Venkatasubba Rao concert hall, which seats 1,100 people. The auditorium gets filled to capacity with South Koreans living in Chennai. Considering there are more than 3,000 Koreans who have made Chennai their home, this should not be a surprise. Chennai is getting exposed to South Korean music, dance, art and films. It is not just South Korean art and culture that people in Chennai are getting used to. Today, there are six authentic Korean restaurants in the city. There are another four in the city's outskirts where Korean investments are located. *Kimchi* (a Korean dish) is no longer a strange word to the Tamilian who is getting increasingly exposed to international cuisine.

This influx of South Koreans into Chennai is a 20-year-old phenomenon. It all started when Hyundai Motors decided to enter India and set up a manufacturing facility in Chennai. Hyundai Motors India was established in 1996 in Irrungattukottai near Chennai with an investment of a little over $600 million. Today, it is the second-largest car manufacturer in the country. Hyundai said when it came to India that it wanted to make India a global hub for the export of its cars. A statement the company has lived up to.

When Hyundai decided to invest in India, it did a thorough market survey. It had to choose between Pune and Chennai. It decided on Chennai as the city had a port. *"At that time, there were 100 engineering colleges in Tamil Nadu. The state offered impressive human resources. South Indians were also seen as more hard-working than the North Indians,"* says Shin a Korean entrepreneur who has made Chennai his home.

Initially, twenty Koreans moved in. They were coming to a country they knew little about, and there were huge hurdles like language and the weather. *"Many were reluctant to come to Chennai,"* smiles Shin who has lived here for almost 20 years. *"The Westerners play golf and give up when the temperature crosses 40 Celsius. The local people can play up to 45 Celsius. But Koreans and Japanese play even when temperatures shoot above 45 Celsius. We don't give up."*

As a result of this attitude, what started as a trickle has grown to 3,000 plus. Sriperumbudur where the Hyundai factory is located is almost a Korean township now. There are ancillary manufacturers and 200 sub-contractors, all from Korea.

Hyundai came soon after the American multinational Ford decided to set up shop in Chennai. It was Ford's arrival which was to make the city the largest automobile hub in the country. Mahindra-Ford which was the largest of the new automobile projects which came up in the mid-nineties chose Tamil Nadu over Maharashtra to locate its main assembly plant and Tamil Nadu has never looked back. Sleepy Chennai won over all its rivals.

After almost a year of wooing Ford and the Mahindras, Tamil Nadu pulled off what was considered a near-impossible feat. The TN government signed an MoU with the Managing Director of the new joint venture John Parker, and RK Pitamber, Managing Director of Mahindra and Mahindra (M&M), to set up a plant in Chennai. At that time the projected investment was around ₹1,500 crore, not counting the investment in the hundreds of ancillaries that were to be set up around the state-of-the-art plant. The ecstatic bureaucracy gave Chief Minister Jayalalithaa full marks for her initiative in bringing the project to the state.

This was indeed a major coup for Jayalalithaa because her rival, Manohar Joshi, the Maharashtra Chief Minister, was as assiduous as her in his pursuit of the project. He met senior officials of the Ford-Mahindra team at least twice to lure them into putting up the plant in Pune. Apart from the vastly superior quality of lobbying by the Tamil Nadu bureaucracy, the Enron fiasco worked against Maharashtra. And as for Tamil Nadu, its generosity in locating the project of another US giant, DuPont, after it was thrown out of Goa, worked in its favour. Of course, M&M which has most of its large manufacturing facilities in Maharashtra (and some Shiv Sena unions), in an effort to avoid displeasing the state government, worked out a plan to assemble the Ford Escort cars at their Nasik plant and the Ford Fiesta in the new plant near Madras.

The entire exercise was a rare instance of cooperation between the state government and the private sector. For instance, C Ramachandran, the then Industry Secretary, got Suresh Krishna of Sundram Fasteners (TVS group) to talk to old friend and M&M chairman Keshub Mahindra. The Madras-based auto component industry played a major supportive role. KV Shetty who was a Director in India Pistons then, said that they worked in sync with the government. They made all information available at any given point.

The state was in dire need of a major automobile project. Although a large proportion of auto component manufacturers of original equipment were based in Chennai, Tamil Nadu had not attracted a large project in decades. Ramachandran had been knocking at various doors like Maruti (when it was talking about a third plant), Telco for its small car project and M&M.

When Tamil Nadu first approached Mahindra-Ford, the joint venture had already shortlisted three locations—Gurgaon, Pune and Chennai. Chennai was the last choice as Ford felt that the market was in the west and the north and locating a plant in the south would increase its costs. The state launched into an all-out marketing effort. *"We put together a highly professional multi-media presentation on the state which left a very favourable initial impression,"* said M Raman, Director of Tamil Nadu Export Promotion and Guidance Bureau.

Then Ford sent a 200-query questionnaire covering all aspects of Chennai like climatic conditions, social conditions, etc. The Ford management had 40 parameters which a site had to satisfy. They included factors like access to railways, port, flight connections, proximity to national highways, vendors, labour, political stability, bureaucratic support and so on.

Tamil Nadu was able to provide 300 acres of prime industrial land which fitted in with the parameters. "*They were so particular. They wanted us to make sure that there was no other industry within twenty kilometres which will create dust pollution because of their ultra-modern paint shop,*" said S Arvind, Chairman, Tamil Nadu Industrial Development Corporation. The government also assured uninterrupted power and water supply. Factors like hospital facilities worked in Tamil Nadu's favour. The government with the help of the American Consulate immediately started work on an international school, to satisfy Ford. It was also rumoured that Jayalalithaa herself spoke to senior officials in the US government in Washington hoping to use their clout to persuade Ford.

Within a few months, twenty Ford teams arrived in Madras. When a team from Ford Germany was worried about flooding in the low-lying areas, the government immediately flew down a neutral consultant, Mott Mcdonald from the UK, and produced a report which satisfied Ford. Almost two decades later in January 2016 the Ford factory did get flooded.

These quick reactions had a positive impact. The really tough negotiations began when Tamil Nadu did not compare favorably with Maharashtra on sales tax. Although the state was giving sales tax exemption and deferral schemes, the Mahindra-Ford team felt that as the maximum sales would be outside TN, interstate sales tax should be reduced.

All these negotiations resulted in a new policy for super mega projects. They changed the industry profile of Tamil Nadu irrevocably. Once Ford and Hyundai moved in, the state realised it was on to a good thing. Ever since, Tamil Nadu has given special incentives to organisations who are all investing more than ₹4000 crore in the state. Today Chennai is set to emerge among the top five auto clusters globally, as one of the world's largest destinations for the automotive industry. There are companies making bicycles, cars, trucks, earth moving equipment, rail coaches, and even battle tanks present in the city. It has become the home for many major global automobile manufacturers. Apart from Ford and Hyundai, German premium automaker BMW, and Franco-Japan joint venture Renault-Nissan have set up manufacturing facilities in the city and its suburbs. It is become common for heads of these multinationals to come to Chennai to inaugurate a new facility of a vehicle. Nobody bats an eyelid.

It is not only auto manufacturers who are making a beeline for Chennai. Auto component manufacturers like Visteon and Delphi produce more than 25 per cent of their components here. Domestic players like the two-wheeler manufacturer TVS Motors, Enfield (which was revived after tractor maker Eicher took it over) with its iconic brand Bullet, and Japanese Yamaha all have their manufacturing base in Chennai. Hinduja group flagship, the commercial vehicle maker, Ashok Leyland has been in Tamil Nadu since independence. The country's second largest tractor manufacturer TAFE is based in Chennai. USA's Caterpillar, Japan's Komatsu and South Korea's Doosan have chosen Chennai to establish large earth moving equipment manufacturing plants.

Hyundai Motor India exports more than 40 per cent of cars manufactured at its Sriperumbudur plant to European countries using the Chennai port. Recent entrant Renault-Nissan adopted a similar strategy for its car 'Micra', destined for both the domestic market and exports to over 100 countries in Europe, the Middle East and Africa. The alliance partners' manufacturing facility in Oragadam has an annual production capacity of four lakh cars, from where Renault has started exporting its SUV Duster to UK. Renault had to choose between Maharashtra and Tamil Nadu to put up its Indian plant. It settled for Chennai. People from Renault's global operations come to Chennai to take lessons on how to start up a plant and apply it to other countries. The Indian operations are seen as a major cog in the global alliance manufacturing hub.

Ford India too recently expanded its manufacturing capacity to two lakh passenger cars per annum besides setting up a separate engine plant making 2.50 lakh units per year (mainly low displacement engines). Currently it exports its compact car 'Ford Figo' to 50 markets in the world through Chennai and Ennore port. Ford has been ramping up India operations to create an export hub for small cars and engines.

In tyre manufacturing, the State has succeeded in attracting major investments from firms like Michelin, JK Tyre, MRF and Apollo Tyres. The total installed tyre manufacturing capacity of the Chennai region is set to exceed 1,600 metric tonnes a day. This will make Chennai the largest tyre manufacturing centre in the country and one of the largest in the world. Chennai has emerged as the tyre capital of India.

A lot of vehicle design and related research and development facilities have been set up in Chennai. The National Automotive Testing and R&D Infrastructure Project has made a large investment in Chennai. The testing facility will give vehicle manufacturers a range of facilities including to test, design, safety emissions and performance standards. Hitherto, they had to go all the way to Pune for validating such parameters. At present, Chennai has five major R&D and vehicle development centres promoted by auto majors including Daimler, Renault-Nissan, Visteon, Mahindra and Ashok Leyland. As a result Chennai is also emerging as a knowledge hub for the global automobile industry.

THE RETAILERS OF MADRAS

Selling Middle-class Dreams

Organised retail was pioneered in the South. Retail is is another one of Chennai's home grown success stories. Before the mega malls made their appearance and branded goods started to flood the market, enterprising retailers came up with their innovative selling methods and successfully survived all sorts of competition. Since 2000, many newcomers have arrived. Everybody is surviving, doing well and are ready to face new challenges.

The retail revolution of the last years of the 20th century also began in Chennai. The man who was behind it was Pradipta K. Mohapatra who came to Chennai when the RPG Group acquired Spencers. He became the Chief Executive. Food World was launched in Chennai in 1996 giving new meaning to retailing groceries. It was the country's first stab at organised and modern retail. Mahapatra says, "*Any retail revolution is driven by the middle class.*" Chennai by the mid-nineties had sufficient number of middle class customers. RPG Group also launched Music World and Health & Glow. These were the first mass retailing models in the country.

According to real estate consultancy firm Jones Lang LaSalle's *Indian Real Estate: A Review Of 2013 and Outlook for 2014* report, Chennai witnessed the strongest retail real estate absorption in the first three quarters, at 53 per cent of net rentals and property purchases across the country during the period. In the all-India retail market, the South is the largest and Chennai is the biggest.

An *Economic Times* report on Feb 7, 2013 has this to say:

Chennai's T Nagar is said to be South East Asia's largest high street shopping space. In an 800 metre radius there are around 185 plus textile/garments shops spread over 5.5 lakh square feet. There are jewellery stores spread over 2.5 lakh square feet. According to the World Gold Council 70-80 per cent of the gold sold in Chennai – the most important gold market in the southern region – is from T. Nagar. The southern region contributes to 45 per cent of the 800-tonne annual national offtake. Every year, at least 50,000 sq. ft. of retail space is being added. Footfalls are more than 5 lakh during a normal weekday. It goes up to more than 2 million during weekends and 10 million plus during Diwali and other major festivals. During the festival season, sales in big textile retail shops crosses ₹1.5 crore in a day.

According to guestimates the turnover inthis area is likely tobe at least ₹20000 crore a year. Official estimates put it at a much lower ₹10,000 crore two years ago. Even if one goes by this figure it is still double that of New Delhi's Connaught Place, Mumbai's Linking Road and Bangalore's Brigade Road, which is supposed to be around ₹4,000–6,000 crore.

One of the oldest and respected names in T Nagar is textile retailer Nalli. During Diwali it is standing room only at Nalli Silks, the huge multi-floor silk sari and textile store located there. Before Nalli opened branches all over the country, a must-visit place for all Chennai visitors was this shop either to buy saris or silk materials. A certain generation worries about the fact that nobody is wearing saris any more. But Nalli, especially the showroom in T Nagar, stocks mostly saris. Almost 93 per cent of its merchandise consists of saris at its Tamil Nadu outlets. To get a proper perspective, the show room in Chennai is 30,000 square feet and is packed with clothes. Saris account for 50 per cent of the women's wear market in India. Silk saris account for a sizeable percentage though the younger generation prefers lightweight saris, say people in the trade.

Nalli Silks was started by the grandfather of the affable and totally unassuming current owner of the shop, Nalli Kuppuswami Chettiar, in 1928. It was all of 400 square feet. Nalli is the family name.

His father's untimely death brought the young boy to the shop at the age of 12. He could not go to college. He had to take charge of the shop, when he was 20. This was in 1961. The turnover of the shop was then ₹28 lakh. In 1966, it touched ₹1 crore. It was a great personal triumph for him. Chettiar had this burning desire to make Nalli the number one in textile trade. By 1992, the turnover had reached ₹100 crore. Today it is around ₹500 crore. Till 1984, Nalli was a debt-free organisation. Chettiar went in for bank borrowing for the first time in 1985 when he decided to open a branch in Madurai. Today Nalli has 22 branches. It has shops in all the major cities of Tamil Nadu, three outlets in Chennai, two each in Delhi and Bangalore and one each in Mumbai and Hyderabad. Additionally, it has a store each in the US and Singapore. It has 2,500 employees.

With the retail revolution happening in the nineties, Nalli has big time competitors in T Nagar itself. There are shops like RMKV, Pothys, Kumaran and Chennai Silks, all in multi-storeyed buildings and stocking fancy women's clothes. Chettiar is not particularly bothered. *"We have a separate identity and that will keep us on top"*, he says. He points out that Chennai population has exploded and there is place for everybody. Nalli became a popular brand purely by word-of-mouth publicity. There has been no multi-crore brand building exercise. Nalli hardly advertises. There have been a couple of exceptions, like completing 60 years or opening a major new branch.

It is not that Chettiar is unaware of the power of branding or advertising. He may not have a management degree, may not speak English, but is widely travelled and widely read. For him, customer relations are more important than anything else. Chettiar firmly believes that caring for customers is what sets his shop apart from the rest. "*When I started, there were mothers who came to buy saris for their daughter's weddings. Now, I am selling saris for their great granddaughter's weddings. The relationship continues. They may buy from other shops, but for something as important as a wedding, they will turn to Nalli.*"

There was a time when more than 90 per cent of Kancheepuram silk weavers were supplying to Nalli. The handloom tradition in the country and particularly in the south has survived because of shops like Nalli. But things have changed rapidly with the arrival of the automobile companies in that area. The weaver's children have been hired by companies like Hyundai, picked up from their houses, supplied meals and dropped back. Untrained labour gets ₹10,000 a month in comparison to the ₹5,000 they were making earlier. The young are no longer school dropouts. Everyone is clamouring for education. Weaving is not an attractive profession anymore and Chettiar is seriously concerned about handlooms fading from our lives.

Now, Nalli buys products from all over the country. There are at least 20,000 master weavers who supply to Nalli. Many may not match the quality of the master weavers of Kancheepuram. But some traditions still survive like the tie-and-dyes of Gujarat and Rajasthan, and *ikkat* and *pochampalli* of Orissa. Chettiar is still in charge of purchases for the shops in Tamil Nadu. In other states he now has people selecting fast moving goods.

Do chains like Nalli have a future? Going by the crowds fighting to catch the salesman's attention, one can say that shops like Nalli will be around for a long time, giving a tough fight to competitors who are Johnnies-come-lately.

One of them is Chennai Silks, one of the big ones in T Nagar. It has textiles, accessories and jewellery spread over seven floors. A Kulandaivel Mudaliar from a small village near Tirppur was a weaver of dhotis. He set up a 10x10 sq. ft. showroom in Madurai in 1962 to sell Khadi material. He had eight sons and everybody entered the business. Hailing from Tiruppur the family got into the garment business as job workers. Then they invested in a few machines and started exporting in a small way. Today, the family is one of the largest exporters from Tiruppur employing 25000 people. *"We are completely integrated now. We cultivate cotton, have spinning mills, knitting, printing and embroidery machines,"* says A Ravindhiran, a family member who manages the Chennai operations. The promoters have always thought in terms of scale.

A large multi-brand showroom was set up in Tiruppur in 1978 followed by Erode and Coimbatore. They were called Kovai Kumaran Silks. The shops started retailing jewellery as well. In Madurai and Namakkal, the shops sell only jewellery. It was time to move to Chennai in 2000. The name of the showroom was changed to Chennai Silks as there was already a Kumaran Silks.

Chennai Silks has set up a showroom in Kochi as well. There is a boutique store of 2000 sq. ft. at the Hyderabad airport. Chennai remains the largest. There are on an average 2000 foot falls every day. During festival seasons it can go upto 20000. The rebate season is during the Tamil month of *Aadi*. *"Last year we outsold everybody,"* says Ravindhiran. How did Chennai Silks manage to do that? *"We have interesting discount and gift schemes. We imported Samsung phones directly from Singapore as giveaways for purchases above a certain amount. We also get discounts from suppliers. Yes, profits come down. But it is made up by the volume increase in turnover. So we don't really lose out."*

The Chennai Silks group provides direct and indirect employment to about 40000 people. The Chennai showroom itself employs 1000 people. It provides hostel facilities for about 500 employees from outside Chennai. *"We provide food for all our employees. It is the same for everybody, including me,"* says Ravindhiran. The group has more than 10000 suppliers. Jewellery is sourced from Coimbatore which is the centre for this business in the South. There are at any given time five lakh pieces of various kinds of textile products in the stores.

Every two months somebody is sent to China to source merchandise. *"We get fabrics, garment accessories, denims, women's tops from China"*, says Ravindhiran. A lot of lower income family youngsters are moving into the labour market. These huge showrooms provide them with affordable and stylish clothing. *"We stock both designer clothes and affordable ones"*, says Ravindhiran.

To manage the numbers Chennai Silks has a full-fledged IT team and its own ERP software. There are 60 people working for the IT department. The group has 83 wind mills and is putting up a solar plant to produce 10 megawatts of power. It has acquired 200 acres for this purpose. It also has a pre-cast construction division. *"We built up one lakh sq. ft. in 80 days, near Kangeyam,"* says Ravindhiran.

The Chennai Silks group has no debts and does not approach banks or institutions. It does not want funding from PE investors or angels. It is going to set up two more showrooms in Chennai suburbs. So what is the group turnover? *"Around ₹3000 crore"*, smiles Ravindhiran. He is being modest.

Saravana Stores is another success story which chose catering to the lower middle class as its niche. Brothers S Selvarathnam, S Yogarathnam and S Rajarathnam, who came from a village near Tuticorin in the southern tip of India, started their careers selling vessels. Eventually, they diversified into selling clothes, food, electronics and jewellery. The group's revenue (they do not disclose figures) is estimated at about ₹2,500 crore. Thousands of people come here from all over Tamil Nadu, by train and bus in the morning, shop till they drop and get back in the evening. There are wash rooms, eateries and resting places for them in the multi-storey buildings.

Kishore Biyani of the Future Group has said in many interviews that his inspiration came from watching a store in Chennai's Ranganathan Street sometime in 2000, when he was figuring out how to start a retail chain that would sell almost everything that an Indian household consumes and offer them at a discounted price. His consultants would tell Biyani to study hypermarkets in the US and Europe and local businessmen would tell him that it would not work here. *"That's when I came across Saravana Store. I noticed hordes of people walking in through the day. The store had five floors and a basement. To many, it may be a shopper's nightmare, but lot of customers just loved it. Saravana served as a template to build upon the idea of Big Bazaar. We developed a model that could be replicated and turned into a pan-Indian chain."* he told *Business Today*.

The group started its first jewellery showroom in 2003, calling it Saravana Thanga Nagai Maaligai. Saravana recently launched Saravana Elite—another jewellery store also in the busy T Nagar area close to where its huge shops now stand. It has well-designed interiors, parking for customers and imported jewellery to attract young buyers. With Elite, Saravana has become a little more upmarket. Saravana's promoters are keeping up with their clientele who are moving up on the social ladder.

Chennai retail is not just T Nagar. There are entrepreneurs who have watched and contributed to the growing aspiration of the Indian middle class for a better lifestyle for many decades. Vivek & Co, VG Panneerdas & Co and Vasanth & Co are three good examples of how organized retail grew in Chennai. The owners of all three migrated to Madras in the fifties and sixties with little or no capital and certainly without any formal training in the nuances of marketing. Native intelligence and a burning ambition to make good was all they had going for them. Today, their modest beginnings are a thing of the past and they all have large format multi-storey showrooms. The range of products they sell is vast.

The pioneer amongst them is VG Panneeerdas who, along with his brother VG Santhosham moved to the big city to seek his fortune in the fifties. Today VGP has four large retail outlets in Madras, six in Bangalore and eight in smaller towns in Tamil Nadu. The VGP brothers started as tea-stall owners. Their customers were largely from the lower income group who did not have the means to purchase what they wanted. In 1955, recalls Santhosham (Panneerdas is no more), the brothers struck upon the idea of selling timepieces on an installment basis. Each timepiece was priced at ₹16, with a down payment of ₹ 4 and six monthly installments of ₹ 2. They went door to door on their bicycles offering this deal.

The response was overwhelming. Soon their customers started clamouring for more goodies. A few years down the road, the brothers felt the need to establish a showroom. Scrambling around for funds, the enterprising duo rustled up ₹10,000 to purchase their first retail outlet at Saidapet, which in those days was considered a downmarket suburb of Madras.

Business grew steadily. A major turning point came when the VGP brothers landed the Murphy radio agency in 1957 (eternally grateful, Santhosham named one of his sons, Murphy Das). For the next ten years or so, VGP consistently won the first prize for Murphy's all-India sales. The brothers found various innovative ways of promoting their products. They were the first in Madras to hire wall space along the railway stations to advertise. They conducted what they call 'mobile fairs' – they filled mini vans with treasures like wall clocks, pressure cookers, and irons, and roamed the rural heartland.

Over the years, many VGP employees have branched out to set up their own outfits. The most well-known is H Vasanth Kumar of Vasanth & Co. *"My inspiration is VGP,"* says Vasanth. In the early seventies he began his career as a door-to-door sales canvasser for VGP. By 1978 he decided to strike out on his own. His capital: a bicycle and a ₹8,000 loan. Today, he has showrooms all over Chennai and Tamil Nadu.

The innovative tack that Vasanth took was to go for institutional sales of consumer durables by tying up with a finance company, the Coimbatore based Sakthi Finance. Vasanth's big breakthrough came when he sold 900 colour TVs to Ashok Leyland for ₹90 lakh. Riding the boom, Vasanth was able to get bulk orders from government departments and co-operative stores. The boom was short-lived, and ended when buyers began to default on payments. Lessons were learnt, he had made his fortune and has not burnt his fingers with bulk orders again.

BA Kodandaraman, Chairman & Managing Director, Vivek Limited (which is the largest of them all), has been in the retail business for almost 50 years. Vivek has been in the forefront of many innovations that have become the norm today. It is the largest retailer of consumer durables, electronics, IT, and telecom products in the region. Kodandaraman pioneered the concept of

New Year sale when products are offered at cost. Hire purchase was introduced for the first time by Vivek.

The company went into a fast-track growth phase after 1991, instead of being threatened by the economic reforms and the markets opening up. Kodandaraman knew that global brands would enter the market, and that the consumers were going to be demanding. Between 1965 and 1995, Viveks had only three showrooms in Chennai. In 1995, the company planned on adding 30 more showrooms in three years. Today, there are 50 showrooms in Tamil Nadu (in 17 cities) and Bangalore. From a beginning with 250 sq. ft., Viveks has grown to 3 lakh sq. ft. of showroom area. Its retail brand is stronger than some of the brands it houses, says a McKinsey study. All the showrooms are large-format, fully-air conditioned stores.

Vivek & Co was set up by Kodandaraman's elder brother, an electronics engineer, the first one in a rice trading family from Kolar to go to Bangalore for higher education. He was spiritually inclined, was a disciple of the Ramakrishna Mutt and wanted to provide employment and make people's lives more comfortable. He wanted to do it in Chennai, which was a major move for the family. Unfortunately, he passed away very young and the parents wanted to continue what he set out to do.

Kodandaraman and his brothers stepped in. Those were the days when there was such a limited range of products to sell. The only transistor radios available were Bush, Murphy and Nelco. There was a shortage of everything and the customer simply did not have a choice. People were scared to buy a gas stove or pressure cooker. They thought these new contraptions would burst.

Says Kodandaraman, "*We have seen the trade grow from shortage to plenty. Manufacturing was easy then, but selling difficult. This has been turned on its head. We have seen so many things happening in these 50 years. This is my strength. We have experience, knowledge and information. These three are equal to power and money. We understand products, customers and value.*" Kodandaraman believes that this is what differentiates Viveks from its competition. The quiet confidence comes from the fact that every other household in

Chennai has been a customer of Viveks. The knowledge acquired over selling to three generations has helped anticipate competition. *"Whatever happens in the rest of the world has to happen here also. We all travelled, saw what a shopping experience really was, and were ready to bring it here. When lifestyle improves, everything changes."*

Viveks has more than 100 trained professionals who are provided with cell phones and transportation to provide service to customers. The division takes care of installation of all products sold at Viveks and offers extended warranty. The service backbone is provided by the service centre, which has 400 employees. Viveks has tied up with the Vector Consulting Group to revamp its supply chain.

Kodandaraman says that new product introductions are happening at super speed. There are simultaneous global product launches. The multinationals are setting up stand-alone showrooms. Then there is the threat from e-commerce. *"Although we are on many platforms, we are waiting and watching to see how the e-commerce business pans out. We will meet the challenges as we have done for fifty years,"* says Kodandaraman.

THE SUCCESS STORIES OF THE NINETIES

K PANDIARAJAN OF MA FOI—TAKING HR ALL-INDIA

When K Pandiarajan, an MBA from XLRI and his wife Latha, a Chartered Accountant decided to launch a recruitment firm, they named it Ma Foi. *"We were thinking of various names and I came up with Ma Foi which means my world. We wanted a global sounding name,"* says Latha. The Pandiarajans registered Ma Foi Management Consultants Limited on 15 August 1992.

Their timing was perfect. India had opened up. A lot of MNCs were rushing into the country. Jobs were being created *"The concept of outsourcing was catching up very fast,"* says Pandiarajan. Pandiarajan got into the HR space when he got admission into XLRI, Jamshedpur, after getting his engineering degree from PSG College of Technology from Coimbatore. He comes from a small village close to Sivakasi, which is known for its match making industry. Many families set up cottage industries and the children in the family rolled matches. *"We were not starving, but we had to come back from school and get to work."*

Pandiarajan was a class topper who was encouraged by his family to focus on studies. They were willing to make sacrifices to help him pursue higher education. *"A new door opened for me when I got admission to the PSG College at Coimbatore. I was one of the few Tamil medium students to be admitted there. Though English was a challenge initially, I caught up pretty soon."* He did his post-graduation from Guindy Engineering College in Operations Research. He was persuaded by a friend to try for an MBA degree. He got into XLRI, Jamshedpur which opened more doors. *"I got into the HR area unknowingly and that triggered the entrepreneur in me. In my village, everybody is an entrepreneur. Entrepreneurship is in my DNA."*

He spent six years working for MNCs such as the BOC group and Deutsche Babcock when he got an opportunity to join V Krishnamurthy, former chairman of Maruti and SAIL, who had promoted the IDEA group of companies. *"I worked with him for three years and he gave me a lot of opportunities."*

In 1992 a lot of MNCs came to the country and out sourcing as a concept was catching on. *"An American expert, commissioned to put out a fire that had broken out in an oil well in Andhra needed 35 engineers to assist him in the project. The Australian HR firm appointed to hire these personnel recruited 35 engineers, of which 31 were Indians. An Indian oil major paid their salaries!"*

"The Australian company received a fee of one million dollars for the assignment, higher than the annual income of India's top human resource enterprise. The episode made a strong impact on me. I could not reconcile myself to the idea that a foreign company earned such huge revenue out of a transaction involving an Indian company and the Indian engineers it hired."

"The staffing industry was very small in India and it was huge in the rest of the world. That's when my wife Latha and I decided to start a company to enter this niche. Ma Foi was launched with a capital of ₹60,000 in a small room with one phone in a building owned by Latha's father."

By the end of the year, four of their friends put in ₹10,000 each and the investment went up to ₹1 lakh. Ma Foi started by placing engineers, middle-level and managerial people overseas especially in the Middle East. Pandiarajan had had enough exposure to the oil and gas industry and he was able to put together a database.

When they put their first advertisement in the paper with their phone number they were quite tense. They need not have been. The phone didn't stop ringing. Latha was just helping out in the beginning. She came in full time a year after the company was set up. *"I used to take down details of the callers from morning till sometimes midnight. It was exhausting, but also exhilarating,"* says Latha. *"In 1992, when we sent a draughtsman to Singapore, his entire village came to see him off."*

Ma Foi believed in having personal interaction with the candidates. *"We met them, chatted with them, had coffee with them and gained a lot of insight. When we launched, the Gulf and Far East recruitment market was booming. When things were going well and twenty engineers were ready to go to the Gulf, Babri Masjid happened. All their visas were cancelled. These engineers had resigned their jobs to go to the Gulf."* It was 8 December 1992. And Ma Foi's losses ran into lakhs. *"It was a tough phase and we had to pledge property, jewellery. But when we came out of the struggle, we expanded into all kinds of things."* After weeks of tension, the visas arrived in the first week of January.

Latha recalls how frugal they had to be. Getting a one lakh overdraft was difficult for an HR company. Says Pandiarajan,*"We decided not to collect any fees from the job seekers. We did not want to be associated with those unscrupulous elements taking people for a ride"*.

Pandiarajan was very clear about what he wanted. He wanted to scale up. *"Nobody listens to you if you are not large."* He did not want Ma Foi to be just a staffing company. He wanted to it to be in recruitment services and HR consultancy. Hastha Krishnan, a market research professional who joined the company in 1993, says that Pandiarajan sold a dream to her. She grew with the company and was one of its senior employees till it changed hands.

By 1994, more and more MNCs had started to enter India. Many green field projects were coming up. Pandiarajan did not want to restrict Ma Foi to only providing manpower to companies abroad. He was quite clear that he had to expand in the country as well. When Apple Computers opened an office in India in 1994 and decided to hire 300 employees, Ma Foi got the assignment in spite of tough competition. It was a huge opportunity. Advertisements were released across India in all the leading magazines, asking for applications for jobs in Apple to be sent to Ma Foi. The campaign gave the company great visibility. It could attract a lot of talented youngsters. Around the same time, salaries in the Gulf region started falling.

Till then Ma Foi had not done any such large recruitment in India. It had only dealt with the secretarial side. With that one assignment from Apple everything changed. Ma Foi made a name for itself by providing complete services to newcomers, including help them find locations. It set up offices in all the big cities in the country and started seriously looking at domestic recruitment and sectors like IT, finance and banking.

In this phase Ma Foi became a closely held public limited company. *"We took equity from friends, relations who put in their savings from running small match units. We promised them 20 per cent dividend every year"*. It is a promise they kept up by building the 20 per cent dividend in their costs.

By 2000, Ma Foi had become the largest company in HR services in the country. It was the only company in recruitment services to get an ISO quality certification. It went on to get BVQI certification as well. The only major survivors in the business after 2000 were Ma Foi and naukri.com. They both had different models. Naukri had taken the centralised technology path while Ma Foi covered a wider canvas.

Ma Foi jumped onto the dot com bandwagon which was the rage in the new millennium. This move attracted a lot of VCs to the company and it got funding from three VC funds with international linkages. This was not a good move.*"Entering the dotcom business was a mistake. We were struggling with our model which was affecting our balance sheet. Thankfully we understood that this was not working. We pulled out of the dotcom model very soon and convinced our VCs that we will use what we had got (around ₹8.5 crore) in the brick-and-mortar model. We spruced up our offices and added more people."*

There was need for more funding for the next phase of expansion. In 2002, Ma Foi set up their first overseas office in Dubai. After understanding how the overseas market worked, they had two choices: either to go for an initial public offering or to look for a global strategic partnership. Pandiarajan decided to opt for a strategic partnership with global major Vedior in 2002. Vedior, one of the world's leading specialist staffing companies from Netherlands, was looking at the Indian market. "*We had to ask our 276 shareholders to sell their equity to Vedior. They were reluctant. It took us three months to persuade them to do so.*" The Rajans themselves diluted their share holding to 24 per cent of the equity when Vedior came in. "*Vedior treated us as a fellow entrepreneur*", says Pandiarajan.

It was a good association. Vedior was a multi-brand company and it saw itself as a federation of companies. It allowed Ma Foi a lot of flexibility. During this phase Ma Foi set up 105 offices. "*We were in 15 countries. We went through the franchisee route to tier II and III cities in India. We were in all state capitals, except the North East.*"

Vedior was subsequently acquired by Randstad Holding NV in 2008. Randstad is the second largest HR services company in the world. "*Randstad operates as one country, one brand.*" It was time for the Rajans to exit."*We felt it was time to leave gracefully after 20 years. We were mentally prepared for this move after Randstad came in,*" says Latha. Ma Foi had kept up a growth momentum of 64 per cent a year for twenty one years, had found jobs for several lakhs of people, given employment to a lot of young graduates, and created entrepreneurs.

Pandiarajan stepped down in 2010 and Latha in 2011. They are now 'Ma Foi Strategic Consultants Pvt. Ltd.' and have ventured into non-staffing solutions like strategy, research and education verticals, with an investment of ₹25 crore spread over a period of three years. They also plan to set up a chain of management schools—Ma Foi Development Programme School (MDPS).

Pandiarajan has also followed his passion to become a full time politician.

In August 2015 after the non-compete period was over, the Pandiarajans returned to HR by launching CIEL HR Services to provide solutions leveraging technology and analytical strengths they have built up. CIEL too is a French word, meaning the Sky!

BHARAT MATRIMONY—INNOVATOR PAR EXCELLENCE

Bharat Matrimony completed 15 years in 2015. With over three million marriages, the company serves 20 million people across the globe and has been ranked India's Most Trusted Matrimony Brand by The Brand Trust Report 2014. *"We want to be the custodians of marriage in India"*, says Murugavel Janakiraman, the founder of Bharat Matrimony quite seriously. About competition, he says. *"All segments in this business have been pioneered by us. Everyone follows. We are the leaders."* For instance it was his idea to start *elite.com* for the rich. If the wealthy want to meet other wealthy prospects, they have to cough up ₹1 lakh to register! *"The rich also need help,"* he says. He now has *assisted.com* for those at the bottom of the pyramid.

Murugavel was the first member of his family to go to college. He grew up in a blue-collar tenement in North Chennai. He was a bright student. He is today able to laugh about his struggles when he was put in an English medium school for his plus 2 classes.

His maternal uncle, the only educated member in the family asked him to do Chemistry in college so that he could get a job easily. As it happened he got admission into BSc (Statistics). He had not even heard about Statistics. He put in hours of hard work, conquered the subject and also started taking part in inter-college competitions. A degree in statistics made him eligible to pursue MCA (Master of Computer Application). *"Till then I had never touched a computer. I applied for a seat in Madras University. I was one of 15 students selected. If I had got into the chemistry course, I may have been working in some lab on a monthly salary of ₹10,000."*

When Murugavel was doing his masters he realised that he had excellent programming skills. He gained confidence and found himself a job in Singapore in 1994. *"It was the first flight I had taken in my life"*, he says. He moved to the United States in 1997 as a consultant working for a multinational.

By this time, the internet was emerging as a major force. In his free time he set up a portal for the Tamil community living in the US. This was a free site. *"I started working at home after office hours, leveraging the strong cultural bonds that united the Tamils living abroad. I offered the daily calendar on my website to Tamils used to tearing the day's sheet on their calendar. I offered them what they were used to back home, reminding them of Indian festivals, auspicious days, the daily fortune, and so on. Till then, all websites for Tamils were meant only to register their views. Mine was the first site that was useful to them."*

Some of his friends were beginning to look for brides in India. *"I made it possible for them to register their personal details on the net for their prospective brides. The first marriage as a result of my service took place within three months. Technology had dramatically cut short the normal lead-time of months, even years for Indian marriages. I established a portal called tamilmatrimony.com, without realising this was going to be the turning point it in my life."*

Murugavel started noticing how many hits his matrimonial service was getting. That triggered the idea of a matrimonial portal based on a revenue model. The dotcom bust gave him the opportunity to return to India. *"I lost my job and so the decision became easy."* He launched TamilMatrimony from a small apartment in Chennai with three employees in 1999. He realised that most Indian families no longer wanted to operate with limited choices. TamilMatrimony became inclusive of all communities and soon became BharatMatrimony.

"In the beginning, it was a one man show. Once I introduced a membership fee, I started earning up to ₹200000 per month. I opened offices in the US and Chennai for starters. It was the first step in my progress. That decision of mine opened many doors for me." Murugavel tied up with all the major portals like Sify, Rediff and MSN, which gave him a lot of visibility at minimum cost.*"We were able to monetise the additional traffic.", he says.* Then he branched out all over India and the portal started to service all communities and languages. He introduced offline concepts like door to door collections, and big marriage melas in large spaces.

He was among the first to get Private Equity funding from Yahoo. He then diversified into *indiaproperty.com* and *clickjob.com*. Mistakes were also made.

"In 2006, we raised around ₹40 crore but in a year blew it all up, because we didn't have the understanding of how to use it efficiently. So we were left with hardly any money and were trying to raise the second round.

Finally, I had to pledge my house to borrow some money. It was a very challenging time. When we finally managed to get the next line of funding in 2008, the economic meltdown happened and we started losing money again. We couldn't raise a third round. We had a rough time for four or five months and at the end of it emerged stronger."

Murugavel has shut down the jobs portal. He now has a separate CEO for *indiaproperty.com*. His focus is totally on matrimonial services. There is an IPO in the offing, sometime soon. According to PE circles, the company is being valued at very high figures.

BharatMatrimony became profitable by 2009. In the last few years Murugavel has launched several marriage related businesses such as Tambulya offline shops which offer return gifts, a directory of matrimonial services, wedding expos and so on. His mobile apps have had more than 500000 downloads.

Marriage is a very big market in India. Over 10 million people are getting married every year, which means close to 40–50 million people are actively looking to get married at any given time. The company hasn't even catered to 10 per cent of this market; hence the potential to grow is huge. Murugavel fully plans to exploit this potential. "*We have scored on various parameters like scale, size, revenue, business model and success. We will build a better Bharat through happy marriages!*"

CAMS—BACKROOM POWERHOUSE

Chennai based CAMS is the largest professionally managed, institutionally owned, SEBI regulated entity engaged as an IT enabled service solution partner to BFSI (Banking, Financial Services and Insurance) players in India.

V Shankar the founder is from IIT, Chennai. He is one of the very few engineers from his batch who actually stayed back in India. He went on to get his MBA from IIM, Calcutta. Then he joined Hindustan Lever and went through Commercial, Project Management and Sales Management functions and was responsible for systems initiatives in these areas.

In late 1987 he gave in to his instinct to turn an entrepreneur. He left a promising career in Hindustan Levers and started his first business in computer hardware. Computers were just being introduced in India and there was a tremendous governmental initiative to set up domestic manufacturing capability. Shankar's first startup was in the area of assembly. This venture did not progress beyond a point since India's environment then did not facilitate any manufacturing activity.

Then Shankar turned to computer education. This was a more promising venture, and for a period of three to four years in the early '90s, CAMS Software Education Centre Private Limited was one of the premier establishments in South India, rivalling NIIT in market share. The area of Computer Software came into focus at that time, and Shankar's next startup was in the software industry, initially for the domestic market.

As Y2K approached, the market for computer software started to swing around to the overseas market to the extent that by the 2000s there was almost nobody with credible credentials to service the domestic market. That is when Shankar decided (in a contrarian approach) that the domestic financial services marketplace was to be his focus, and the area of operation was to be in managed services, not just IT services.

Says Shankar, *"The Indian financial services marketplace went through a renaissance in the period 1997–98 to 2006–07, with far reaching changes in regulation, products and supporting infrastructure."* Financial businesses, always early adopters, started taking advantage of technology and networking to facilitate their business. Shankar founded CAMS (Computer Age Management Services Pvt. Ltd.) to provide what are now known as platform based services to the Indian financial industry.

It was a struggle in the beginning. *"We tried to support manufacturing doing their stock accounting. They wanted to do it themselves. Working for BPOs meant pure cost arbitrage which did not require much intellectual content. Locating a financial services company in Chennai seemed like a major disadvantage as all the action was in Mumbai. We just had to be better."* Chennai did have some advantages. Real estate at that time was cheaper. IT professionals were available.

It was slow progress. At this time nobody was really managing a customer's experience. By 1992–93, mutual funds (MFs) entered the country. MFs are not a onetime experience like an IPO. This is an open ended instrument where the customers buy and sell all the time. MFs have to take extra effort to keep customers happy and retain them on a sustained basis. *"At that time the state of intermediation was quite pathetic,"* says Shankar. *"A position opened for trusted and professional intermediaries. People were also getting smarter with larger incomes."*

This opened the door for Shankar to step in. *"MFs gave us a role between manufacturing and investment. By and large MFs are commodity products. The differentiation at product level is entirely technology dependent. We effectively built product features and product differentiation to the clients."*

What does CAMS do? The demat system for stocks that commenced in 1996 and became significant after 2000 comprises of the depository participant (e.g. banks, broking firms etc.), which handle the customer interface and these roll up into the two depositories which maintain the master accounts of customers. This book entry system for holding records of share ownership eliminated the need for holding and exchanging physical share certificates.

What CAMS launched in 1995 was effectively a demat system for Mutual Funds. Till then, MFs were held as certificates. These were not suitable to efficient trading because of the same problems that physical share certificates had. When Open Ended Mutual Funds were launched in 1994, CAMS, in association with the MFs, decided to issue Units in uncertificated (demat) form. In this architecture, CAMS held the master accounts of the customer, while CAMS' own branches acted as the customer interface (Participants). Over time, a variety of entities, including Index Fund Advisors (IFAs), banks etc. started acting as additional customer interfaces.

This architecture not only preceded, but proved at least as resilient as the widely appreciated Demat system for shares; in fact from the beginning it supported a T+2 settlement and has graduated to a T+1 settlement for over a decade now, something that the stock market is still aspiring to. These refer to the *settlement* date of security transactions. Furthermore, all this was achieved at a transaction cost that was between 10 per cent and 20 per cent of the overall transaction cost of the stock market.

Around 2000, Shankar had to deal with some major competition when all the global banks with their colossal net worth entered the country. "*We were terrified. Fortunately they could not crack into this market as local knowledge and local connections were very important to make a breakthrough. When Fidelity wanted to go with Citibank, we challenged that and we won.*"

The next round of competition came from Indian companies, NSDL (National Securities Depository Limited) and CDSC (Contingent Deferred Sales Charge). They are seen as government bodies. However, equities and MFs are completely different animals. They were unprepared for the change. *"This is an ongoing battle. We are holding our ground"*, he says.

In 2000, the HDFC Group invested into CAMS in a significant manner, helping it to accelerate growth. In 2007 the company accepted a PE investor to further facilitate growth. In 2014 India's premier stock exchange, the NSE, took a significant position in the Company.

CAMS has just been granted a licence to offer repository services to the insurance industry. Shankar hopes he is on the cusp of another tremendous expansion over the next decade.

After the broadbasing and professionalizing of CAMS (it has 400 offices and 4500 employees), Shankar has focused on his second passion, viz. Angel Investing. As a member of The Chennai Angels and the TiE, he actively participates in the process of Angel Investing, which among other things includes the mentoring and supporting budding entrepreneurs.

"I am really a product of liberalisation," says Shankar.

Those who came from outside

Tamil Nadu becomes a favoured destination

THE OUTSIDERS

Redington India

Redington India is India's largest distributor of electronic goods with a turnover of more than ₹20000 crore. It has a strong presence in 23 countries, is associated with over 120 leading global IT and telecom brands and has more than 32000 channel partners. It also has 76 sales offices, 102 warehouses, 105 own service centres and 235 partner service centres. Redington handles 100,000 tons of goods per annum through multimodal agencies to enable road, rail and air transportation. After running slightly behind the huge multinational Ingram Micro, Redington reached the number one position couple of years ago. It has been distributing Apple products such as iPads, Macbooks, iPods and of course, the iPhone and some other electronic brands.

The company's Founder Managing Director R Srinivasan has always maintained that it is possible to take on a multinational and succeed in India and also in some of the emerging markets in Asia, the Middle East and Africa that too based in Chennai. "*We give credit but also collect intensively. In businesses where there isn't much investment in technology or a long gestation period, Indian companies have a big advantage,*" says Srinivasan. "*Indian manufactured goods or services have been popular in some of the emerging economies even before the Western companies entered the picture. Countries like Turkey and Egypt are absolutely the right markets for us to look at."*

"There are a lot of Indian managers in the MNCs in these places. The gap between Indian companies and the MNCs exists only in terms of funding or investment in technology," he says. Srinivasan is an engineer with an MBA from IIM, Ahmedabad. After stints in Coca Cola and Reader's Digest in India, he worked in Indonesia and Singapore. He founded Redington in the early 1980s in Singapore for specialised trade in personal computer components, focusing on the market in India and the Middle East. Singapore is an intensively competetive international market.

Moving from Singapore to India and not the other way round was the right thing to do. *"My co-promoters are the Singapore-based Kewalram Chanrai group. I put in 15 per cent and they gave me bank facilities in lieu of which they got shares."* Srinivasan does not believe in promoters having a substantial shareholding in a company. The companies he admires are L&T and HDFC. *"With a substantial shareholding, the promoters are not answerable to any one before going public. Answerability alone brings discipline. Our senior managers have stayed with the company for a long time. It is important that they get shares in the company. We have been liberal in sharing the shareholding. People start a business with the idea of making a lot of money. But if you see it as a large canvas to paint, shareholding does not really matter."*

When India opened up, Srinivasan could sense the kind of potential the country offered. Redington India was launched in Chennai in 1993. Its proximity to Singapore, port facilities and the availability of quality staff made him choose Chennai. The company went public in 1997. *"We are comfortable with our margins in India. Our investors are happy. We have consistently given 20 per cent returns to investors. I think of the old Hong Kong airport where landing in the middle of the city flying over rooftops was a hair raising experience. Having done it again and again the pilots never failed. Nor have we. In the last 6 to 7 years we have increased and expanded margins by changing the product mix."*

The reason for growth as a constant has also been due to Srinivasan's ability to read the market in advance and to spot opportunities. Redington is the distributor of all BlackBerry smart phones in India. *"Four years ago nobody thought BlackBerry would have such a high demand in India when we tied up with RIM. What was thought of as an office productivity product became a consumer product."* He thinks Microsoft's Xbox for gaming will become very popular in the next two or three years.

Srinivasan says that while the competition looks upon itself as an IT products distributor, Redington is a supply chain service provider. *"Coke was just a carbonated drink till the day it decided that its business was to quench someone's thirst. When you have a long pipeline, it need not be used just to transport water, it can also be petroleum."* As he explains, in the supply chain, you have logistics, finance and after sales service. *"We are disaggregating each of these businesses to create separate companies. Redington and others will be their customers"*, he says.

In 2008, Redington launched its finance company Easyaccess Financial Services.*"This company was set up only to finance the channels. Originally, it was meant only for Redington. Now Redington is trying to leverage it for other businesses on the assumption that some of its customers may want its full services."*

The logistics business was spun off recently. With year on year growth of 25 per cent, the Indian logistics management and services business is one of the fastest growing in the country. Redington started its first state of the art automated distribution centre in Chennai in 2009–10. *"It makes sense for companies like Apple to hand over their distribution to us. They can concentrate on their brands and products and we will move them across the industries. As long as the product is cartonable and is unique in numbers, we are in business. Wherever there is conventional distribution based on cash transaction our model won't work. We have IT digital products, consumer durables, gaming consoles and so on in our portfolio. The German company Dorma, which makes door handles and hinges chose us to transport their goods. We don't handle FMCG or Pharma customers yet."*

Srinivasan feels he can keep up his growth rate by constantly introducing new products. "*We deal across products and across platforms. We are really brand agnostic and platform agnostic. IT products now cater to both lifestyle and computing segments. People see the Apple iPhone or the iPad as consumer products. The HP notebook is a computing product which is also a content creating product. The iPad is a content consuming product. Today most of us have a content creating product at the work place and content consuming product at home. Growth will come from one or the other during difficult times.*"

VA Tech Wabag Ltd

"*Water treatment is the next sunrise industry,*" says Rajiv Mittal, the Managing Director and Chief Executive Officer of VA Tech Wabag Ltd. It is the largest water solutions company in India which is based in Chennai and has a turnover of ₹2,000 crore. "*We shouldn't be confused with infrastructure and construction companies which build water pipelines. We are a technology company. We are the only company in total management of water services.*" Wabag is a multinational, operating from Chennai, implementing projects in 19 countries. "*Half of our order-book is from outside the country,*" says Mittal.

Mittal came to Chennai in 1996. A chemical engineer from Bombay University, he started his career with Hindustan Dorr-Oliver Ltd. He was working in the UK, and joined Wabag in 1995. The company sent him to India to set up a strategic business unit in water. "*We made a major breakthrough that year when we got an order from Reliance for their Jamnagar refinery project. We executed the largest effluent treatment plant in Asia in 1997. When I came back from the UK, the water business was unheard of in India. I had to do a lot of aggressive selling. What we offer is life-cycle solutions for water: sewage treatment, effluent treatment, sludge treatment desalination, and reuse for industrial and municipal corporations. It is not a sexy business,*" he laughs.

The water treatment division, Wabag, was one among the four units of Deutsche Babcock. In 2000, the Austrian conglomerate, VA Tech, acquired a 100 per cent stake in Wabag, forming a new company known as VA Tech Wabag. Wabag India became a wholly-owned subsidiary of this company. *"I had to boost the morale of the employees, reassure the existing and prospective customers, and also vendors and bankers. Other Deutsche Babcock divisions in the country were winding up operations and the employees were feeling very insecure,"* Mittal says.

It was a difficult time for the company. Mittal managed to carry out ongoing operations seamlessly and put the company on the growth path. In 2003, VA Wabag's turnover was ₹100 crore, the only company in the water business to achieve this figure. *"The following year, we made ₹200 crore."*

Just when things were settling down for Mittal and the company, another change took place. VA Tech decided to sell its Indian subsidiary due to business compulsions. Siemens took over the entire VA Tech group in 2005. Soon after, Siemens decided to put on the block all the overseas companies of the Wabag group. The German and French subsidiaries were making losses. The Indian company was doing well. *"So, Siemens was very keen on selling our unit to make up for the losses in Europe. We started getting a stream of prospective investors, some of whom filled us with dismay. I decided to try and acquire Wabag India and put an end to so much uncertainty. With the support of ICICI Ventures, I put in a bid, competed with eight multinationals, and emerged the winner,"* Mittal recalls. It was an audacious reverse acquisition and Wabag India became a true-blue Indian multinational—the wholly-owned subsidiary was now the principal. *"We got 70 million euros as bank guarantee from ICICI Ventures. Today, we are a debt-free company,"* the man who made it all happen says.

Wabag has put up a desalination plant in Nemmeli, in the southern outskirts of Chennai, in 2013 to augment water supply to the city by 100 million litres per day (mld). Tamil Nadu, with its perennial water shortage, was the first state to go in for desalination to meet drinking water needs. The desalination plant is situated 35 kms. from Chennai. This is the largest desalination plant for drinking water in the country. The Nemmeli plant's project cost is ₹1,033 crore. A seven-year operate-and-maintain clause is a part of the project agreement. Mittal says that water from this plant is very affordable and is available at 2.5 paise per litre. Desalination of sea water for drinking has become more viable in the last 6–7 years, explains Mittal. *"With our large coast line—and agriculture taking up 80 per cent of our water resources—desalination may be the way forward,"* Mittal contends. Wabag has put up many smaller desalination plants for industrial use.

"Our international business managed and operated out of India has started paying off. We are putting up a challenging desalination plant twice the size of the one in Chennai in Oman," Mittal says. He is confident that the company will end the year very well in these difficult times. *"We have been winning international bids funded by multilateral agencies and have entered Turkey and the Philippines,"* he notes.

"People have to change their mindset about recycled water. Singapore uses recycled water for bathing, cooking, everything," Mittal states. He goes on to explain how precious water is going to become in the coming years. He quotes scary figures. *"There is going to be a demand-supply gap of over 50 per cent in our country,"* he claims. *"Demand for water is expected to rise from 1,500 billion cubic metres(bcm) against a projected supply of 740 bcm. Municipal and domestic water demand will double and demand from industry will quadruple by 2030."* No wonder Mittal calls water a sunrise industry.

Medall Healthcare Private Limited

Raju Venkatraman, Managing Director and CEO, Medall Healthcare Private Limited, says that an ultra sound test is the safest and cheapest diagnostic tool available, but there are not enough people available to do it. In India, only doctors handle ultrasound while most other countries train high school graduates. This is one of the many frustrations the MD of Medall (Medicine for all) faces in his quest to provide premier healthcare services to the diagnostic and radiology imaging requirements of a diverse range of customers. *"Would the IT revolution have happened if the government had insisted that only computer engineers can work in the industry?"* he asks.

Venkatraman is a serial entrepreneur who lived the American dream but never lost sight of his desire to give back to his country. He started two companies in the BPO space, scaled them up and sold them. Now he is all charged up providing affordable healthcare particularly to tier II to VI cities. *"It is not a non-profit venture,"* he says.

Raju is a chemical engineer who graduated from IIT Madras in 1981. He opted not to go the US to pursue further studies like most IIT graduates did in those times. After getting his MBA from IIM, Ahmedabad, he got his dream job in Cadbury when he was recruited as a management trainee.

In 1985 Raju got a green card because of his sister living in the US and decided to move there.*"The prospect didn't really excite me. Cadbury kept me busy. My career was taking off. However I was disillusioned with the India of the '80s. I did not have a clear vision of where I will be in the next 20 years. I was scared of becoming a corporate junkie. I really had nothing to lose and was ready to try and learn something new."*

As soon as he landed in the US, he took up a job for minimum wages of $3.65 per hour in Sears Department Store, much to the horror of relations and friends. *"I sat at the sales counters and it gave me a great exposure to the mindset of people. I met a professor at this time and helped him put together a small IT company. I learnt how to scale up from this experience."*

He had been applying for jobs and got an offer from EDS which was merging with General Motors. EDS retained its identity within GM and Raju got several breaks during his stint there. Initially, he was sent to Buffalo to the insurance division. *"Those were intense computer days."* Soon he was shifted to Detroit. *"EDS could spot talent very quickly. In less than three weeks they could see that I could conceive solutions."* He built their imaging business, set up an imaging lab, and a solutions centre.

EDS was trying to get a break through to Apple by bidding for a project which finally went to Accenture. Raju told the CTO of Apple to call him if they could not implement the project. Apple's CTO called him in 8 months. Raju's insights into solutions helped

EDS win many deals. However he was beginning to feel that EDS's bonus policy was not working in favour of somebody like him. "*I realised I won't see my potential financially in EDS.*"

Raju set up a venture called Vetri Systems in 1991 with a capital of less than $10,000. He took an advance against work. He started a subsidiary in India in 1993 to do back office processing for healthcare insurance for some of the large insurance companies in the US. Seven years later Raju sold the venture to Lason, a provider of document management outsourcing services. By this time he had scaled it to a 2,500 employees, $26-million IT and BPO Services organization. Angel investors made a return of 12 times. Raju continued with the company for three more years. Shortly after that he moved back to India and wanted to do something meaningful. He joined a non-governmental organisation, but soon realised that he was not cut out for that. "*Their lack of governance shook me up.*"

Raju's second venture—RevIT, an anagram of his first business, Vetri, was launched in 2002. This was focussed on healthcare and high-end claims processing. He raised venture capital, scaled it to a 1,500+ organization within two years and sold it to ICICI OneSource in 2005. He had delivered 84 per cent IRR to investors.

Raju stayed with the company for four more years. "*Our vision was the same.*" In these four years the company grew to a turnover of $400 million with 25000 employees. "*It was a great experience. We opened offices in Ireland, Philippines and Argentina. The scale and speed of thinking was remarkable.*"

In 2009, Raju decided to quit. "*I wanted to do something in rural India, something in healthcare. I travelled all over the South for six months before setting up Medall. I covered all the districts in the state. I looked at affordability, accessibility, availability of technology and resources.*" He started Medall by acquiring Precision Diagnostics in Chennai in 2009.

Today it has more than 120 diagnostic centres offering a comprehensive range of integrated diagnostic services including imaging and path lab services and more than 350 collection centres across the South. Medall serves 3.1 million customers annually and has expanded to Maharashtra. "*We were awarded the 'Emerging Diagnostic Services Provider Company of the Year' by Frost and Sullivan in the year 2011. We are the largest Integrated Diagnostic Services Provider in the South and the fourth largest diagnostic brand in India according to industry sources.*" The centres have state of the art equipment and technology and have several quality certifications.

Raju's vision is to serve the entire population from the poorest of the poor to the urban rich. "*We offer preventive health checkups to over 600 corporates and insurance clients along with wellness packages to general public. It is time we moved towards preventive care rather than cure. Most patients lack knowledge of critical parameters like BMI (Body Mass Index) and HDL (High Density Lipoprotein).*"

What next? "*Maybe something in agriculture,*" he says.

AGS Health

Devendra Saharia, Co-founder and President, AGS Health was a young investment banker doing mergers and acquisitions for technology companies in San Francisco during the late 1990s. While working for Merrill Lynch during the years of the internet boom, he witnessed several fortunes being made. "*I saw the mania that took over the world; companies would be bought for billions of dollars and within months they would be worth nothing.*" That experience shook him up and he wanted to move to India and be a responsible entrepreneur.

He checked out several cities in the country to start his venture. He ended up choosing Chennai. Founded in 2000, Ajuba International provided billing and revenue cycle management solutions to healthcare providers such as hospitals, physician groups, durable medical equipment companies and academic medical centres in the US. Pioneers in the onshore-offshore industry model, they drew on the expertise of people with significant experience in US healthcare, in both the US and India. Saharia built an award-winning business model that gave customers the best of both worlds; onshore service levels at offshore costs.

Saharia exited Ajuba in 2011 and launched AGSHealth, again in Chennai in 2012. He is once again targeting the American healthcare market. He already has three centres in Chennai. "*We are doing high end work with technology and analytics orientation,*" he says. "*Chennai has a diverse talent pool. There is hardcore engineering talent, hardware talent because of the automobile industry and also a vast IT talent pool. Chennai is ideal for companies who combine IT services with technology.*" It has been winning the Rising Star award in the 2013 and 2014 Global Outsourcing 100 List awarded by by the International Association of Outsourcing Professionals (IAOP)

Saharia says that the company has focused on four components to build world-class delivery capabilities:

People: The 1,400 employees are trained in various aspects of US healthcare. Many of them have been sponsored for certifications from leading industry bodies. Experts work in specific functional areas in a combination of onshore-based customer relationship and offshore-based service delivery.

Processes: AGS has achieved ISO 9001:2000 and 27000 certification for process excellence, data security and compliance with key legislations such as HIPAA and FDCPA in the US. It runs more than 20 in-house workshops and programmes for its employees at all levels annually. These are complemented by sponsorships to US-based certifications, external management workshops, conferences and seminars and assignments abroad for top performers.

Leadership: The company runs quarterly Leadership Development Programs (LDP) and Management Development Programs (MDP) which are anchored by the senior management team and include experts from the industry.

Technology: The company deploys top end technology in all aspects of the business, with built-in disaster recovery and business continuity solutions and houses offices in best-in-class buildings (e.g. Tidel Park in Chennai). The implementation of several tools to automate workflow processes has increased productivity and improved turnaround times.

The journey has not been smooth. The 9/11 attack on the World Trade Centre threw a massive spanner in everybody's plans for success. *"This incident impacted sentiments towards outsourcing, especially to offshore service providers. There was virtually no new business for two or three quarters. We managed through those difficult times primarily by being prudent with our costs and running a tight ship."*

There were other pressing, local concerns too. For any BPO to function efficiently, the liaising between onshore and offshore talent is all important. It means creating proper rapport, understanding, and trust between both the parties. *"We started Ajuba right after the internet meltdown; prospective employees wanted to be convinced that our business was real! We were also a new company in Chennai and an unknown employer brand. It was a tough task to build the team because we had to share our vision for the business and set realistic expectations for the candidates."*

A major challenge faced by most BPO service providers is how to curtail the attrition rate. Saharia has taken several pro-active steps to reduce attrition and its negative impact. The company proudly mentions employee engagement, pay-for-performance practices, and improved work-life balance for employees through several measures. *"Many employees who quit for higher studies or who joined other companies have come back and joined us saying that they value the family feeling and team spirit they experience with us."* says Saharia.

Coimbatore: The Wonder City

OLD AND NEW

Coimbatore is one of the most entrepreneurial cities in the country. Almost everybody from Coimbatore aspires to be an entrepreneur. They may be working for somebody, but will also be making simultaneous plans to start something on their own. The story of Coimbatore deserves a book of its own.

The city used to be called the Manchester of India because of the textile mills that came up there. Many of these mills were set up by the pioneering industrialists of Coimbatore. They also sowed the seeds for Coimbatore becoming a leader in the light engineering industry. Today, Coimbatore is not just textiles. It has foundries, pump and motor manufacturing, auto ancillaries and wet grinders. At various points Coimbatore has been called the foundry capital, the pump capital and the wet grinder capital of India! The city continues to be a hotspot of entrepreneurial activity. All kinds of new businesses spring up in Coimbatore constantly.

The two communities, the Kammavar Naidus and Kongu Vellalas (Gounders) who laid the foundation for Coimbatore's dynamic growth have not been celebrated enough. They have been typical South Indian businessmen, low key, and averse to publicity. None of them have aspired for monster growth. The pioneers from both these communities were agriculturists turned traders who then blossomed into full-fledged industrialists.

To start with, these pioneers were cotton farmers. They did not have huge land holdings. PS Govindasamy Naidu, the founder of the PSG Group set up the first Indian owned textile mill in the city. He inherited about 14 acres of land, of which more than half were dry lands. He started trading in cotton and tobacco. The family slowly established a sizeable cotton trade with many of the mostly British-owned mills. They acquired land, which they irrigated with the help of oil-powered engines and were the first to use tractors in their farms. A ginning factory was established in 1911.

Govindaswamy Kuppuswamy Naidu set up a small ginning unit even earlier in 1906 that used a pair of oxen to pull the rollers on the gins. He had to shut down his mill but went on to establish one of the largest textile units in the South, Lakshmi Mills, several years down the line. At that time Coimbatore had not become the Manchester of India and there was only one textile mill set up by Robert Stanes. Lakshmi Mills was a ginning factory till 1933 when it became a full-fledged textile mill.

PS Govindasamy Naidu, had four enterprising sons—Venkatasamy Naidu, Rangasamy Naidu, Ganga Naidu and Narayanasamy Naidu. The First World War was a bad time for the PSG family. Trade slowed down and Govindasamy Naidu passed away. Ganga Naidu persuaded the family to establish a spinning mill and they set up the Sri Ranga Vilas Ginning, Spinning and Weaving Mills in 1922, the fourth mill in Coimbatore.

The PSG brothers were the first (in 1931) to use electric power from the Pykara Electricity System, replacing the older technology of generating power through steam engines. The family has many such firsts to its credit.

Coimbatore understood Corporate Social Responsibility decades before the phrase became familiar. The PSG brothers took a decision to divide their wealth not into four parts, but into five, with the fifth to be willed to charity. The PSG family in 1921 set up the Sarvajana School so that village children would have access to education. Says S Gurumurthi, commentator on political and economic affairs, *"It is the industry which set up educational institutions in Coimbatore and not vice-versa."*

Rajshree Pathy of Rajshree Sugars and Formula One racer Narain Karthikeyan are prominent members of the family. As Rajshree says, the PSG family produces girls, the Lakshmi Mills family produces boys and they marry each other. She is married to Lakshmi Mills' founder's grandson Pathy. The pioneering families remain connected to each other. The PSG families today run industries, educational institutions and hospitals.

Coimbatore evolved as a light engineering power house because the entrepreneurs wanted to make equipment for agriculture and textile mills. Narayanaswamy from Pappanaickenpalayam loved machines. In 1922 he set up a workshop to repair sugarcane crushers and cotton ginning machines. He found it difficult to find suitable castings for his workshop. The story goes that he travelled to Cochin (now Kochi) and studied the operations of the crucible furnace of the Cochin shipyard. Two years later he set up the Dhandayuthapani Foundry. Today there are about 700 foundries in the city.

The story of the pioneering industrialists of Coimbatore will not be complete without a mention of the fabulous GD Naidu who was known as the Thomas Alva Edison of India. He was a serial entrepreneur and a serial inventor. He designed and invented all sorts of products such as super thin shaving blades, a distance adjuster for film cameras, a fruit juice extractor, a tamper, a recording machine, and a kerosene run fan, among others.

Naidu began his transport business in 1920 acquiring an automobile coach. He drove it between Pollachi and Palani. In a few years, his United Motor Service (UMS) owned the most efficient fleet of public transport vehicles (600) in the country. In 1937, the first motor to be produced in India was brought out from Naidu's UMS factory. This was the country's first indigenous motor which Naidu developed with D Balasubramaniam even before the Kirloskar brothers.

These were the people who made Coimbatore what it is today. Credit also must go to Robert Stanes the Englishman who came to Coimbatore when he was seventeen and set up many industries and a school in the city.

The founding families of Coimbatore may not make it to the top 100 list compiled by business magazines and papers. They have however not faded away. There are several offshoots of the older institutions which produce world class products. Take the example of LMW founded as Lakshmi Machine Works in 1962 by GK Devarajulu to produce spinning machinery locally in collaboration with Reiter of Switzerland. His son Jayavarthanavelu built it up to be the market leader a position which it has never lost. Today, his son Sanjay runs LMW and its associated companies.

This low-key company is possibly the world's largest spinning machinery manufacturer. It has more than 60 per cent of market share in India. Says a leading yarn manufacturer, *"If Indian spinning industry is today internationally competitive, LMW is one of the reasons."* Many outside the textile industry may not know that every spinning mill in the country is bound to have at least one LMW machine. It has no Indian rivals. It manufactures the entire range of spinning machinery. It is not only the leader in the domestic market, but also the top exporter of textile spinning machines. But it never gets its due outside the industry, as it is closely held and does not have a large body of share holders.

The KG Group started as a cotton-trading venture by K Govindaswamy Naidu in 1932, has evolved into one of the most highly integrated companies in the textile industry. The Group has also set up hospitals and educational institutions and is into real estate as well.

What may not be well known is that it is also one of the largest terry towel manufacturers (Sharada Towels) in the world. The KG Group is the recipient of Frost & Sullivan award for creating a world class product, and several best exporter awards from the government and best vendor awards from leading retailers worldwide. Its trademarked brand Microcotton is placed in over 20,000 retail stores worldwide. Sharada has offices in New York and warehouses in USA and Europe.

Coimbatore has many such world class textile units who quietly go about doing their business. Textile industry sources single out mills like KPR mills and Ambika Cotton Mills. KPR

Mills, a vertically integrated apparel company with international accreditations for quality control is a relative new comer which was set up in the eighties. Ambika Cotton Mills which also came up in the eighties is one of the established players in supplying yarn to almost all premium shirt manufacturers around the world.

Coimbatore's textile tradition continues in different shapes and sizes and the industry is no longer the stranglehold of the Naidus.

The founding families have grown and have diversified into different areas. Elgi Equipments was established in 1960 by LRG Naidu as an air compressor and garage equipment manufacturing company. Over the years, the company has grown its product portfolio to fit the changing market requirements. The company is a global leader in compressors.

Elgi Ultra Industries also from the same group has proved to be a most innovative company, reflecting the spirit of Coimbatore's passion for engineering and manufacturing. Even in a highly competitive segment like home appliances, the Ultra brand wet grinder commands a premium in the market. Coimbatore has around 600 small and medium companies making grinders and parts. Elgi Ultra Grinder is the beautifully designed up market product in this lot.

Pricol Limited was founded in 1972 by N Damodaran and LG Varadarajulu. It makes automotive electrical and electronic products. It has been a leader in dashboard Instruments for many years. Pricol like other largish Coimbatore companies has a global presence and exports to around 40 countries.

The Gounders

The Gounders entered industry a little later than the Naidus in Coimbatore. They too are agriculturists turned traders turned industrialists. VC Vellingiri Gounder set up Gnanambikai Mills in 1935. Two decades later two other mills, Sri Karunambikai Mills of AV Ramana Gounder and Sakthi Textiles of N Mahalingam were established.

Sakthi Textiles was the first company to come up in the Sakthi Group, and Mahalingam who passed away in 2014 was one of the grand old men of Tamil Nadu industry. He set up industries, educational institutions, and was a noted philanthropist. He actively helped and encouraged people to become entrepreneurs. Mahalingam's father P Nachimuthu Gounder laid the initial foundation for the group. He started his business by hiring out bullock carts and ended up starting Annamalai Bus Transport (ABT) with 14 buses in 1931. Mahlingam took the group forward and the group expanded into textiles, sugar and auto components among other things. Sakthi Sugars is one of the larger sugar companies in the country.

Today the ₹6000 crore Sakthi group which has seen its share of ups and downs has learnt to cope in spite of the sugar industry dragging it down every few years. Mahalingam's eldest son Manickam who did his MBA from Ann Arbor after getting his engineering degree from Chennai is now focusing on auto components particularly for the export market and has started manufacturing from Detroit!

Family patriarch Mahalingam in his customary style urged his young cousins to start something on their own. The Bannari Amman Group was founded by SV Balasubramaniam, and he worked for Sakthi Sugars for 21 years coming to work as soon as he completed his graduation. Balasubramaniam started with the business he knew best, sugar. Today, Bannari Amman is a well diversified group with interests in manufacturing, trading and service activities. Manufacturing and trading include sugar, alcohol, liquor and granite. Group's turnover is around ₹3000 crore.

Some of the Newcomers

The major pump industries in Coimbatore are Suguna Pumps, Sharp Industries, CRI Pumps, Texmo Industries, Deccan Pumps and KSB Pumps which are global. Let us look at one of them, CRI Pumps.

This low-profile Coimbatore company is probably one of the country's largest pump manufacturers, with a wide range and a global presence. When technocrat K Gopal borrowed ₹10000 in 1961 to set up his own business, he surely did not dream that his small foundry in Coimbatore, making valves for agricultural pumps, would grow into the ₹1300-crore pump major it is today. He knew how to get the Group to move forward. Two years before he died in 1980 when he was just forty-nine, he got into the pump business. It was quite a late entry, as Coimbatore was already getting to be known as India's pump capital.

It innovated many times to reach the position it is in today. CRI Pumps has a long list of firsts to its credit: it pioneered 100-per-cent stainless steel pumps; and when problems erupted in the 1980s due to voltage fluctuations with its agricultural pumps, its biggest business then, it developed pumps that could work at voltages as low as 250V to 300V. That decade also saw groundwater levels falling. Most of the manufacturers were making mono block pumps. CRI invested money and time to become pioneers in submersible bore-well pumps, which is now a big business not only in the domestic market but with exports to 60-plus countries, including the US, a first for any Indian manufacturer, with both UL and CE certifications. It was also the first to get IS0 9001 certification and ISI approval for energy-efficient pumps.

CRI has a patent for its floating impeller technology, which has a rotating device in the pump that sucks up water, nearly doubling the effective height from five metres to nine metres with the same power. And after eight years of research, it created a submersible motor that uses a resin filling for cooling instead of water or oil, with a built-in lightning arrester. It is one of the very few in the world with its own stamping unit for startors and rotors. It also runs an international standard training centre.

The founder's four sons Velumani, Soundararajan, Rajendran and Selvaraj got into the business one by one as they finished their studies. CRI's unique selling proposition, Soundararajan had said in an interview to *Business India* magazine is its approach to selling and marketing. *"We study the market at the field level and give products for the very difficult and adverse conditions that exist in India,. We also have very strong relationships with our dealers, We took the initiative to break out of the wholesaler chain and go direct to the dealer.*" CRI was the first pump manufacturer to take this step. "*We have invested a lot of time and money in our 4,500 dealers who have more than 100,000 mechanics. We invited every one of them, from as far off as Ludhiana, to Coimbatore giving them train tickets and accommodation for five or six days in a hotel while they attended a training programme here.*" There is also a complete design scheme for the dealership, with assistance from CRI to build their showrooms to a uniform standard.

Another pioneering effort of the CRI group was to develop, with the help of TCS, a special software to help select pumps. "*We stuck to our knitting, without going in for diversification just for the sake of it,*" Soundararajan says. "*All our profits are ploughed back into the business.*"

The company has now started manufacturing PVC and CPVC pipes, designed for higher durability, which will have application in pumping and plumbing systems. It has invested ₹120 crore to set up two state-of-the-art pipe manufacturing units at Gandhinagar in Gujarat and Hosur in Tamil Nadu. "*Making a foray into pipes segment is part of an overall business development strategy arising out of our five-year Vision 2020 by when we target to have a turnover of ₹5000 crore compared to ₹1,300 crore in 2014–15. We could foresee an opportunity in the pipes segment, and we want to be an integrated pumping solution provider,*" says G Soundararajan, Vice-Chairman, CRI Pumps.

CRI Pumps has also started acquiring foreign companies. A recent acquisition was Fabbrica Italiana Pompe Sommergibili Srl (FIPS), an Italian company engaged in waste water pump technology. It bought Pipes & Process Systems Ltd, in UK which makes a range of industrial pump products. Soundararajan has said that CRI Pumps would continue to invest in capacity building and research and development. "*We will look to acquire value added pump manufacturing companies in the developed countries and take both—the inorganic and organic route to grow,*" says Soundararajan.

Apart from Pricol and the Elgi Group, there are around 20–25 tier I auto component makers in the city and more than 100 tier II and tier III component suppliers here. RSM Autocast is a first generation auto component company which believes in green technology.

RSM Autokast

RSM Autokast Ltd is the flagship company of the RSM Group, which has diversified interests in auto components, castings, sheet metal components, horticulture and wind power generation. It is best known for its design and manufacture of brake drums for commercial vehicles. It is one of the largest suppliers of this component in the country. RSM is the only company that caters to OEMs, exports and the aftermarkets. It exports to 30 countries under its own brand name.

RSM Autokast was set up by K Kasturirangaiyan in 1996. Almost its entire power requirements for manufacturing activities are met by its windmills located in Tamil Nadu and Karnataka. The total installed generating capacity is over 6 MW. Says K Ilango, the founder's son and deputy managing director, *"My father believes passionately in green energy"*. Kasturirangaiyan is one of the founding members of All India Wind Power Association and was its chairman for many years.

Habasit Iakoka

A textile machinery company which is thought of very highly is Habasit Iakoka. This is the story of a typical first generation entrepreneur with strong values from Coimbatore. He also thinks outside the box.

N Subramaniam, Managing Director, Habasit Iakoka was the first to go to school in his family. He comes from a small village near Coimbatore. Most of the people in and around his village worked in textile mills, including his father. *"We had no footwear, we went hungry, but education was paramount. My good grades got me into engineering college*". Subramaniam completed high school and went on to pursue Mechanical Engineering at PSG Tech in the city.

He spent a few years working for a chemical unit in the North and then moved back to Coimbatore to join Shanthi Gears in 1981–82. Subsequently, he worked with the Elgi Group for a few years. In 1987 with some friends, started Iakoka Syntrans, for manufacturing synthetic spindle tapes at a time when the market was predominantly using cotton tapes. They started 'Iakoka' with a capital of ₹1 lakh in 1987.

Says Subramaniam,"*We started customising belts for different machines at a time when all machines had standard belts. This brought us recognition. We appointed excellent agents and offered a share in our profits. We converted every order into a repeat order. We turned our backs on quick profits based on reduced quality.*

"*We did not poach customers from our competition through subterfuge or undercutting. Every order was won on the basis of quality. We attended to complaints giving personal attention.*" In three years the company became the market leader, with an annual profit of ₹4 crore. The world leader in the product line is the Swiss company, Habasit. Subramaniam asked them for an agency arrangement in India and they offered a joint venture instead.

This is one of the most successful joint ventures in the textile industry in India. From a turnover of ₹4 crore in 1996, the company recently crossed ₹100 crore. With three manufacturing facilities, 300 employees and over 23 dealers across India, Habasit Iakoka is the market leader in the product segments in which it operates. It is the largest manufacturer of Synthetic Sandwich Spindle Tapes for textile machinery applications in the world.The company enjoys a domestic market share of 60 per cent for spindle tapes with 10–15 per cent of the turnover coming from exports.

Says Subramaniam "*We give employees the same importance we give our customers. We sack workers who demand dowry from their brides. We offer monthly incentives to employees who take care of their wives' parents as their permanent house guests. We do our best to help them educate their children. We are determined to enhance the desirability of our employees as life partners.*"

Roots

In a country that uses the horn obsessively somebody had to think about going into horn manufacturing. K Ramaswamy decided to do so. In 1970, he started a small company for the manufacture of auto parts with three employees. He took almost a decade to develop the now famous Roots Electric Horns. The company was already making a name for itself in the air horn market with the first-of-its-kind electric air horns.

Today, Roots is the eleventh largest auto horn manufacturer in the world. Another group company is Roots MultiClean Limited which was conceived to deliver world class mechanised cleaning solutions to the Indian manufacturing and service industry. A technical partnership with Hako, Germany, opened up global market opportunities. Today it is a market leader in India and is known globally.

Some Who Thought Differently

Kovai Pazhamudir Nilayam

Kovai Pazhamudir Nilyam the largest vegetable and fruit retail chain in the South, is really a remarkable Coimbatore rags to riches story. The first outlet was opened in 1965 by N Chinnaswamy and his younger brother Natarajan. Chinnaswamy started life working in a fruit shop in the '50s. *"I did not want to go to school. So my father got me a job at his friend's fruit shop at Annur when I was twelve. Within days, my father passed away, leaving behind my mother and three younger brothers. My day would start at five and I would leave the shop only at 9 in the night,"* says Chinnaswamy. Selling fruits was becoming part of his DNA. It is small wonder that the Reliance and Birla groups have not been able to take on Kovai Pazhamudir Nilayam in this retail niche.

A few years down the line when he was eighteen, Chinnaswamy joined a neighbourhood spinning mill, which allowed him to save some money. He bought a cart and started selling fruits after his day was over at the mill. *"My younger brother Natarajan too became a mill worker. After the eight-hour shift, we would take turns and sell fruits,"* he says.

In due course he realised that customers seemed to want a shop from where they could buy fruits at any time of the day. Chinnaswamy gave up the cart for a rented shop at Peelamedu in Coimbatore. The brothers did not give up the mill jobs. They were able to put aside some money to grow the fruit business. Seven years later, they used their savings to open their second shop, next to a hospital compound to offer fresh juices as well.

Seeing the great response they got from the customers they decided to branch out. When others started following their fruits-vegetables-juices model, the brothers decided to name their outlets Pazhamudir Nilayam. The next two outlets opened in quick succession and there was no looking back. Today there are more than 40 outlets; eight are company-owned while the rest have been given to local franchise partners. They soon plan to have 50 outlets in Chennai alone, *"To maintain a distinct identity, we have named these stores 'Kovai Pazhamudir Nilayam',"* says Chinnasamy's son, Dorairaj.

Pazhamudir has mastered its sourcing strategy, which ensures that only the freshest produce reaches the outlet. *"We don't buy directly from the farm. We leave this to the agents, who source from the farm, grade the produce and send it to us,"* says Dorairaj. This helps the promoters save time, minimise wastage and improve productivity.

In 1983 itself the family divided the business among the four brothers with the elder brother ensuring that his younger siblings got the shops with the higher turnovers. Their children are educated, tech savvy and are taking their companies forward in different ways.

Natarajan's son Senthil Natarajan has launched an online store for fruits, vegetables, and groceries targeting customers in Chennai. 'I Buy Fresh.com' takes orders online and via phone and delivers the products within 24 hours. He is now looking to raise PE funds for rapid expansion. Palaniswamy Vanchimuthu and Kavitha Vanchimuthu launched Boomerang Gelato in 1997. Kavita is Chinnaswamy's daughter. They wish to establish Boomerang's presence in London soon.

Since inception they have opened up 16 outlets of which six are in Coimbatore and the rest across several cities in Tamil Nadu including Erode, Salem, Tiruchy, Karur and Tirupur. *"Five of the 16 outlets are owned by us. We are looking at a franchisee model to expand rapidly"*, says Vanchimuthu. *"Expansion apart, we are also keen to have two signature stores for gelato."* The promoter couple—Palaniswamy and Kavitha attended the first leg of the 2015 Gelato World Tour at Singapore. Their caramel and almond crunch was accorded the second place from among sixteen entries around the world.

Suguna Foods

GB Sundararajan, Managing Director, Suguna Foods Limited started life as a trader in the poultry industry. In 1986, Sundararajan and his brother Soundararajan set up a poultry farm with 200 egg laying birds (layers). In 1988, they went in for Suguna's first feed mill to meet the feed requirements of the neighborhood poultry farmers. Suguna was the first to realise that the future lay in organised contract farming. This has helped the company and thousands of rural entrepreneurs who are now Suguna's contract farmers. This was in 1990.

Suguna Foods at last count reaches over 8000 villages, more than 20000 farmers, 100,000 channel partners, and millions of consumers every day. It operates across India and offers a wide range of poultry products and services. The fully integrated operations cover broiler and layer farming, hatcheries, feed mills, slaughter house, processing plants, vaccines and exports.

Suguna has also set up a chain of modern retail outlets under the brand Suguna Daily Fresh. It currently has one take away outlet in Bengaluru called Suguna Crisp and Crunch. The company wants to open 2000 outlets in the next five years. They will be franchise driven and the focus will be on small outlets.

Suguna Foods has a turnover of ₹5400 crore and hopes to double this figure in the next three years.

Ampere

Ratan Tata, Chairman Emeritus of Tata Sons, recently invested an undisclosed amount in Ampere, a Coimbatore-based electric vehicle manufacturer founded by a woman entrepreneur, Hemalatha Annamalai. Tata made the investment along with Ampere's existing investor, Forum Synergies. Ampere sells electric vehicles—cycles, scooters, trolleys—and special purpose vehicles for the differently-abled in Tamil Nadu, Karnataka, Kerala and Maharashtra. Hemalatha says she will use the funds to scale up operations and hire talent.

Hemalatha has an MBA from the Royal Melbourne Institute of Technology, Australia, and a bachelor's degree in computer science and engineering from Government College of Technology, Coimbatore. She does not have a manufacturing background. She turned entrepreneur when she was twenty seven. Her first few ventures were in professional services, technology training, tours and ticketing and an international consultancy for talent acquisition. As a serial entrepreneur, Hemalatha has spent more than a decade creating and driving entrepreneurial ventures.

Hemalatha used her savings to launch Ampere in 2008. Ampere designs and makes chargers, motors and controllers. The company has developed its own method to revive old batteries and offers after-sales service.

"Our vehicles are designed to suit Indian rugged conditions and it was well appreciated by Mr Tata," Hemalatha told the media. *"In 2000, China sold 40,000 electric vehicles. In 2015, they are selling 32 million vehicles. Why not India?"* she asks. *"We want to use the investment to scale up our operations and take our company to the next level. We want to strengthen our products and focus on large-scale production and make it faster, better and cheaper. In the electric vehicles industry, executions are challenging. We want to make a difference to it. We have started our talent hunt for sales, marketing, and R&D."* she has said in an interview to *The Hindu* .

The Ampere Mitra series, the three-wheeler load carrier, is totally indigenous. *"It carries loads up to one tonne and the battery requires about 6-8 hours of charging. Our customers, especially from villages, are happy. The four primary components of the vehicle are the battery, motor, controller and charger. Sixty per cent of our components are indigenous and we are working towards making it 100 per cent."*

Ampere focuses on rural areas as farmers use two-wheelers to transport chicken feed, eggs and grains. The firm's vehicles are part of a waste management project in the Kurudampalayam panchayat in Coimbatore. Hemalatha after this fresh round of funding is brimming with ideas to build a world class company and grow much faster.

The Start-ups

Those who returned to their roots

Anand Purushothaman—CEO, Payoda

Born and raised in Coimbatore, Anand Puroshothaman completed his engineering degree from PSG Tech. He took the usual path followed by many engineering graduates and pursued his master's in Industrial Engineering—Human Factors from Clemson University, South Carolina and took up a banking IT job in New York.

Anand worked for over 15 years in Wall Street firms. He was a key technologist in various start-ups, notably Tradeweb, an online trading platform. He spent eight years in Tradeweb. The company founded with $20 Million was acquired for $2.5 billion. This helped him make a fortune thanks to his stock options. He set up Payoda Technologies in 2005 in the US with $50000. He shifted operations to India in 2006.

Starting with only 10 employees Payoda has more than 600 employees now and is growing fast. His customers include a few top global financial firms in the US, leading insurance companies in the Middle East among others. Anand hopes to make Payoda a billion dollar company in 2020. He is also convinced that he can build a world class IT products business from Coimbatore.

Rajiv Srihari—CEO, KitUp

Rajiv Srihari owns and manages KitUp which gives a total automobile experience to those who love their cars. It is a store, a workshop, a business, that offers car lovers a chance to get their dreams come true by giving them customised colour, interior, music, revved up engines and jazzed up exterior for their beloved machines.

Rajiv's romance with cars began quite early when he used to experiment with cars owned by family and friends, styling their car interiors and experimenting with audio equipment. It helped that he was a science and math prodigy in school. After a mechanical engineering degree from PSG, he went to the US to do his post graduation in Industrial and Operations Engineering from the University of Michigan, Ann Arbor where he finished *summa cum laude* (highest honour) scoring a four out of four GPA (Grade Point Average).

"After achieving top academic honours, and having worked with my professor in consulting assignments I was all set for a good career in the US. I was an only child. So I decided to return home." He took up a job with the LMW group. During his spare time he started styling cars and enhancing car audio experience. What started as a hobby, turned into passion and led him to set up KitUp.

The exteriors are where Rajiv's engineering expertise comes to life. Without harming the character of a particular make, Rajiv gives the cars a unique look. Each time a car comes into the Indian market, KitUp starts on a die (mould) for it. The process takes around two and a half months. *"Once the die is made, then all it takes us is a few days to get your car ready,"* he says. Rajiv does all the designing. With more than 500 dies for most of the Indian makes, he has a large client base.

KitUp over the years has styled over a thousand cars with clients coming to him from all over India. He now wants to set up experience centres in Chennai and Bengaluru.

Vinod Narsiman—MD & CEO, Indsil Group

The first businessman in the world to set up and successfully operationalise a ferro chrome smelter (to manufacture chromium alloy for applications in the stainless steel manufacturing industry) is from Coimbatore. Vinod Narsiman, has set up a ferro chrome smelter with an annual 150000 tonnes capacity in the Sultanate of Oman.

Vinod plunged into businesss right after getting his MBA in the US. After receiving top honors in finance and getting offers in investment banking, he returned to India with dreams of building a successful business.

Betting big on the Indian auto industry, he moved aggressively investing significant capital into an auto component manufacturing business bringing advanced Danish technology into India. The business never took off and he sold this business out to focus on the challenges faced by the family stainless steel business, learning all about metal ore smelting plants and captive power generation plants.

Vinod's business mantra back in 1996 was to pursue high growth by exploiting opportunities in potentially high growth industries and markets where you bet big, invest in delivering high quality and differentiated products, and make huge returns. Reality turned out otherwise. He has now learnt to make profits from manufacturing commoditized products under extreme pressures of highly volatile prices, escalating costs and cut throat competition fighting for non-exclusive raw materials.

Today, Indsil's business in Oman has already delivered an operating profit which is twelve per cent above the global competition. After twenty years in this journey, growth to Vinod is all about business and organisation evolution, continuously building a competitive advantage and winning in the industry at a global scale. He is now working on a double pronged growth strategy of moving upstream into becoming a chrome ore miner cum seller in the international market and moving downstream into manufacturing stainless steel.

Homegrown entrepreneurs

Sanjay Kondaas—CEO, Kondaas Automation

Sanjay Kondaas took up a sales job in the consumer and commercial electronics business and he seized the first opportunity to start a business of his own with a single objective—'Make more money'.

"During my school and college days we faced money problems and I wanted financial independence both for myself and my family

*members."*Sanjay comes from a farming family. He chose to do computer science. He took up a sales representative job selling basic electronics products in and around the Coimbatore region.

In 1995 Sanjay launched Kondaas Automation as a dealership business focused purely on sales and servicing of UPS, inverters and batteries. In a few years he expanded the scope of business to include product assembling and packaging and created the first series of products with brand name Kondaas.

Today with over 30,000 users, Kondass Powerlite is the leader in power invertors, UPS systems and servo stabilizers. Kondaas offers comphrehensive power solutions. Kondaas products are conceived and developed at its world-class R&D centre and manufactured at its state-of-the-art plant on completely automated process.

Says Sanjay, *"After a few years I wanted the Kondaas brand to become associated with something unique, special and I sensed a tremendous potential with the emerging solar power market."* In 2003, Kondaas Automation launched its line of solar products and in ten years has expanded to solar water heaters for consumer and industrial applications, solar powered street lights water pumping system for agro farms, and solar powered hybrid inverters and batteries.

In 2013, Kondaas launched the first of its kind solar power experience centre in Coimbatore where all of its solar products are in use and the entire power to run the shop is generated from solar energy. Sanjay takes pride in bringing clean energy in the lowest cost possible and by offering highest quality of service to his customers.

V Parthiban—CEO, Bull Machines

Parthiban comes from a business family in Coimbatore and after having graduated from PSG College of Technology in 1997 with a Diploma in Mechanical Engineering, he was certain that his future was in entrepreneurship. To him entrepreneurship meant innovation.

In 1997, he started Bull Machines to manufacture farm equipment as tractor attachments. The first vehicle mounted with the first attachment broke into two pieces. It was a huge learning experience. Parthiban and his engineers and technicians had mounted the attachment in the European way. Indian operating conditions were different resulting in the failure of the gear box.

"Innovation is about designing machines indigenously within constraints such as lowest cost, tough operating conditions and low-skilled operators. After many trials and errors, we created several unique tractor attachments, and won a patent as well."

Parthiban advocates the 'Go Direct' model for bringing truly disruptive innovations to the market. The manufacturer works directly with the customer and in the early stages explores a co-creation model bringing the customer as a partner in the product design, development testing and upgrade process. This strategy adopted by Bull Machines initially meant no takers among the mainstream tractor manufacturers such as Mahindra, John Deere and Escorts. However, increased satisfaction among their target customers created a strong pull and Bull ultimately gained recognition. A testament to this achievement was Mahindra's willingness to co-brand the tractor plus attachments product line, giving Bull an equal partner status, especially after offering to buy out the brand at a pittance.

CLUSTERS IN TAMIL NADU

There are more clusters in Tamil Nadu than anywhere else

CLUSTERS

Tamil Nadu has business clusters which have come up all over the state right under the government's nose as they often do. A couple of entrepreneurs start something new when agriculture fails, several others jump into the business with family and friends backing them, and within a few years an industrial cluster develops. These have nothing to do with government promoted industrial parks and SEZs. In many cases, the government does pitch in once the cluster has developed.

Tiruppur

Says S Gurumurthi, in an article in *Business Line* about Tiruppur: "*By 1990s...Tiruppur was a world leader in the knitted garments industry. The success of this industry is striking...What is behind the story of this development? The capital was raised within the Gounder community, a caste relegated to land-based activities. The entrepreneurs relied on community and family networks...These networks were viewed as more reliable in transmitting information and enforcing contracts than banking and legal systems that offered weak protection to creditors' rights. The community network which promoted entrepreneurship based on self-learning also trained new entrants to the knitwear business and customer management*".

The first generation entrepreneurs from Tiruppur who were making vests for the local market saw an opportunity in knitted garments and they moved in. Tiruppur's direct exports started with Italy. Everyone talks about Verona, a garment importer from Italy who came to Tiruppur in 1978 through Mumbai exporters to buy white T-shirts. A lot of job workers were manufacturing garments for merchant exporters. Verona recognised Tiruppur's potential and came again the following year. He was the man who brought European business to Tiruppur. On seeing the quality, others soon followed suit. In 1981, the European retail chain C&A came to Tiruppur. Gradually, other stores approached the exporters. A handful of manufacturers exported garments worth ₹15 crore in 1985. The next couple of year was a windfall for Tiruppur and exports touched ₹300 crore by 1990. Today it is about ₹18000 crore.

Tiruppur exporters started exporting to the US and European countries without even knowing English or European languages. They slept with their fax machines next to their beds.

Tiruppur is full of rags to riches stories. Take the case of Viking International Ltd.

Eswaran who is a school dropout is the founder of Anand Hosieries, Anand Textiles, Viking Knitters, Viking Textiles, Viking Net Process, Premanand Textiles and other industries. Coming from an agricultural family Easwaran headed to Tiruppur when the family faced difficult times during a drought. *"I went to Tiruppur to work in a hosiery factory. Tiruppur is ten kilometres from Anaipudur, our village in Coimbatore. I walked to work every day, dreaming about the day I could afford to take a bus."* After struggling for about three months he landed a job on a weekly salary of ₹2.

Easwaran's father bought him a rusty, old, second-hand bicycle. He greased and cleaned it everyday and soon learnt to take it apart, overhaul it and put the parts back together like an expert. That was how he ventured into business. In time, he bought ten bicycles and hired them out. The next move was to open a grocery store.

Then he decided to start a banian (vest) manufacturing unit. He had saved ₹2000 and his grandmother who was always a support gave him her jewels to pledge. Having worked for a garment factory, he knew how to manufacture high quality undergarments. Easwaran like other entrepreneurs like him found a place to rent and installed a sewing machine there. *"I worked day and night. I was the boss and I was the worker. I had no time for home, for my hometown. Nights merged into days."*

He travelled for the first time by train, went to Bombay, knocked at the door of agencies and found business. *"The orders we bagged on that first trip exceeded our expectations. I had to employ ten people in a matter of months."* The order book was full. When his friend, the marketing manager cheated him, he decided to takeover marketing himself. He did not know English. He did not know how to operate a bank account. He managed. *"The customer wanted quality products. I needed orders. I managed the transaction well without English. I slept at railway stations. I ate at every street food stall in India. I travelled on the rooftops of buses. My only dream was to collect orders. My dreams made all my hardships bearable."*

Easwaran set up a unit to make vests in 1963. It started doing well and Easwaran was ready when the export market opened up. His small unit has expanded to the Viking group of companies. Viking has grown and grown and is today one of the top manufacturers of knit wear for exports and local markets. The export companies are all ISO 9001 certified.

Then there are others who set up ancillary units for the knitting industry and have since scaled up. Sundaram comes from a small village about eight kilometres from Tiruppur. Dropping out of school in the third standard when he was ten, he joined his uncle's workshop. He set up his own unit at the age of twenty-one. He made a beginning by manufacturing small engineering items. He then started manufacturing calendaring machines in 1991. He was doing well when he happened to see a demonstration of a newly introduced compacting machine by a foreign company. These machines are used in the hosiery industry to remove shrinkages in fabrics. He realised that he could make better machines at a cheaper cost.

Sundaram struggled to produce this machine spending more than sixteen hours a day in his factory. He sought the help of academic and research institutions for clearing doubts. He approached banks for funds and was turned down. His mother gave him some money to start his business. He borrowed from local financiers and he came out with his first machine in 1998. The price of his Nova machine was one-third of the price of the US company then controlling the market. His foreign competitors were astonished to see this machine. As a result, they had to reduce their original prices to be competitive.

Sundaram made regular improvements and innovations. For example, in the process area of component heating, he introduced oil heating instead of the usual water heating. His major international competitor had to adopt this method subsequently. Currently, P.S.A. Industries Private Limited promoted by him, is the leading player in India leaving his competitors way behind. He gets enquiries for his machines from different parts of the world, including Europe.

Sankagiri and Tiruchengode

The Sankagiri transport cluster in western Tamil Nadu is the second largest centre for lorry traffic in the country. Some 90 per cent of the Sankagiri truck owners were originally agriculturists. They now own the largest population of Taurus vehicles in the country. According to *Indian Models of Economy, Business and Management*, a book by Prof. P Kanagasabapathi, seven out of ten people in Sankagiri are now involved in transport-related activities.

Take Tiruchengode in Namakkal district. In the 1960s, a severe water crisis forced Tiruchengode's farmers to join hands to buy a rig to dig deep bore-wells. But seeing the rising demand for borewells, they successfully turned this into a business that soon spread over to Karnataka, Andhra Pradesh, Maharashtra, Madhya Pradesh, Rajasthan and Odisha. Today Tiruchengode is the largest provider of bore-wells in the country, according to Prof. Kanagasabapathi.

There are close to 4,000 rigs owned by people in and around Tiruchengode. Nearly 500–1,000 rig trucks are added to the industry annually, while 20–30 per cent of the old and worn-out trucks roll off the road. The average life of a rig truck is 10 years. By utilising the rig properly one can get back the investment in 3–4 years and, thereafter, make profits.

Most of the rig owners (with minimum education) started as rig operators and became owners. They go away to drill bore wells till the rainy season sets in and then come back to service and repair their equipment. Spare parts of the rigs are sold on the pavements of Tiruchengode like consumer products are in other towns. Tiruchengode started with rigs, and then it moved onto power looms and is now involved in different activities such as textile mills and paper manufacturing.

Entrepreneurship in these places is dynamic, not restricted to one business, says Prof. Kanagasabapathi. It was noticed in a number of clusters such as Rajkot, Coimbatore, Sivakasi and Tiruchengode that the entrepreneurs initially started with one activity and later diversified into different areas, sometimes even unrelated ones.

Sivakasi initially started with the match industry. Later it diversified into fireworks and then printing. Almost all these clusters are built by the entrepreneurs themselves through their own initiatives and efforts

Sivakasi and neighbouring Virudhunagar are dry and arid areas. When the crops failed Ayya Nadar and Shanmuga Nadar decided they had to have an alternate avenue of income. They ended up promoting the first match unit in 1923. They went to Calcutta to learn the trade of making matches. Sivakasi started booming. It makes 80 per cent of India's safety matches, 90 per cent of its fireworks and has 60 per cent of the offset printing solutions business. Its printing industry, which was initially started to cater to the needs of the local match and firework units, has grown to such an extent that even cheque books of foreign countries are printed here.

Srinivas Fine Arts

Srinivas Fine Arts is one of the landmarks of the town of Sivakasi and its founder R Chockalingam is one of those who brought state-of-the-art printing technology to Sivakasi. Printing orders come to Srinivas Fine Arts not only from the rest of the country, but also from Britain, France, Germany and China. The company employs thousands of workers.

Chockalingam's father had a soda factory, which did very well. Then his father ventured into the manufacture of detergent soap. This was doing well too, but could not survive after liberalisation which is the story of many cottage industries. Whatever his fortunes were, his children were brought up to work hard. "'*You must work hard and earn your keep,' my father told us. If you are born in Sivakasi, you are no stranger to hard work. Children may play truant at school but would willingly go to work.*"

Chockalingam had to drop out of college and join a match factory. He learnt the basics of business there. His boss was his mentor from whom he picked up administrative skills. Chockalingam used to work eighteen hours a day. He spent a few years working for his mentor who started his own small business. This was in Tirunelveli. Inevitably differences erupted and Chockalingam had to look for a job again. He found himself overqualified for that job market.

He returned to Sivakasi and with the experience he had gained, was able to infuse life into his father's soda company. He found this tiny business quite limiting. He decided to set up a printing press without knowing much about the business. "*My decision to enter the printing business was impulsive. I had never ever seen an offset printing press.*" All he knew was that every small product was getting branded and required labels.

He started getting orders to design brand labels and print them. *'I had arranged with some Sivakasi printers to get my designs printed. With an investment of just ₹125,I bought five reams of paper and farmed out the printing of labels. I earned a net profit of ₹15 from my initial venture."*

From this truly humble beginning and several hard lessons learnt on the way, Srinivasa Fine Arts moved to making diaries in the '90s. *"When we predicted the spread of the diary habit in India, people laughed at us. We started to see the economy picking up and knew that keeping a diary would become important and lead to efficiency. We incorporated details of auspicious hours for those who believe in such things. We also designed diaries to double up as calendars. We chose the brand name 'Nightingale'."*

Chockalingam wanted to establish the Nightingale brand in the stationery industry like the Penguin imprint in books. Nightingale diary entered the market offering the utility of the traditional Indian calendar in a sophisticated product. It was received very well. Corporate houses started ordering diaries as gifts for clients and employees. The office diaries of many MNCs are made in Sivakasi. *"We export diaries to England, the country that introduced diaries to the world. We have spread out to several parts of the world, strengthening our bases in the Netherlands, Poland, Russia, Malaysia, Singapore, Rwanda, Kenya and several Arab countries."*

When Srinivasa started strengthening its diaries with case binding, it was seen as expensive. Indian diaries used inferior binding that made them cheaper but also short-lived. Misjudging the customer, manufacturers hesitated to change the pricing pattern.

When he went in for the manufacture of notebooks, Chockalingam aimed for international quality. For instance, he consulted mathematics experts and his graph notebooks were error free. The smallest error in the design could have cost the students heavily. *"Other graph notebooks had such inaccuracies while the graphs in our notebooks were precise. It was a marketing triumph for us"*, he says.

The printing presses were all in Sivakasi but the paper distributors were in Madurai, even though imported paper from Tuticorin port reached Madurai via Sivakasi. *"I believed that taking up paper distribution would be the natural next step in the business. I swiftly acted on the idea. Today, we handle 5000 tonnes of paper a year."*

Chockalingam installed his first demi printing machine in September 1964. Today Srinivas Fine Arts has implemented the latest technologies in pre-press, printing, binding, print finish and packaging which enables the company to fulfil every unique requirement and demand. It offers a host of customised services. Its new manufacturing facility is a greenfield project, spread over an area of 63 acres with a built up area in 19 acres. The hi-tech facility is equipped with state of the art automated machinery and the latest German cutting edge technology making it one of the world class manufacturing facilities in Asia.

The organisation is ISO 9001: 2008, SA 8000: 2008, FSC certified. FSC stands for the Forest Stewardship Council, which is a non-profit organization devoted to encouraging the responsible management of the world's forests.

"Quality is our watchword. My fifty years' experience has taught me that business comes to you, if you maintain quality", he signs off.

Karur

Generally, it is assumed that the banking and financial institutions could be successfully promoted and run only by highly qualified people. But there are a number of banks promoted by the local communities across the country. In Karur, which was made the headquarters of a district only a few years ago, people belonging to the local Vysya community had promoted two scheduled banks, namely Karur Vysya Bank and Lakshmi Vilas Bank when the country was still under the British rule. In the earlier periods, banks were mainly promoted by the trading communities. But there have been exceptions. There is a highly successful bank promoted by a traditional non-trading community in the South—the Tamil Nadu Mercantile Bank (TMB) set up by the Nadar Mahajan Sangam.

It is one of the banks in India consistently declaring high rates of dividends from the beginning. The bank declared a dividend of 1000 percent during 2006–07 and proposed 5000 per cent dividend during 2007–08. Above all, a record interim dividend of 9000 per cent was proposed in October 2011. All this, inspite of the bank slipping out of the hands of the promoter community and their protracted legal battles to get it back.

Namakkal

Namakkal is about 375 kilometres south-west of Chennai. Visitors to this small town find the place buzzing with activity, full of markets, residential areas, hotels and educational institutions and the latest high end cars plying the roads. Namakkal is well known in the automobile industry for its body building workshops for commercial vehicles. Trucks, trailers, tankers and rig units are sent here from all over the country to have their bodies built. Trucks and rig units built here get exported to other countries as well.

What may not be so well known is that Namakkal is also the country's second largest egg producing centre, Hyderabad being the first. India is the third largest chicken egg producing country in the world, next only to China and USA. India produces around 75,000 million eggs a year.

About 80 per cent of the layer farms in Tamil Nadu are concentrated in and around Namakkal town. Namakkal region is a dry semi-arid zone where agricultural operations cannot be carried out economically, due to rocky soil and shortage of water. By dedicated hard work and entrepreneurship, the poultry farmers have successfully established a large poultry pocket in this area and Namakkal has come to be known as the 'Poultry City'.

Poultry farming in Namakkal became serious business in the early-seventies when a farmer started out with 100 layer (egg laying) chickens in a thatched poultry shed. A few farmers started preparing their own feed as well. The production took off in the early-eighties when the breeders started rearing poultry under tiled roofs. Many aspiring entrepreneurs rushed to set up layer farms. This resulted in many problems like over production, exploitation by traders, non-availability of superior hybrid layers, frequent disease outbreaks, lack of scientific knowledge in poultry rearing and quality feed preparation.

To overcome these problems, the government of Tamil Nadu started a veterinary college in Namakkal in 1985 to serve the local poultry industry. It also helped that the National Egg Co-ordination Committee (NECC) was set up during 1982, to fix a fair price for eggs and to avoid exploitation by middle men.

As poultry farming was proving to be profitable entrepreneurs started expanding their layer capacity and dropped other livestock and agriculture operations. They also started preparing their own feed and got into direct marketing to reduce production cost and improve profit margin. The poultry farms are no longer under thatched sheds. They have moved to modern multi-storeyed buildings. This has resulted in the closure of small farms. The number of farms has come down from more than 5,000 to around 1,000 farms; but the total poultry population has increased from 7.5 million in 1991–92 to 54 million during 2012.

Tamil Nadu accounts for 20 per cent of the eggs produced in India of which 80 per cent comes from Namakkal region. However the export of eggs and egg powder is highest from Tamil Nadu. Almost 95 per cent of the export of shell eggs from India is from Tamil Nadu. More than 1000 million eggs are exported to mostly Afro-Asian countries from India of which 950 million tonnes come from Namakkal.

Exports start picking up during winter. Namakkal egg exporters have always been conscious of quality and make sure that the uniformity in size is maintained, says NS Kesavan MD, NS Exports and also a representative of Namakkal Egg Merchant Traders Association. Separate batches are maintained for export and domestic markets. Larger sized eggs produced by older chickens are off loaded in the domestic market.

Egg exports face a lot of competition from China, Pakistan and Iran. It is a cyclical business. Its fortunes are tied up with production costs, mainly the feeds. The feed requires soya and maize. If the cost of these products shoots up in the local market, then export competitiveness suffers. The poultry farmers are unfazed. The other exporting countries also face similar problems. The domestic market has been steadily picking up. Prices of eggs have been keeping pace with inflation.

An entrepreneur has set up a plant to generate power from chicken droppings to combat the power crisis in the state. *"If the total poultry litter in the district is collected daily [6,000 tonnes] and processed, nearly 16 MW of power an hour can be generated, with 1,000 tonnes of manure and 10,000 litres of liquid biofertilizer as by-products,"* says Salai Sivaprakasam, executive director of Subhashree Bioenergies (P) Ltd.

Sivaprakasam's plant extracts energy from poultry excrement. It started with a capacity of 2.5 MW, later scaled up to 3.76 MW. The bird droppings are collected daily from several places and brought to the factory, where it is fed into a processing unit. It emits methane gas that is converted into electricity with a patented technology. The slurry, generated as residue, is sold as manure and liquid bio-applications to farmers.

The company has got approval from the Union government under the Clean Development Mechanism (a Kyoto Protocol component) since the plant helps to trap greenhouse gases that would otherwise be emitted by the litter left in the open, says Sivaprakasam. *"The industry has been growing exponentially. Can you imagine how much litter is being created?"* asks Sivaprakasam. He says modestly that he is doing his bit for power generation, green environment and job creation (he employs 100 people).

Leather

One of Tamil Nadu's well kept secrets is that it accounts for almost 50 per cent of India's leather exports, and 40 to 45 per cent of footwear exports. The value of exports from the state was a little over ₹11000 crore in 2012 13. A pair of branded shoes you pick up in high street London is in all probability made in Ambur, in Tamil Nadu's leather belt.

The leather industry in Tamil Nadu goes back to colonial times. For many years leather export meant export of basic material i.e., tanned leather. A cluster of small and medium units sprung up in and around the North Arcot district. The tannery effluents polluted the river Palar and the river water is no longer potable and cannot be used for agriculture. Many attempts have been made to reverse this and zero-effluent units are the norm now. Although the leather industry says that effluents will no longer pollute the river, it is going to take many years and a lot of effort to breathe life into the Palar again.

The Tamil Nadu leather industry started reinventing itself in the seventies. This was when the government started looking at the potential of exporting finished leather goods. Finished leather was a big jump for those who had just started making semi-finished goods. Some small scale units fell by the wayside. It also paved the way for larger units which could think of scale. *"Then we moved to shoe uppers which is no big deal technology wise. The shoe manufacturers helped us make the transition,"* says Rafeeque Ahmed, Chaiman of the Farida Group, Chairman, Council of Leather Exports and Federation of Indian Export Organisations, who is the voice of the leather industry. The group's tannery was among the first to set up an in-house effluent treatment plant. Ahmed, who has been president of the All India Hides and Skins Tanners and Merchants Association as well, was also instrumental in setting up a common effluent treatment plant in the district in collaboration with the state government.

The next step was moving from shoe uppers to finished shoes and this was a different story altogether. The original customers were not quite welcoming of this trend. They obviously saw Indians as a threat. The European companies slowly came round to accepting these manufacturers as good suppliers. Italian shoe makers started sending their designers to these dusty little towns to train the people. These designers would spend almost a year in Ambur. Farida used to get food for these foreigners from Chennai. All that has changed now. Groups like Farida have their own designers, posh guest houses and chefs who can whip up anything the westerners want. One can hear locals using Italian and German phrases with ease.

Manufacturers like Farida really took off after liberalisation. The transition from commodity exports to value added exports became easier with the removal of many shackles. Import of machinery and technology became easier. Travel restrictions no longer existed. It was in the early '90s that the large shoe factories came up in the leather belt. This was the time when American and European factories were shutting down. Vaniyambadi, Ambur, Ranipet, Pernampet, Gudiyattam, Visharam and Pallavaram form the leather cluster. Ambur is the town where the large factories have come up. Just next to Ambur is Vaniyambadi with a host of small and medium scale industries. Earlier they did job work for the larger factories. This is no longer possible as the big exporters have to comply with international standards which they cannot do if they source from these small manufacturers. While some small units have had to shut down, many have survived because they are agile and flexible.

The Farida Shoe factory at Ambur is a thoroughly modern place. It is spacious, brightly lit and well-ventilated with high ceilings. It's buzzing with activity. Several hundred men and women, many of them wearing gloves, masks and protective head gear, are busy at the assembly line, sticking the soles, sending shoes meant for Japan through a special x-ray machine and stacking boxes and boxes of finished footwear. It's spotless and—surprisingly for a leather factory—fresh-smelling. There's no odour of hides here; instead, the smell of air freshener lingers. Apparently a finished shoe goes through 350 hands.

The Farida group manufactures 25000 pairs of shoes every day, all for exports. The privately-held Farida group's turnover is more than a thousand crore. It employs about 9000 people. Another little known fact is that more than 90 per cent of the employees are women. Farida Group was the first leather company in the region to employ women. It also provides maternity care, free health care and has set up a crèche in each of its factories. A dual shift policy offers the women flexibility to manage their household chores and continue working. College girls work part time using the opportunity to supplement their family income.

Women dominate the shoe factories in the South. The industry spokesmen say that women are far more disciplined. There have been no labour problems after women started entering industry. What they are not saying is this has increased divorces and alcoholism among men. Women however are here to stay.

When the Chinese set up their shoe factory, Lotus in Cheyyar, it took them five years to figure out how to adjust to Indian working conditions. They faced a strike in their second year. Now they employ a large number of women as well and are happy. They are going to scale up and increase volumes. The South Koreans are planning to set up a factory in Tamil Nadu. Won't these developments pose a threat to the local industry? Ahmad does not think so. He feels that inviting these large manufacturers to set up their factories here will bring more customers to the country and the local industry will also get more business and learn from these outsiders.

Irshad Ahmad, son of Rafeeq Ahmad and the Managing Director of the group (who got his MBA from Italy) feels that the time has come for the leather industry to decide which way it is heading. There is competition from smaller countries like Bangladesh and Vietnam. Labour laws in India are very restrictive. Vietnam attracts more FDI than India in this industry. *"We have to decide whether in spite of these road blocks we are going to get more aggressive, build our own brands and make a mark in the world"*, he says.

SMALL TOWN SUCCESSES

Every City has its Success Story

Entrepreneurship can be tucked away in unexpected corners in Tamil Nadu. It happens even if there are no ecosystems existing to help set up a business and no Angels and PEs stepping in to fund a project. Sheer passion and the desire to succeed have propelled emerging entrepreneurs from second and third-tier towns in Tamil Nadu to succeed, says R Ramraj, who set up Sify. He is now mentoring many budding entrepreneurs. Among other things, he is an advisor to The Indus Entrepreneurs (TiE). A Silicon valley based organistion to foster entrepreneurship

TiE Chennai is one of the best performing chapters of the global organisation with 55 branches. TiE Chennai decided to look for active entrepreneurship beyond Chennai and took steps to attract nominations from all parts of the state a few years ago. It held road shows in Coimbatore, Tiruppur, Salem, Erode and Madurai; it reached out to a larger number of entrepreneurs and identified potential nominees for the awards. A look at some of those identified and a few others as well, all from small towns.

Sakthi Masala

When he started his business in 1975, PC Duraisamy, the founder of the Erode-based Sakthi Masala, was trying to sell a concept as much as he was trying to sell spice powders and curry powders. Duraisamy was a small-time turmeric trader in a village, Mamarathupalayam, a sleepy little town 10 kilometres from Erode in southern Tamil Nadu. Then he began selling pure spice powders like turmeric, chilli and coriander. This was not easy in those days since housewives preferred to make their own masala powders. He started marketing the powders under the concept of easy cooking. As it happened women started entering the work force in larger numbers around this time and these readymade powders came in handy.

Duraisamy's wife Dr Santhi, a Director in the company, has been a pillar of strength for him. Duraisamy started with an initial investment of ₹10,000 in a 300 sq. ft. space. Sakthi Masala today occupies a space of more than 30 acres, employs 1,000 workers, has a turnover of more than ₹350 crore (these privately held companies do not reveal exact figures) and the Sakthi brand of spice and curry is an all-India name, with a flourishing export market as well.

Sakthi Masala manufactures over fifty varieties of spice and masala powders, over a dozen varieties of pickles, flour, papads, ghee and sunflower oil. The company employs mostly women and differently-abled persons from the rural areas. It uses modern technology in drying the raw materials. Solar heating channels, the largest in Asia, are used to dry the raw materials uniformly and hygienically. The Duraisamys have won many awards in various categories, for entrepreneurship and their community activities. They are now talking about setting up a food park.

"Almost all our purchases are cleared by family members, to ensure that we buy the best possible inputs so that our products are of impeccable quality," says Santhi. The farmers do not mind, because they don't need to deal with middlemen, and they get

paid directly. The company buys 36,000 tonnes of inputs every year. *"If you ask me to describe the reason for our success in one word, it is quality,"* she has said in an interview to *Business Today*.

"There was no specific machinery for the production of spices and spice blends. Through experience and suitable changes in the process, we were able to produce and package spices and spice mixes that retained the aroma and flavour," she says. *"We had to arrive at the perfect blend of tradition and technology."*

KPN Travels

The Swedish commercial vehicle manufacturer Scania delivered the first inter-city bus in the country to KPN Travels headquartered in Salem in January 2014. The Scania Intercity range of coaches were launched to offer highly reliable multi-purpose coaches for medium and long distance luxury travel for the Indian market. *"The luxury coach is the product of knowledge gathered from studying the needs of long-distance bus passengers in India. Scania Metrolink HD is based on renowned Scania virtues such as robust design, maximum passenger and driver safety, leading fuel economy and a long and trouble-free service life"*, says a press release from Scania.

KP Natarajan loved buses from his childhood. His family moved from Tiruchengode to Salem to escape a drought. *"We were marginal farmers who ploughed leased land. My father wanted me to become a police officer, but I wanted to be a bus driver. I enjoyed watching buses all day long as they carried loads of passengers. My school was opposite the bus stand and I used run away from school to watch buses. I looked at the drivers with admiration. Whenever I had money, I got into a bus and stood near the driver's seat in order to observe him."*

He dropped out of school in the seventh standard. *"I took it as Lord Ayyappa's blessing when my brother and his father-in-law bought a bus. I joined as its cleaner and I was very happy. I lit agarbathies in the morning and cleaned the seats last thing at night."*

Natarajan gradually learnt to drive the bus. *"Driving was heaven."* he says. Soon he learnt to do everything from fixing punctures to repairing the engine. Next he took a bus on lease and started a tourist service. It did well. *"I then bought a bus with funds I borrowed from my father and by pledging my wife's jewels. I named my business KPN with the first letters of my grandfather's, my father's and my names. Today, the transport business is not all that remunerative. The stock market and real estate are more profitable options. You can lose a fortune if you don't pay constant attention in the transport trade. Our business is intertwined with the good times and bad times of our passengers. Transporting them safely to weddings and birthdays, funerals and new jobs is more important than profits. Our passengers make our business reasonably profitable."*

Natarajan was the driver and owner of the first KPN bus. *"I hate it when there are no seats available for the passenger to sit. I am particular that bus travel should not tire the travellers. We can carry a handful of extra passengers if we stopped everywhere and allowed standees. To me, that was a sure way of losing passengers' confidence. I don't believe in either soliciting passengers during the off-season or hiking the fare during the peak season. I am honest and sincere. Those who do honest business face problems galore. KPN Travels goes more often to court from the Salem magisterial court to the Supreme Court to fight for justice than any other travel company. I love every fight."*

More than 250 luxury buses run in the four southern states under Natarajan's supervision. He wakes up every morning and goes to sleep every night managing KPN Travels, KPN Parcel Service, KPN Petroleum or some other company connected to the transport industry. Catering to 7,000 passengers and handling 18,000 parcels a day, Natarajan never takes a break.

KPN put headrests in its buses to relieve the strain on the necks of passengers. When one of the customers wrote in the suggestions book about the need for comfort for the back as well, pushback seats were introduced. *"We have tried to improve the aesthetics of the interiors of our buses. 'Air buses', buses with air suspension systems to reduce jerks inside the bus, were our innovation, the first of its kind in India, introduced with the help of the TVS group. I understand that the name 'air bus' has found a place in the dictionary. We introduced air-conditioned buses. We reduced the number of seats to enable sleepers in our buses. We risked loss of revenue and succeeded in providing comfortable journeys at night."*

There were more innovations to follow. KPN introduced a computerised reservation system. *"We were the first to computerise, keeping our record of being the first to introduce any revolutionary improvement in the industry. No passenger ever has to pay a premium for our tickets, in season or off season. We introduced a foolproof online reservation system. We opened the reservation a month before Deepavali and sold 7000 tickets in ten minutes. Today we have lakhs of registered customers, showing their trust and respect for us."*

"The driver is the heart of the transport business. No one with less than ten years of experience is appointed as a driver in KPN. You have to be recommended by one of our drivers to get in as one", he signs off.

Others

Education is big business in the smaller towns. Some of these colleges have incredible infrastructure, says Ramraj, who has looked at several. Take an institution like Mahendra Engineering College near Namakkal, set up by the Mahendra Educational Trust (MET). The college was started in 1995 with three branches of engineering—Computer Science, Electronics and Communication and Mechanical and it is affiliated to the University of Madras. Today, it offers several undergraduate and postgraduate programmes in engineering, computer applications and applied sciences. The student strength has grown from 180 in 1995 to about 2,500 in 2008. The total built-up area of the current facility is 31,970 sq. metres.

The Mahendra Educational Trust was established in 1978 by Bharath Kumar, a well-known educationist and philanthropist from the region. Dr Sridhar Mitta, an IT industry veteran and an internationally recognised expert in the effective management of multinational R&D in Information Technology, is closely associated with the institutions. The college is working with him to set up rural BPOs.

D Navaneetha Krishnan started the Shri Kannan Departmental Store (SKDS) in 1989 in Erode with his partner T Tanushgaran

(Chairman of the group). It was then a very small *kirana* store that could be managed by just two people. Krishnan's vision was to create a chain of shops in Tamil Nadu. In Chennai, he was working in a coffee powder shop and he learnt the modalities of setting up a departmental store. His vision was big but he had to put together the funding to make his dream come true. When he set up a store in Erode in 1989, he strongly believed that giving the best product at the cheapest price possible to the customer was the way to go. In the early days, Krishnan used to work for 20 hours a day and SKDS saw continuous growth for a straight 72 months.

After many ups and downs, he started his first branch in the year 1996 in Erode. Today, there are 35 branches in many districts of Tamil Nadu with an employee strength of 4,500. "*We always believed we can grow every day, we can face any competition and we can win over our customer's heart,*" says Shivaji Siddharth, Krishnan's son. "*We are now working on expanding branches to other states. Taking the company public is also on the cards.*"

Another example is that of Lion Dates. It is the single largest and trusted supplier of dates in the country. The company was set up in 1978 in Trichy by P Ponnudurai, whose education ended in class 10. The son of a landless farmer from Tiruchi in Tamil Nadu, who later went to Sri Lanka, Ponnudurai started working in a small provision shop when he was just ten years old. When his parents were sent back to India in 1974, the seventeen-year-old continued working in a provision store in Tiruchi at a monthly salary of ₹85. "*But right from childhood I wanted to have my own business. So I got a bank loan of ₹4,600 through a lawyer friend and started a small provision store, but with my having no experience, it failed and I was left with a debt of over ₹4,000.*"

He then started distributing a washing powder brand (Sabina), which meant visiting a lot of big and small shops. He noticed that dates were popular and fast moving, but were badly packaged and nobody thought about their quality. He started importing dates from the Middle East and slowly built up his reputation and business.

Ponnudurai has no hesitation talking about the English tutor he had to employ, paying him a daily fee of ₹100 for three years to learn the language, after a terrifying trip to Mumbai in 1992. *I wanted to enter the Mumbai market to expand my business. So I went to Mumbai but was too scared to go outside the hotel as I knew only Tamil. I was asked to take a train to Masjid Bunder and meet a commission agent. Luckily the agent spoke Tamil.*" Not only that, he also ordered from Ponnudurai half a tonne of dates, and gave him an advance as well.

In 1996, he was importing 34 tonnes of dates from Oman (the year he really took off) and today he imports 8000 tonnes from Oman, Saudi Arabia and Tunisia. From being just a distributor of dates, he has created value addition through setting up plants for date syrup and syrup-based products. Ponnudurai has put up four factories. "*I found it difficult to get labour in Tiruchi so my production centres are in villages around Tiruchi,*" he says. He has given employment to about 1,000 women in four nearby villages.

With his salary and income from sale of Sabina and dates, he soon wiped off his debt. After a while, the sale of dates went up to 500 packets a day; "*As I did not have a shop, I'd pack dates at home and personally deliver to shops and stores,*" recalls Ponnudurai. Gradually he extended his sales to Chennai, being supported by Sabina distributors. Slowly he expanded his business to Madurai and Thanjavur and he started advertising on radio.

When it came to finding a name for his product he took just five minutes to do so. "*I asked myself who is the most powerful being in the world and the answer that came to me was the lion, who is the king of the jungle.*" As dates are packed with iron and vitamins, he thought this would be the most appropriate brand name to depict strength. But he didn't have the money to print labels "*...as I had to give order for a minimum of 10,000 labels, I took the lion's picture from a political party's election symbol!*" He has stuck to the name and symbol ever since.

In 1995 he was invited by a Muscat Government factory that had made a lot of date syrup but did not know how to sell it. "I *thought if it can be mixed with milk, then it would become a healthy drink... a good tonic for children and adults."* He personally began to experiment with mixing of date syrup with milk at different temperatures. *"A few times the milk curdled, or the drink tasted horrible. But then I found that the syrup mixed in lukewarm milk really tastes good."*

The sales of the date syrup picked up but then the Muscat factory closed down in 2000. He knew a Keralite working there, so after consulting him he put up his own production plant and the product started doing very well; *"People like to have date syrup not only with milk but also with idli or dosai,"* he says. Another Lion product is honey; he first tried to make honey with dates, but that didn't do well. The shopkeepers said 'give us plain honey,' and he did, branding it Lion Honey. Ponnudurai has also started marketing Lion Oats. *"I import in bulk from Australia and that is doing well. My eldest daughter, who is now in the US, has joined me and marketing oats was her idea,"* he says.

The bulk of the company's datescomes from Iraq (through Dubai) and Muscat. *"I was the first one to get black dates from Muscat. Then I started importing from Iran, Egypt, Tunisia and Algeria. Now I have started importing Jordanian dates; they are very good but very costly at ₹1,200 a kg. Iraqi dates cost only ₹100 a kg."*

As other players in the dates business are small, he estimates he has about 80 per cent of the market and thinks he owes his success to *"hard work, dedication, and my belief that I should not sell something that is not good for the health of the people."*

Ramraj Cottons

Dhotis are big business in Tamil Nadu. Although dhotis are woven and mill-made in the other southern states as well, they remain small in operation compared to what they are in Tamil Nadu. Dhotis have always found a market in the South. People wear them at home, at religious functions and on traditional occasions. Dhotis are also seen as a poor man's attire as one can buy dhotis for as low as ₹50. So one enterprising young man who grew up in a village near Coimbatore decided that it was time to make the dhoti a fashion garment. In fact, he has actually managed to sell the dhoti to even fashion-conscious young men. All his products are pure white including accessories like shirts, undergarments, handkerchiefs, belts and even cell phone cases. But he makes sure they are high quality. From politicians to bridegrooms, everybody wears his dhotis.

KR Nagaraj, the founder of Ramraj Cotton, comes from an agricultural family and he had to work in the farm after school. When he was still in school, he saw a well-dressed man in an Ambassador car wearing a white shirt and dhoti. He found out that the man owned a textile business. It made an impression on him. Nagaraj decided he could also travel in a car if he entered the textile business!

Nagaraj had to work very hard to make that a reality. In 1976, he started working in a small shop, selling dhotis. Soon, he started his own dhoti business with three friends. He could raise only ₹15,000 towards his share of ₹25,000 by getting some money from family. The total capital was ₹1 lakh. Another ₹10,000 came as a loan at 24 per cent interest from one of the partners. But the business failed and Nagaraj found himself with a whole lot of unsold dhotis. Undaunted, he decided to launch Ramraj Cottons in 1983. He was only twenty-three and the company was set up in Avinashi. He was a one-man show going from Avinashi to Tiruppur every day to sell dhotis made by others.

When he wanted to go into manufacturing of his own dhotis soon after, it was impossible to get a bank loan. Like many entrepreneurs of Tamil Nadu, he set up his business with help from family and friends. He has not gone public. Nor has he got PE funds. Profits have been consistently ploughed back into business.

Nagaraj chose to stick to dhotis based on his conviction that quality dhotis will surely find a market. Those were the days when dhotis were low priced use-and-throw products. Nobody thought of quality, but only profits. Nagaraj decided he would make profits by increasing the price and not sacrificing quality. He started selling better quality dhotis at ₹115. He decided to stick to white as he did not want to pollute the environment with colour dyes.

In the first year, on a turnover of ₹9 lakh, he made a profit of ₹1.14 lakh. His instinct that quality will create demand turned out to be correct. By 1990, Ramraj Dhotis were available in all the southern states. Nagaraj started advertising quite heavily to promote the dhoti as a garment which men can wear with pride. Till then, dhotis used to be tucked away in the bottom shelves of showrooms. *"We made sure they were displayed prominently and given pride of place in showrooms"*, he says. By 1995, Ramraj Dhotis were on TV. The TV campaign started projecting men of substance such as businessmen, actors and stylish youngsters flaunting the dhoti. Today, Ramraj Dhotis are popular with most Tamil politicians.

From 1999, Ramraj went into the manufacture of white cotton shirts, with prices ranging from ₹600 to ₹6,000. He is also diversifying into products like readymade pure silk shirts, women's wear, linen shirts, new premium inner garments, T-shirts and kidswear. Nagaraj has also set up retail stores to sell his products. He wants to focus more and more on youth. Cricketer Ashwin Ravichandran is the brand ambassador to attract the young.

"Of the 10,000 looms in the Coimbatore region, about 8,000 are with the company doing jobbing work," says Nagaraj. Ramraj Cotton employs around 6,000 people. Every day, 1.5 lakh metres of dhotis are woven and 2,500 varieties of dhotis are sold annually. Out of the 1,000 dhotis sold in the state, 700 are from Ramraj Cottons. It makes 30,000 pieces of shirts (all white) in a day. It has invested around ₹50 crore into its facility. At present, almost 50 per cent of the turnover comes from Tamil Nadu. Kerala is also a large market, but the preference there is for unbleached dhotis. The dhoti business accounts for 70 per cent of the turnover while the rest is contributed by shirts and other items. Nagaraj is now entering the rest of India through the franchisee route. Will dhotis sell in the North? They wear dhotis (panch) which are 4.5 to 5 metres. In the South, it varies between 2–4 metres. He is not yet ready to talk about his turnover. He drops a broad hint that it will be around ₹1,000 crore soon.

These entrepreneurs have understood that they have to strive for global standards even if they do not go global. All have expansion plans and dreams. Do they have scalable models? Will the second and third generation share their passion?

THE CK FAMILY—ALL PATHBREAKERS

In small town Cuddalore a school teacher/farmer possibly did not realise when he started retailing popular products in tiny sachets for one time use for the local market that he was pioneering a revolution and that the sachet was going to become ubiquitous. With a strong entrepreneurial streak in him, Chinnikrishnan had set up a small scale unit to repackage generic drugs. He started selling pharmaceutical drugs in sachets. He had a large family. He advised his sons to be job givers and not job seekers. He understood the Indian consumer. He wanted the common man to have access to what were then seen as rich people's products. That was the rationale behind one-time sachets. According to family legend his wife used to slice the plastic sheets with a kitchen equipment to make the sachets.

Three of his sons turned entrepreneurs following his footsteps, with varying degrees of success, but all have been pathbreakers in their own way. The sons who adapted to the India which opened up to enterprise in the nineties have survived and are trying to reach the top in their chosen fields.

Storm in a Sachet

In the late '70s CK Rajkumar, Chinnikrishnan's son was considered the sachet pioneer. A qualified medical doctor, he entered business on his father's death. His father had left the family a legacy of a shampoo formulation and also the concept of packaging goods in a sachet. According to Rajkumar, shampoo was a low-tech product that was eminently suited for small-scale manufacture. His only innovation was therefore the packaging.

Rajkumar named his shampoo *Velvette* and sold it in sachets in the South from 1979. The sachets literally swept the market when they were first launched. The uniquely packaged Velvette, priced at ₹1 per sachet, outsold many established names, picking up an astounding market share of 16 per cent in the southern region.

Rajkumar's beginnings were humble. He used to pedal around on a bicycle trying to hawk his product in the early days. Velvette was clearly aimed at the segment which was aspiring to use shampoo but was intimidated by the price and fancy bottles. Velvette's low price pack induced those who used soap to wash their hair to try out and eventually switch to shampoos.

Until 1987, Velvette remained only a regional brand, despite a marketing tie-up with Voltas in 1981. The turning point was when Godrej came into the picture and took up Velvette's distribution and marketing in right earnest. In 1988, Velvette went national. It gradually expanded its range to six varieties. At one point, there were more than 100 units manufacturing Velvette shampoos.

By 1991, Velvette's 16 per cent market share in the south almost caught up with the market leader, Hindustan Lever. Clinic scored 19 per cent and Lever's other brand, Sunsilk had a 16 per cent share in the south. Velvette became the subject of many case studies.

The market leader was not amused. When Rajkumar became a little audacious in his packaging, the giant struck. It secured an injunction from the Madras High Court against three small time shampoo manufacturers who supplied to Pharma Care Ltd., Rajkumar's company. Godrej Soaps Ltd. the then distributor of Velvette, was named co-defendant. The multinational claimed that Rajkumar had played dirty by cloning the design, colour and logo of their heavily advertised and successful shampoo brand *Clinic Plus*. The court ruled in Lever's favour. Velvette was asked to withdraw the offending pack and restrained from using the four features that were distinctive to Clinic Plus.

One of the reasons why Velvette could take on the MNCs was the excise advantage small scale industries enjoyed over larger manufacturers. Velvette's success spawned a host of new brands made by small entrepreneurs whose cheap products began to nibble into the market share of the established names.

Though not particularly profitable, Lever, which then paid an unbelievable 110 per cent excise duty, was forced to enter the booming sachet market in 1988. At ₹2.50 for a 10 ml sachet, Sunsilk was pitched against Velvette which had managed to hold its price down to a rupee. Subsequently Sunsilk reduced its pack to 5 ml, pricing it at a rupee to match Velvette's price. *"My success really lies in making Hindustan Lever come down to one rupee. I feel I have helped the Indian consumer."* said Rajkumar.

Things changed after the reforms. Rajkumar could not hold on to his model beyond the nineties. Velvette had also built successful brands like *Nivaran 90* (a popular herbal cough drug, which accounted for a large chunk of the company's turnover) and *Memory Plus* a memory enhancing herbal pill. However, in the late '90s, the company slipped into the red, thanks to growing competition from bigger brands and the lack of a strong distribution network. The association with Godrej had to be terminated after Godrej chose to tie up with Procter and Gamble.

Rajkumar tried many ways to hang on to his Velvette products. There was talk of the Kalpathi family who were the promoters of SSI, the IT training company, taking over Velvette. This fell through. Rajkumar tried tying up with Wimco, the match maker and NEPC, both of which do not exist anymore. Nor did a distribution arrangement with Amrutanjan work out. By the end of the decade, Velvette was just a memory

CavinKare

CavinKare has always been seen as the proverbial David and Goliath story. But will David end up becoming a Goliath? The David here is CK Ranganathan, Rajkumar's younger brother who also started selling shampoos in a sachet with an investment of ₹15000 in 1983 and also dared to take on the multinationals, Lever and P&G, the leaders in this segment. Ranganathan's company, CavinKare today has a turnover touching ₹1500 crore. Ranganathan has survived many crises and is confident that CavinKare will end up an Indian multinational.

Ranganathan, a fresh graduate entered the family business with his brothers when his father passed away. Soon he wanted to branch off on his own. He had clear and different ideas about how to do business.

He started Chik India as a small partnership firm. The partners were his mother and grandmother. Chik India started off by offering a single product, Chik shampoo. Ranganathan created a mild stir in the sachet shampoo market, by selling his Chik brand of shampoo at a much lower price than other shampoo sachets which were selling at ₹2. He targetted rural and small town customers. He offered his sachets at an unbelievable price of 50 paise. How could he have made any money?

Ranganathan says he didn't start off with 50 paise pricing. He introduced the sachet at 80 paise. Only by 1988 did the 50 paise pricing happen. And that is when the multinationals sat up and noticed him. This was one regional player who was there to stay and also was giving them a good run for their money. With the volumes he had built up by then, his margins became quite healthy in spite of the low price.

From the time Ranganathan decided to strike out on his own he was quite sure he wanted to have his own distribution network. He did not want to piggy back on some larger manufacturer's set-up (his older brother had burnt his fingers badly by tying up with Godrej). *"I also realised that you can't rely on the product alone. Quality and strength of the products are very important. Consumer differentiation is equally important. I had a basic product, the shampoo. I played around with that,"* he says. He has stuck to quality and product differentiation in whatever he has done.

"I introduced the concept of fragrance which seemed revolutionary then. If you opened the sachet, the entire room would be filled with fragrance." It obviously appealed to his target consumers. This was a period when the small company had no money for advertising. But understanding that the concept of fragrance worked, Ranganathan targetted the stockists. *"When we went to visit them, we use to spray fragrance outside the packs. The stockists couldn't help noticing the lingering fragrance."* They did this till Chik shampoo became an established name.

But what really worked was the offer of 'bring empty sachets and take shampoo sachets in return' offer. His competitors sneered. They said he was giving away sachets as charity. But Ranganathan proved his critics wrong. Sales zoomed from 35000 sachets to 12 lakhs. *"Initially we took any sachet, but after three months, we restricted it to our Chik sachets. But the idea had caught on, and it didn't make any difference to the popularity of the offer."* says Ranganathan. With increasing cash flows the company finally got some funds for advertising. The next step was the introduction of floral fragrances like rose and jasmine. The sales rose to 35 lakh sachets. *"From then on there was no looking back"*, he says.

Talking about cash flows, it took Ranganathan three years to get a bank loan. *"My auditor told me to pay taxes and on time. Not to indulge in any evasion.Actually that helped me with the banks. After all I didn't have any collateral, no godfather to back me. But the challan from the Income Tax department convinced my bankers that I was a profit making company and they could take a chance with me."* Once bank credit became available, things became much easier.

In 1991, Ranganathan named his company Beauty Cosmetics and started to professionalise his set-up in earnest. He started putting together systems and practices and creating a good environment for professionals. *"I always believed in paying salaries higher than market rates in the South."* This attitude towards salaries helped when the then Finance Minister Manmohan Singh's budget withdrew the excise concessions for small scale units. The excise advantage of 105 per cent disappeared overnight.

This jolt actually strengthened Ranganathan's resolve to accept the challenge and survive. The budget shock came in February. He gave a hike of 40 per cent to his staff in April. It gave them confidence in the survival of the company and the resolve to fight. He also took a firm decision not to make inferior or me-too products. He is happy that he took these decisions in 1995. The company started doing very well.

Ranganathan turned his attention to food business in a small way by selling pickles in sachets. He went into it in real earnest in 2003 when he acquired Ruchi pickles, Maa fruit drink in 2008 and Garden snacks in 2009. Ranganathan is convinced that there is a great future in the dairy business. In 2009, he bought a small dairy farm in Kanchipuram. He has been scaling up by buying small units.

Ranganathan has had his share of disasters. In 1992, he went into the mineral water business which was a complete drain on resources. *"We got into it too early. It was not viable. We pulled out fast."* A few years ago he set up a restaurant business. He realised quite soon that it was an owner-driven business and withdrew from it.

In trying to go pan India again mistakes were made. *"We have tended to view any place outside Tamil Nadu as a different country. We have remained isolated because of the language barrier. When we opened our sales office in Delhi we sent a very dependable Tamilian to run the operations. This was another one of our disasters. Then we recruited a proper sales manager from Delhi. There has been no looking back. I learn from my mistakes."*

CavinKare has been closely held since its inception. In 2013 for the first time it has raised ₹250 crore from ChrysCapital, the private equity fund to put its growth plans in place. It is now going to push its premium products where margins are higher, will look at export markets, and take the dairy business national. Ranganathan will focus on personal care, dairy segment and food and beverages to fuel growth.

"I am investing in R&D and people. It is going to make a huge difference," he says.

Naturals

Chennai-based Naturals hair and beauty salon has almost 400 outlets. It is the largest chain in India in the beauty business. Its co-founder CK Kumaravel is Rajkumar and Ranganathan's younger brother. He is ambitious. He is launching salons all over the country. He wants to double the number of his salons in a couple of years. To get brand recognition and make an impact outside the South, Kareena Kapoor has been roped in as Naturals' brand ambassador. It is already the largest chain in India in the beauty business.

The first Naturals salon was set up in 2000 by Kumaravel's wife Veena. She wanted to do something of her own as their children were in school. Her husband helped her set up the first parlour. In 2000, Chennai did not have many good salons. People ran beauty parlours at homes or one had to go to a five star hotel and spend a fortune. The rationale behind Naturals was to give 5-star quality with 3-star pricing when people visited a parlour. The initial idea was to use only natural products—hence the name Naturals—but that idea was impractical because it was not a feasible option if Naturals had to scale up.

Kumaravel, the third entrepreneur from the family was struggling with the Raaga range of products he had launched in 1993. He had introduced Raaga Herbal Shikakai powder. It did very well and he wanted to expand rapidly. He extended the range under the Raaga brand to hair oil, soap, and amla-based chewing products. None of them did well. Kumaravel says that he was clueless about going to new markets. He was also facing technical problems when he wanted to scale up production. He finally shut down the business and sold the brand to his brother Ranganathan.

The salon business picked up. Naturals was turning out to be a natural fit to a rapidly changing city. The first salon was unisex and Kumaravel had his doubts about this concept working in conservative Chennai. To his surprise Chennai did not bat an eyelid. By 2003, Kumaravel had wound up his business and was fully involved in Naturals. Expansion became a problem. Banks were not willing to fund the beauty business. *"They thought a loan of ₹60 lakh was excessive to start a beauty parlour. They could not think beyond ₹3 lakh."* After knocking on 53 doors, the 54th bank manager saw merit in Naturals.

By 2006, six salons had been opened. *"We were making profits. We were comfortable. When we wanted to expand many people told us not to do so including people from L'Oreal. Then I read 'Rich Dad Poor Dad' by Robert Kiyosaki and Sharon Lechter. This influenced me a great deal and I knew we had to move forward. I am addicted to growth. My earlier failures were due to my wrong strategies."*

Kumaravel decided he would use the franchisee route to grow. The inspiration came from Anita Roddick of Body Shop. Body Shop went global by acquiring franchisees. *"Anita Roddick is my role model."* he says. This turned out to be quite tough. Naturals advertised in the papers for franchisees. *"We got 340 applications. They had to fill a form based on what I learnt from Body Shop and 33 replied. Of the 33, only three showed serious interest. Once I connected with them, they too lost interest. Naturals was neither a big brand then nor was an MNC. Franchisees were required to put in ₹30 lakh and it seemed a big amount. People were not quite convinced about the beauty salon as a business."*

Kumaravel then approached the wives of friends and relatives. He convinced several of them to be Naturals' franchisee partners. *"Women are very good franchisee partners. They are usually hands on and are perfect for hospitality and beauty business. They are more grounded than men and do not get carried away. Today 70 per cent of my franchisees are women."*

With Naturals salons becoming visible everywhere in Chennai the business really took off from 2010. Kumaravel is committed to network marketing. *"Franchising is using other people's money and time responsibly."* The franchisees are 50-50 partners. Kumaravel starts a new salon and Veena manages the staff. The franchisees take care of day-to-day operations.

Veena and Kumaravel oversee HR, training, new projects tie-ups and the introduction of new services. Naturals salons feature all well-known international beauty care brands like L'Oreal, TIGI and Kerastase. All the new trends are followed and the salons give what Indians want. *"It will take MNCs years to adapt to India,"* Kumaravel states.

Naturals has gone more upmarket over the years. There is a Naturals Lounge (premium services), Naturals W (exclusively for women) and Page 3 (luxury services). Kumaravel is test marketing an exclusive salon for men called Star Cuts in Coimbatore. He has opened two outlets there. The local Barbers' Association protested. The irony is that the association president's son is an IT professional and there is a serious manpower shortage. *"I told them that we will help them expand and grow."*

Kumaravel is setting up an academy to train people in the styling business in Chennai. The 20,000 sq ft space will take in 1,800 students. Short-term and one-year courses are being offered. *"I can absorb all of them,"* he says. Naturals has 300 salons in the south. *"When we launched, Lakme had 130 salons all over India. Now they have 210. We see as our competition YLG in Bangalore and Enrich in Mumbai. After roping in Kareena Kapoor, we got a lot of enquiries and are setting up at least four salons outside the South every month. Once this number reaches 100, growth will have its own momentum."*

Naturals' turnover is now touching ₹300 crore. *"I am not looking at growth in turnover now. I am looking at 1,000 women entrepreneurs, 3,000 salons and 50,000 jobs in the next six years. We also want to be the largest salon brand in Asia."*

THE MAN WHO BECAME DAIRY KING

RG Chandramogan, Managing Director of the Chennai-based ₹3000 crore Hatsun Agro Product group, has the largest private sector dairy unit in the country. Its Arokya milk is the largest private sector liquid milk brand in India. The company has three major divisions, ice cream, milk and milk products and milk-based ingredients. Hatsun's Arun Ice Creams is one of the leading ice cream brands in South India.

According to Chandramogan, the Verghese Kurien model of co-operative milk farming was the most innovative in its time. Kurien was the one who made it possible for the organised industry to buy milk from the marginal farmer. In spite of expenses involved in chilling, problems of perishing and transportation, there is good value addition in dairy industry.

Chandramogan, a great admirer of the Amul model, feels that every system, however successful it has been at one point, requires a change. When Dr Kurien launched the Gujarat Co-operative Milk Marketing Federation, rural India was very different from what it is today. The focus was on poverty alleviation and survival. The co-operative milk movement was one way of helping the suffering farmers. Agricultural waste could be fed to animals besides providing some income for the farmers. The situation today is different. Chandramogan says that we have to start working towards rural prosperity. Rural poverty is no longer the issue.

Chandramogan comes from a village near Sivakasi. He discontinued his education early on to support his family. His family sold some property for 13,000 rupees with which he started Arun Ice Cream in 1970. He was twenty-one then. The factory was just an unassuming little place in a Chennai suburb, where three or four people worked and manually produced about 20 litres of ice cream per day. Ten paise candy was their first variety of ice cream and it was sold through push carts. After 10 years of struggle, success came his way. From 1981, Arun Ice Creams started growing and in 1991 Arun recorded a turnover of ₹3 crore.

As he has strong rural roots Chandramogan had the urge to do something in the villages. He started Arokya milk in 1995. "*We were procuring milk for our ice creams and so this idea came about. We now manufacture butter, milk powder, ghee and curd. We are associated with 3,50,000 farmers and buy milk from 8,5 00 villages. We operate from nine different factories and our people travel 4,20,000 kilometres to collect and distribute milk,*" he has said in an interview to *Business Line*.

Hatsun goes straight to the farmers to procure milk. There are around 8,500 Hatsun Milk Banks (HMBs) covering over 10,000 villages with each HMB receiving milk from 3.2 lakh farmers everyday. With the help of milk analysers installed, the HMB tests the quality of milk from each farmer using Fat and SNF (Solid Not Fat) as parameters, and then factors that with the volume of milk delivered, into the calculation of the amount to be paid. The company makes it a point to pay the farmers on time—a track record Hatsun Agro has maintained for over two decades.

The milk is collected from the HMBs and taken to the Hatsun Milk Chilling Centre, where it is tested again for parameters. After this, further samples are taken for advanced testing. Only after the milk samples match the stringent quality norms are they sent to the dairy. At the dairy, the milk is put through more tests before taking it up for further processing.

Hatsun plans to set–up 40,000 units of dairy farms with 30 animals per unit yielding 300 litres of milk per unit per day. The main requirements of these model farms are: five acres of land for farm and fodder production, a minimum of 30 animals which can go up to 40, adoption of soil-based fertiliser application and scientific farming techniques, and partial mechanisation of the farm. Hatsun will give its inputs on animal selection and their health care, calf rearing, farm management and productivity and monetary assistance (arranging to help them get bank loans, insurance for farm animals). Most importantly, the farmers will get an assured income of ₹40,000 per month.

In 2012, Hatsun started yet another ice cream brand, *Ibaco.* This is the upmarket version of Arun Ice Creams and is based on the ice cream-by-scoop model. Arun is a factory finished product and comes in cones, cups and sticks. As for Ibaco, it's the scoop variety. You walk into an Ibaco parlour, choose the flavour and get it dressed with toppings. Hatsun has gone national with Ibaco.

Early entrepreneurs

Why they failed

BRAVE HEARTS OF YORE

Contrary to popular belief, enterprise thrived in Madras (Chennai) during the '60s and '70s. There were quite a few professionals who wanted to strike out on their own. Several did very well for a couple of decades. They all came up during the era of import substitution. Then they disappeared into the sunset. Let us look at some of the leading lights of that era.

Cutfast Abrasive Tools Pvt. Ltd.

It was seen as the small guy who came in from the cold which would take on giants. A technocrat turned entrepreneur U Mohan Rao, set up a small scale unit to manufacture coated abrasives. At that time there were three multinationals in the market—Carborundum Universal, Grindwell Norton and John Oakely Mohan. There were no abrasive units in the small scale sector as the planning commission had said that coated abrasives could not be successfully manufactured by small scale units.

Mohan Rao, a chemical engineer took the plunge as he had spent many years in the industry working for Ajax Corporation which was taken over by Carborondum Universal, then part of the TI group. Why did he give up a lucrative job? *"To be on my own appealed to me"*, he said then. He started Cutfast Abrasives in

1967 with the help of family and bank loans. He was the first to use totally indigenous machinery which cut down costs. A saving of ₹40,000 meant a lot in 1967. He knew he could not compete with the giants. So he decided to concentrate on a niche product—abrasive belts—and this brought him success. In 1970, Rao floated Cutfast Bonded Abrasives to make grinding wheels, taking on Grindwell Norton.

By 1972, Cutfast had grown to be a medium scale unit. Then Rao had to put up a plant in Gujarat to produce an important raw material. Ironically, his MNC competitors were monopoly manufacturers of the raw materials. Then he went in for vertical integration, trying to manufacture most of the inputs himself. In 1982–83 his turnover was around ₹3 crore.

The mid-eighties were not a good time for abrasives manufacturers. Too many small scale manufacturers had entered the fray making the industry face cut-throat competition. The export market had not yet opened up. Rao remained unfazed. He felt he had invested in R&D to absorb high technology. He thought he could diversify and grow. By 1987, he was hoping to get a turnover of ₹10 crore.

Family disputes, some complacency and the opening up of the economy did him in. Carborundum bought Cutfast out in 1996.

Transcore

N Kannan who set up Transcore in the '70s had the vision to see that television was going to become huge in India. He specialised in TV technology for his Masters from IIT Bombay when televisions had barely appeared in the country. He joined Bush India which had a good R&D set-up then. In that era his work involved adapting foreign samples, redesigning the circuits and indigenising the components. He took the decision to move to his home town Chennai to set up a unit to manufacture passive electronic components.

He learnt the ropes of entrepreneurship by partnering with Mecotronics, a company trading in and manufacturing low technology electronics items. Electronics did not have much scope in the '70s. It would have been impossible to get credit facilities and a good dealer network for a newcomer. You could not be an unknown and start something.

Kannan decided to go in for passive components such as resistors, capacitors, and coils. IFTs and coils are components used in TVs and radios and he saw a lot of potential in these products. It was not a capital intensive project. The initial investment was ₹3 lakhs! Kannan started as a one-man show, grew slowly and steadily in the '70s. Growth picked up from 1975, when TV industry opened up. In 1985 Transcore's turnover was ₹4.5 crores. It became the market leader in IFTs.

Kannan set up another partnership firm to manufacture deflection components for TVs. He also launched a unit in Pondicherry to make micromotors which were used in tape recorders to make the cassettes move.

The biggest problem Transcore faced in 1985 was space. It was looking forward to a great future with the growth of the television industry. Transcore sadly was too small to keep pace with the changes that hit the industry from the 90's and shut down.

Sietex

Sietex was a pioneering effort in the '70s. P Krishnaswami, a professor turned entrepreneur dared to enter the process instrumentation area with indigenous technology. Krishnaswamy studied instrumentation electronics in the Madras Institute of Technology and went to England on a scholarship for practical training in English factories. He also got a post graduate degree from the University of Manchester in electronics. He returned from the UK in 1957 and became a lecturer in his alma mater. He helped out in setting up a few ventures for others till he gave in to his inner voice to become an entrepreneur himself.

In 1968, the State Bank was looking at funding entrepreneurs like him and gave him one lakh rupees under its Entrepreneur Scheme, and soon many doors opened. He set up the first company in the Sietex fold. It was a one-man show with a single product. By 1985, the Sietex group had grown into manufacturing 150 types of analogue and digital instruments with a staff strength of 200, and a turnover crossing ₹2 crore. The senior staff was mostly from MIT and were Krishnaswami's old students. L&T who were sourcing some products from Sietex became its sole selling agent which was a big boon to Krishnaswami. The Government's licensing policy too helped. After giving licenses to Taylors and Keltron, no other company received a license to manufacture process instruments.

In the mid-eighties Sietex was on top of the world. It was setting up new plants, launching new products and was projecting a turnover of ₹20 crore in 1990. It disappeared in the '90s as the founder's family was not keen on running the business. The era of import substitution by adapting dated technology was over by the turn of the century.

Like the rest of the country several Tamil Nadu industrialists got into TV manufacturing. The entire TV industry assembled kits. The government unleashed the kits on anybody who applied for a license in 1982. The TVs had to be available for the Asian Games. There was no respect for technology. When colour TVs were introduced, the component industry changed overnight and most Indian manufacturers fell by the way side. They forgot that in products like television, technology matters more than brand building and advertising.

Solidaire and Dyanora were the two best-selling brands of televisions from Tamil Nadu. They were brand leaders in the '80s. Solidaire was set up by AN Srinivasa Rao who was running a successful unit manufacturing switchgears for power projects. He was looking out for a project which was not so dependent on the whims and fancies of the government. In 1974, he got a license to manufacture 7000 TVs per annum. Those early days were difficult. Everybody and their aunt got licenses to manufacture TVs, including tennis champion Ramanathan Krishnan who promoted Krish TV. The Tamil Nadu government suggested that Solidaire and Krish TV and a third unit called BLRS merge together. This consortium called Tristar Electronics had an annual capacity of 20000 TVs. All this happened before the Chennai transmitter had been erected. There was not the expected demand and the company was not quite ready to market its products outside the state. Sickness crept in.

Tristar Electronics came apart but Rao persisted. By 1978, he was ready to stage a come back with a revival strategy spread over four years. He launched a TV with solid state technology with the brand name Solidaire. This was a runaway hit. Several models were launched over the years. Solidaire made the transition to colour and remained a successful brand through the '80s.

Like almost all Indian TV brands Solidaire could not hold its own after liberalisation.

Coney

In the '80s Coney was a well-known name because Coney cassettes became synonymous with good quality. This brand had a virtual monopoly over the South Indian music market. The Coney story began in the '70s when Ramesh S Jagtiani, a chemical engineer who dabbled in electronics decided to set up a unit to manufacture tape recorders and car stereos. Jagtiani and his partner Gopal Pardasani saw a tremendous future in this industry. Those were the days before the music industry went through cataclysmic changes.

Coney Electronics was set up in 1980 and grew rapidly in the next few years. It had a turnover of ₹2.3 crore in 1982–83, with 70 per cent of the amount coming from cassettes. The company kept adding on to the range making products such as video cassette tapes, two in ones and other '80s favourites. By end of 1982, Coney Electronics employed about 150 people. The company was thinking about setting up a R&D unit.

It focused on the southern market as the octroi and excise duty structure in Maharashtra made its pricing unviable there. Coney was also getting into manufacture of video cassettes in a big way and marketing pre-recorded education and sports cassettes. The promoters had no clue that the industry was soon going to change beyond recognition. Demand for all its products dried up in the '90s. Coney shut down and disappeared without any fanfare.

The new rock stars

Stories of the last ten years. Those who have plunged into uncharted territory

AFTER THE '90s

In many ways, the eighties was a lost decade for Tamil Nadu industry. However, several things were stirring beneath the surface. The growing IT industry spawned many capabilities. Developments in the IIT campus were to have a major impact in the telecom industry and also rekindle the adventurous spirit in young people.

For Dr Ashok Jhunjhunwala winning awards is a way of life. He never seeks publicity for his achievements. This affable, unassuming professor of the Department of Electrical Engineering, IIT Madras is the moving spirit behind India's telecom revolution from 1994 onwards. In the late 1980s, Jhunjhunwala and his colleagues at IIT Madras formed the TeNeT Group (Telecommunications and Computer Networks) with a vision to develop low-cost technologies to enable telecom growth.

In 1993, nobody believed him when he said India could be aiming at 100 million telephone lines in a decade. But with the coming together of technology, government policy, the media and the corporate sector, telecom happened. Jhunjhunwala and his group developed corDECT, an advanced, field-proven, wireless access system along with Midas Communication Technologies, a company incubated by them at IIT Madras.

In the early 1990s Dr Jhunjhunwala and his colleagues dreamed out of the box to bring down the cost of land lines. One of the reasons why India wasn't getting those phones was because the capital and operational expenditures of telecom companies (telcos) were so high that the revenue needed to break even was as much as ₹1,500 a month per rural home. *"Very, very few people in India could afford that. There was no question of reaching 100 million lines in that situation. We realised we needed to replace the copper local loop with something else. Going forward, we saw that a wireless local loop was our solution. That was when we conceived of the corDECT wireless loop. We proved that wireless was the way to go in the future. Wireless brought down the cost of local loop by a factor of 4 or 5."* It was a period of fighting against all odds and of many people giving up their careers to work on this.

Not only was this the lowest-cost wireless system in the late 1990s, its exchange and base station could work at 55 degrees centigrade and it required less than 10 per cent of power as compared to other technologies prevalent at the time. It provided a complete wireless access solution for new and expanding telecom networks, with seamless integration of both voice and internet services.

The other thing Dr Jhunjhunwala has been doing quietly is to mentor young entrepreneurs. He has supported 45 enterprises from IIT Madras. This was even before the word 'start-up' caught people's imagination. He is really the father of start-ups in Chennai. In 1998, he set up the Rural Technology Business Incubator (RTBI) to help enterprises with a social meaning, focusing on rural markets and the underprivileged.

Dr Jhunjhunwala is convinced that nurturing entrepreneurship is the best way to inspire young people. He says they must be willing to make mistakes and face multiple failures before they succeed. When young persons approach him, the first thing he asks is what their immediate obligations are. *"If they have to support parents and educate siblings, their risk-taking ability gets limited."* Today he finds many youngsters (whichever economic segment they come from) are more free from commitments as compared to 15 years ago. A little more prosperity has made this happen. Jhunjhunwala is also pleased that one-third of the youngsters he has trained are women. "*That is transformation for you,*" he says.

Dr Jhunjhunwala is currently looking at energy. "*Energy is going to be a major issue, particularly clean energy. In the next 15 years, we must aim to take care of fifty per cent of the country's power needs with photovoltaic technology. When I say fifty per cent, I don't mean today's demand but the demand which will be there in 15 years. We have to look at specific needs, work in ten different places and make this happen. I am confident we can achieve this in 15 years. And this will take India far ahead of others.*" He is convinced that we need five to six dreams like this for any kind of transformation. Big dreams will connect people who want to be part of the transformation.

Whenever he feels depressed, Jhunjhunwala always thinks about how the situation was in 1981 when he returned to India. He recalls how he was told that he had to wait for years to get his Bajaj scooter. He still goes around in his updated Bajaj scooter in and around the IIT campus.

The Turn of the Century

Chennai continued to remain unnoticed in the '90s. It was still seen as a laid back city where youngsters went to engineering colleges, settled for safe and steady jobs and did not take risks. That image of Chennai started changing a bit only in the turn of the century. Says city based serial entrepreneur Chandu Nair, "*Even in supposedly 'conservative Chennai', a business is no longer something you have to inherit in order to own or run it. Nearly 600 start-ups are coming up every quarter, according to the Registrar of Companies. Chennai ranks among the top 3 cities in India for women's entrepreneurship.*" Nair is a pioneer in the KPO business and he is currently engaged in working with early stage and growth entrepreneurs.

"*In the late 80s, when I turned entrepreneur, an angel had nothing to do with money. A first generation entrepreneur had no one to turn to for assistance, funding, support of any kind. We've come a long way since then and post the dotcom boom, there has been a sea change in the entrepreneur ecosystem in the city and for certain newer industries,"* says Nair.

Nair is a good example of professional turned entrepreneur who has been unfazed by failure. He calls himself an accidental entrepreneur, one who started young and kind of segued into it once he started helping out a batch mate (from IIM-A) who quit his job and went into market research. Before he knew it Nair had turned entrepreneur and joined his friend. Then three other batch mates got together to set up one of India's first specialist industrial market research agencies. This was in 1987. Needless to say there was a lot of opposition from family and friends.

Client commissioned market research was a new concept and the young company took up strategic assignments across specific domains/ industries. It did well and earned more than its peers. However trouble brewed between the partners. Risk taking ability and willingness to stretch differed. In a growing market, the company faced closure.

Nair bought out the partners who forayed into other things. Nair made a fresh start again. Angel investors entered, he changed the company's focus and changed its name. This was the time of the dotcom boom and Nair set up a B2B portal providing content for industry such as News, Features and Articles for various portals, industry reports, product/ market profiles etc. Then came the dotcom bust and the company faced closure again.

Nair then moved towards the Knowledge Process Outsourcing (KPO)business. He calls it his third avatar. He named it Scope e-Knowledge Center to reflect intent. This was a turning point. Funds came from angel investors who exited with six times their investment. He started attracting the attention of venture capital.

Scope got into into STM (Science, Technical, Medicine) databases, content enhancement and organisation, B2B data services and newer offerings such as IP research, medical content and so on. It also made successful marketing forays overseas. Then the focus turned 100 per cent to overseas markets with the induction of overseas marketing personnel.

By 2007, a strategic investor, Quattro BPO Solutions, pioneers in BPO had acquired a significant portion from the VC who made eight times their investment. The strategic partner helped Scope develop newer lines such as library information and technical services and master data management. The focus shifted to more technology related subjects. Greater integration with the parent group in certain areas started happening.

By 2011 Nair and his partners exited selling out to Quattro. *"Our competitors were giants like Genpact, WNS and the like. The company needed deep pockets to grow to its potential. It was the logical thing to do"*, he says.

Chennai Startups

It is still not well known yet that Chennai is seeing several technology start-ups, especially IT products start ups. According to Nasscom, the next wave of growth for the Indian IT industry would be driven by product companies. An entirely new breed of entrepreneur who is making the most of this trend has entered the scene in Chennai. The coming years will determine whether Chennai will evolve as the next big thing in IT products and technology.

Dorai Thodla, an early serial entrepreneur and an engineer from Chennai started two IT companies in India and two in USA. iMorph is his fourth company which he set up in 1999 after he moved to the US. It has an office in Silicon Valley and in Chennai. Thodla who has been shuttling between Chennai and the US says Chennai has changed a lot in the last seven or eight years. He is trying to help create an ecosystem for entrepreneurs as it exists in the Silicon Valley.

Thodla has been working with a lot of start-up groups in Chennai. He is part of the TiE Chennai chapter whose members mentor and help start-ups. He has actively promoted the Chennai Open Coffee Club, a meeting place for young people with ideas. He says it has grown from a few people discussing things in a coffee shop to conducting meetings in conference rooms. Chennai Gigs where all those who want to set up technology companies meet is another group he has promoted and is actively involved in.

Thodla says that there is quite a bit of micro product work going on in the city. There are any number of youngsters doing products for gaming sites, phone games and android games. They earn about a lakh of rupees every month. *"Some of them produce a product every three months,"* he says. There are also a growing number of award winning companies which have a turnover between ₹20 to ₹40 crore a year emerging from the city.

Vijay Anand, better known as The Startup Guy has been around on the Indian startup scene since 2006 and has seen it evolve from really up close. In 2006, he founded *proto.in*, a platform for young startups and entrepreneurs to showcase their innovations. He was Vice-President (New Ventures) at RTBI – IIT, Chennai's Rural Technology and Business Incubator. The Startup Centre was founded in February 2011, and it conducts accelator programmes for start-ups. It helps them incubate their ideas.

As all these mentors say, the ecosystem for start-ups is changing much faster than anybody anticipated.

Howerver Chennai still has a lot of catching upto do. Sarath Naru, Managing Partner, Ventureast, an early-to-growth-stage venture capital firm based out of Chennai, has some interesting statistics to share: Bengaluru leads in terms of angel investors and angel-funded companies; Chennai is way behind. More than 220 angel investors reside in Bengaluru, around 210 in Mumbai but only about 50 in Chennai. The number of companies that received angel funding in Bengaluru and Mumbai was twice that in Chennai between January 2010 and January 2015. Even in terms of incubators, there are only four in Chennai to 12 in Delhi, nine in Bengaluru and five in Mumbai.

K Ganesh, a serial entrepreneur, angel investor and mentor to start-ups, who hails from Tamil Nadu but has made Bengaluru his home and started his ventures there has said in an interview to *Business Line* in May 2015 that Bengaluru benefitted a lot from the reverse migration of Indians who had worked abroad, particularly in Silicon Valley, and of having a large number of expatriates, mainly because of the weather. "*Chennai sends a lot of youngsters to the US, but when they come back, most of them prefer to settle down and work in Bengaluru,*" says Ganesh.

Two of the top four Indian IT companies are headquartered there. Consequently global companies such as Amazon and Google also set up base in Bengaluru. They have been supportive of startups. Such an ecosystem is missing in Chennai.

What is also missing is the buzz, a normal Chennai problem of not drawing attention to one's success. "*Buzz happens only when there are notable exits or large funding. Our entrepreneurs aren't showcasing themselves. There haven't also been too many large second-round fund raises yet,*" says Ramraj.

No one is writing Chennai off. Many investors feel that the next wave of start-ups will be in the SaaS space and it is here that companies like Zoho may be able to set an example for the city and the city will come into its own.

FSS

Nagaraj Mylandla is the Founder and Managing Director of FSS (Future Software & Services), a Chennai-based payments technology leader. Mylandla pioneered this business in the country. What the company does is to power the retail payments initiatives of leading banks, financial institutions, processors, merchants, governments and regulatory bodies across the globe. The Company's end to end payments suite provides the back end to retail delivery channels such as ATM, PoS, Cards, Mobile and internet.

Mylandla did his BSc Chemistry in a government aided college in Chennai in 1979. "*I come from a middle-class family and I went to a government school and college,*" he says. How did Mylandla get into the payments business? After trying to work in the family electrical contracting business for about three years, he got a break when he wrote the CAIIB exam to get a bank job and joined IOB, the public sector bank headquartered in Chennai. "*There really was very little work in those days. I became an active member of the union. I took charge of the canteen, which was catering to 3000 people. I made it profitable. I also started teaching at the staff college."*

From running the canteen in IOB headquarters, how did Mylandla make the leap to payment systems? He was transferred to the forex department and started dealing with a lot of students coming to get their foreign exchange to pursue their studies in the US. He felt that he could also attempt to get admission in an American university.

In 18 months that dream became a reality. Equipped with some savings Mylandla landed in the University of Omaha in the Midwest to do his MBA. This cold Midwestern town was to open up a new world for him. *"I got to work with the Nebraska Small Business Development Centre which helps the air force people to start small businesses. This gave me a great exposure to startups. I then briefly worked for First Data Corporation and ACI which were both electronics payments pioneers, based in Omaha."* All this exposed him to the world of electronic switches and transfers and payment systems.

When Mylandla finished his MBA, US was passing through one of its worst recessions in 1987–88, after the infamous stock market crash (Black Monday). *"I knew it was time to return."* As it happened Mylandla met Gary Biggs in a bar who was nursing his sorrows as he had just been sent back to the US from India as he did not have a visa! Biggs who ran ACI wanted to enter the Indian market with his company's credit card operations technology. One thing led to another and Nagaraj landed the job of selling ACI's specialised switching equipment for credit card providers.

"When I came back to Chennai in 1988, there were no ATMs in the country," he says. Mylandla was able to convince the then Indian Bank chairman M Gopalakrishnan to install an ATM in one of its large branches. By 1991, some slow progress was being made. Mylandla stopped working for ACI and became their agent. FSS was formed as a 50-50 partnership with Harish Murthy of Diebold HMA which sold the machines. In 1997, Mylandla bought over Murthy's share.

A big breakthrough came in 1996 when HDFC bank selected FSS to set up their ATM network. *"Citibank expanded in the US through its ATM network. Aditya Puri, Managing Director of the bank gave us the mandate and ever since we have grown with the bank."* In 1997 UTI Bank (now Axis Bank) came into the FSS fold. *"The next year we lost out to a competitor when ICICI chose them to set up their ATM network. The competition could not pull it off. We got the business after a few months."*

What catapulted FSS into the major league was getting the State Bank of India (SBI) business in 2000. There was international competition. At that time, the SBI had 200 ATMs and about 2000 cards. Today the numbers are 65000 ATMs and 200 million cards. What the Americans did in forty to forty-five years, the SBI has achieved in 15 years.

Mylandla says he has always gone by his gut feel. He realised that this business was going to grow very fast. By 1996 he started hiring more people. *"I knew we had to get into servicing all the networks we were connecting. We started off shoring within the country."* This paid off when Indian Banks Association (IBA) launched the *Swadhan* network in Mumbai to connect 42 banks with one switch.

During the same period a meeting with Nandan Nilekani led to FSS working with Infosys to launch their product Finacle, the universal banking solution. The solution helps banks renew their business by simplifying banking. *"Being identified with Infosys when we did the back end work for about 22 banks gave us a lot of visibility,"* says Mylandla

Then came the dotcom boom and ICICI's KV Kamath and HP's Balu Doraiswamy wanted an internet gateway. *"We built it in three months. It was a non-ATM, non-switching project. We got more visibility."* By 2001 onwards FSS got to be known as a company which banks can work with. *"They started trusting us that we can deliver any new product they wanted to develop. We also decided to build our own products. IBA was not interested in continuing Swadhan. We bought our own switch and 32 banks remained with us. We started competing with Visa and Mastercard."*

By 2002 banks wanted to outsource their non-core business. Slowly over a period of time ATM services have been outsourced to FSS. *"We were 12 to 18 months ahead of others in being ready for mobile gateways and internet gateways. We took a lot of risks, but business came and we are number one today. We do the entire spectrum of payment systems including hosting them. Everything has come as a request from the banks,"* says Mylandla.

FSS delivers end-to-end payment products, services and solutions to more than 100 global customers. In India, FSS's domestic client portfolio of 35 plus banks features majority of public and private sector banks in the country. Today, FSS powers 6 million transactions per day, providing faster and smarter payment solutions to billions of people across 7000 villages and cities in India.

Over the years FSS has received four rounds of funding. In 2014, the Azim Premji foundation invested in the company. *"We are very conservative. We don't borrow."* Right now FSS' turnover is nearly $200 million. Nagaraj is quite sure that he will be running a billion dollar company in a few years. What next? *"I am looking at Africa. My gut feel says that Africa is the place the next phase of growth will come from,"* he says.

TNQ—KNOWLEDGE BANK

How TNQ became one of the largest publishing services company in India and how liberalisation and Chennai made it possible

Mariam Ram promoted TNQ Communications in 1986 after stints in Hindustan Thompson Associates, as JWT was known then, and O&M (Ogilvy and Mather). It specialised in corporate and financial services advertising and communications focussing on businesses entering the financial markets. Among its customers were several large Indian business groups such as the Murugappas and the multinationals Ford Motor Company and Citibank.

TNQ had a good niche in this market till the bigger agencies decided to jump into this business. Mariam was not willing to take on smaller clients with the associated credit risk. She had a Eureka moment when she was visiting Macmillan in Bangalore to see their pre-press units which set her thinking about getting into publishing services. The machines were quite large. Mariam was told not to get into digital publishing till it could be done on PCs. The use of PCs became possible in 1995. TNQ was established in 1998. *"We were late,"* says Mariam. The India Today group, Macmillan and SPS were early entrants.

The big names in publishing are Amsterdam based Elsevier, Springer and Blackwell of UK in that order. Others had already tied up with these giants. Says Mariam, *"When we set up TNQ with just 10 employees in 1998 we knew our aim was to one day become an Elsevier supplier and we also knew that we were probably too late. Rumour had it that Elsevier had closed the door on new suppliers. However Elsevier was the only name we knew amongst STM (science, technology, mathematics) publishers. And we knew of just one person within Elsevier and that was Lee Pierce, unarguably the face of Elsevier in India."*

For TNQ to get a breakthrough with Elsevier was near impossible in 1998. Mariam would not give up. She tracked down five suppliers to Elsevier in the UK. She met Alden who was one of them and was also a printer. The time was just right to approach them. There was a huge cost advantage in offshoring typesetting. TNQ entered into a 50-50 partnership with Alden.

Mariam quickly moved from advertising to copy editing. Initially, ten copy editors who had Master's degrees and PhDs in Science were recruited. When she put an advertisement in the papers there was a lot of response as the salaries offered were high. The work was also far more interesting as these young post-graduates were going to be editing original research work. The next few years were spent in moving further up the value chain and negotiating to do the actual pages. TNQ started making investments in expensive machines for publishing services. Work started coming from English, Irish and American suppliers to Elsevier. The target of course, was to become a primary supplier to Elsevier.

Mariam met Lee Pierce, head of production of Elsevier in 2001 when he was visiting Chennai. He was not particularly encouraging. A junior staff member, who was listening to Mariam's presentation, persuaded Pierce to try TNQ two years down the line. The much needed breakthrough happened after a validation exercise which lasted six months.

Pierce sought countries that offered, in addition to cost advantages, all that STM content production needed—a facility in English, a large pool of graduates, post-graduates, and even doctorates in all branches of Science and Mathematics and software strengths. TNQ had all these.

Edward Luce of *Financial Times* has this to say about TNQ when he wrote his book, *In Spite of the Gods* in 2006. In the chapter *Old India, New India* he says, "*TNQ typesets, formats, stylises and edits some of the world's most complex, scientific journals and other scientific academic publications. Mariam's biggest client is Reed Elsevier, the Dutch based publisher. In 2005 TNQ produced 300000 pages; her target is million pages.*"

It has gone way above its target of one million pages. Its client base has grown rapidly. It is the only publisher doing pages for the prestigious journal, North American Health Science. "*Finding science graduates with a sound knowledge of English in Chennai is no problem. China still doesn't have the English language, the Philippines doesn't have the Science, Ireland is too expensive now. So almost all the work is coming to India. At a time when publishing is in its transition from print to online, TNQ assists its customers in transforming the processes, workflows and the associated technologies. The single-minded mission is, give publishing whatever it takes to produce the highest quality page in the fastest possible time, working with whoever it takes to achieve this—authors, referees, editors, journal managers, publishers, typesetters, host platforms, even our competitors.*"

Over the years TNQ has emerged as a specialist in content-centric technologies. It is now on the verge of becoming a global leader with the Proof Central app it has developed. Publishers of original content need to share the proofs with authors. The authors have to view the redacted typeset manuscript and approve it before it is published. This might sound simple. But the execution of this idea becomes complex in a global, distributed, production environment that involves authors, publishers, and typesetters across time zones. TNQ has invented a novel browser-based technology, which replaces traditional methods of proofing that are fraught with workflow bottlenecks and process inefficiencies. This platform, called Proof Central, now supports over a thousand science and technology journals of Elsevier. This rose to 1400 journals in 2014, accounting for more than 25 or twenty-five per cent of all Scientific, Technological and Medical (STM) Journals globally.

Says Henk-Jan Loor, Project Manager for Elsevier Global operations, *"Proof Central is one of the most exciting technology developments to have been implemented by Elsevier's global production division in recent times. We wanted to be sure that authors would accept the new experience and they have been more than encouraging. We now get proofs returned to us by authors often within two hours after we send them out. It used to take at least two days with the earlier PDF process."*

"The underlying technology has the potential to transform more than the proofing process. It adapts easily to other aspects of scholarly publishing like Peer Reviewing, which is the next big way forward for TNQ," says SK Venkatesan, Chief Technology Officer, TNQ.

For Mariam, Proof Central is just the beginning. She hopes to continue to grow with Elsevier.

ZOHO—A WORLD LEADER IN THE MAKING?

Taking on the big boys

Zoho Corporation founded by Sridhar Vembu in 1996 (when he was twenty-eight) has become the poster boy of IT start-ups which have gone truly global. It has survived and has successfully taken on much larger competitors like Microsoft, Oracle and Salesforce.com with products built in India. Vembu is different. He did not go the IT services way, instead he has built IT products. He has shunned venture capital. He entertains no plans to take his company public and says he is not bothered about Wall Street. Zoho is fast becoming known for its business, productivity and collaboration applications at prices that show his nerve to take on competitors.

Customers use Zoho applications online to run their business processes, manage their information and be more productive without having to worry about expensive or outdated hardware or software. Zoho is emerging as a top player in the CRM (customer relationship management) market, dominated by Salesforce, Oracle and Google for enterprise computing. Zoho has more engineers than any other category of employees, whereas its closest competitor, Salesforce has a larger sales team vis-à-vis number of engineers. The company's flagship product, *zoho.com* is providing stiff competition to Microsoft Office on demand, for its online services.

Being a privately-held company, Vembu does not discuss Zoho's revenue or valuations, but market sources estimate that Zoho's business touches more than $200 million, while it has been unofficially evaluated at over $1 billion in worth. The company has around 1,800 employees (about 1,700 in India; 100 in USA, China and Japan) and it is growing rapidly.

Vembu was always passionate about building products that would make a difference. After completing his B Tech in Electrical Engineering from IIT, Madras, and a PhD in Electrical Engineering from Princeton University in 1994, he served as systems design engineer in Qualcomm in wireless communications from 1994 to 1996.

He knew he had to play a role in the emerging technology industry in India so he reinvented himself as a software entrepreneur. With support from his brother, who was also employed with Qualcomm, and who wanted to return home to India, Vembu stayed in Silicon Valley to set up the foundation of what was to be AdventNet. The company specialised in Network Management. In 2001–02, even though the network business had a huge meltdown during the downturn, and many companies were hit badly, AdventNet managed to keep itself afloat.

The company really started hitting big time when it set up zoho.com, at a time when cloud computing was gaining momentum and offered B2B apps directly to end-users. The first product launched on zoho.com was an online office application, Zoho Writer. Seeing the early success of its online offerings, it increased focus on cloud-based applications, which are becoming an alternative for many today as they drive away the burden of hosting, managing and maintaining applications.

Currently, the Zoho portfolio consists of more than 25 different online services. Vembu emphasises that customers benefit most when products are integrated and it does this by offering a first level of integration across all its services with a single sign-on facility. Since then, it has quickly moved to provide what it calls, 'Contextual Integration', which means that Zoho products try to anticipate all the possible touch points/ overlaps that exist among products.

Since the early days, Zoho has been cost conscious and has been self-sustaining. Take the strategy of Salesforce which acquired ExactTarget, a Zoho competitor, for $2.5 billion. Salesforce, which has nearly 10,000 employees, will add another 1,600 employees of ExactTarget after the acquisition, while all of Zoho Corp has about 1,800 employees. Zoho is already beating Salesforce in internet reach and on the sheer number of new organisations signing up for their platform month after month.

Zoho has integrated over 15 business applications within the Google Apps Marketplace; an online one-stop store for tools to integrate business apps jointly. In this online shop, Zoho is the largest vendor in the Google Apps marketplace. At the end of 2014 the company launched *zoho.in*, a free online suite for Indian users including mobile apps. Its market share in web based office suite business is small. *"Microsoft makes $20 billion profit from Microsoft office. Google is small in web based office suite but is breaking the monopoly of Monopoly. We love Google and we want to destroy the monopoly of Microsoft. We will fight in the office suite business."*

Being cost conscious and frugal in running their development centre is part of its vision of 'hiring locally to design global products' says Vembu. The company has set up Zoho University, a unique education-based employment model that does not focus on college degrees, but recruits bright students from neighbourhood schools in Tamil Nadu into their learning programme. Students are provided with a laptop, unlimited internet access, free meals and a small monthly stipend. Those who undergo the rigorous 18-month training are absorbed into Zoho, and given salaries that are onpar with degree holders from the IITs and other engineering institutes. Over 200 employees out of Zoho University constitute its total strength of 1,700 skilled professionals in India. *"We have a lot of software engineers whose parents might be weavers or other artisans."*

Vembu confirms that his unique engineering-centric model will be the road ahead for the company. Vembu's frugal tactics have helped him avoid venture capital, which he sees as interference and a constraint. *"If a company can do without VC money, it certainly should,"* he reflects. *"If we had taken VC funding initially, I don't think zoho.com would have been born."* He has also been successful in rebuffing attempts to invest or buy out his company.

Zoho is viewing the India market with enormous interest. There are two market trends emerging—one is that Cloud applications are penetrating the Indian market and second is an interesting combination of Cloud and mobile apps taking off. Considering that a mobile phone has limited capability to process a lot of information, it becomes dynamic when combined with cloud apps and this holds great potential for Zoho.

Zoho Corp is the largest IT products company in India. Says Vembu, *"We want to emerge as the largest player in the world, a global tech company based in India."*

FRESHDESK—POISED FOR BIG-TIME

Freshdesk is a cloud-based customer support platform that was founded to enable companies of all sizes to provide great customer service. *"Our goal is simple: make it easy for brands to talk to their customers and make it easy for users to get in touch with businesses"*, says Girish Mathrubhootham, who founded the company in 2010. It raised $31 million in June 2014 from three investment firms including Google Capital, which manages money for the software giant. The financing round was led by Tiger Global Management, which was returning after investing earlier, and included the venture capital firm Accel Partners, also a repeat investor.

This makes Freshdesk the first Indian company to get backing from Google Capital, which has only five other companies in its portfolio. Says Mathrubhootham,"*We are excited to get Google on board. Google being Google, they have access and a different view of thinking in terms of being able to offer security-minded engineers, scale-minded engineers, and Google's product focus and marketing."*

Freshdesk is in a crowded market with some big competition, including Zendesk, which went public in May 2010 after raising more than $85 million in cash. Salesforce has a stake in this space as well with its *desk.com* product, but Mathrubootham says there is plenty of room for competition. He knows they aren't alone, but says it's a big market and they can all find their place. *"In the B2B space there is no place for winner-take-all. There is always space for customer support as a horizontal. There has been a paradigm shift in customer support. Customers want to talk to the company. Customers want to talk to other customers. They also want to tell the world if they are upset. We give a platform for all three."*

The idea for Freshdesk's flagship product came from a comment on a Hacker News post in 2010. The post was about Zendesk, a big player in this space raising their prices 60 per cent–300 per cent and how their users were unhappy about it. How there was a need for a better customer support solution that could scale up keeping pace with companies as they grow. For Girish it suddenly opened a mental door. "*Here was an opportunity sitting right in front of me. I had the domain knowledge, knew that the massive transition to cloud was happening and the spidey sense in me told me that I should throw in my hat into the ring. That was when I decided that I should build something in the customer support market delivered as SaaS."*

Freshdesk looks to help those small businesses with subscription software that makes these business customers more active in their custom support through social media and a broader range of online communications. Those include chat, forums, and conferencing, while still providing the traditional phone and email response.

Mathrubootham had a good career. He was Vice-President of Product Management at the ManageEngine Division of Zoho Corporation. However having always had an entrepreneurial streak in him,he wanted to follow his heart and work on his dream. He managed to sell the idea to his colleague Shan Krishnaswamy, who was overseeing product architecture at ManageEngine.

For a few weeks the founders tried working weekends and nights but since both had families and kids, it was obvious pretty soon that they had to do this full time if they were serious. They both resigned in October 2010 and launched Freshdesk. They had six employees and rented a 700 sq. ft. place in a faraway suburb of Chennai. "*The distance didn't matter. We had other infrastructure problems like water, power connections, parking place and access to food.*" Now they have moved to a swanky IT park.

Freshdesk did not start with any outside finance. It was funded by the founders' personal savings. In addition, they raised $25,000 each from two friends as a convertible note with another $25,000 commitment along the way in July 2011. Within six months of launching, Freshdesk emerged the Winner of the Microsoft Bizspark India Startup Challenge in the Cloud Category. A total of 400 companies from across India had applied for the contest and 15 companies were shortlisted as finalists. Freshdesk was declared the winner and the first prize was a free grant from Microsoft for US$ 40,000. One hundred days after that, Freshdesk celebrated its hundredth customer.

The next year Freshdesk raised $1 million in funding from Accel Partners, launched a new version of its cloud-based customer support platform. It also raised $5 million in financing led by Tiger Global Management with previous investor Accel Partners participating.

All this caught the attention of the much bigger Zendesk. Mikkel Svane, CEO of Zendesk, called Freshdesk 'A Freaking-RIP-OFF'. *"Instead of engaging in a war of words in bad mouthing competition, we decided to present the facts as it happened and let our customers and readers decide for themselves."* say the founders. Freshdesk won the Twitter war with a lot of goodwill from its customers.

Mathrubhootham has explained to Forbes Magazine what Freshdesk does uniquely, "*...is to layer on 'gamification,' game-like mechanics to encourage sales reps. The software has trophies and points that reps can earn through successful interactions with customers, such as one for the person with the fastest resolution times per ticket. Rewarding strong performers in such a system produces more energized and higher-rated service reps.*" Freshdesk now works with 28,000 clients in a freemium model which is a pricing strategy by which a product or service (typically a digital offering such as software, media, games or web services) is provided free of charge, but money (premium) is charged for proprietary features, functionality, or virtual goods. From Pearson Education to Goodreads and Hugo Boss, Freshdesk has a range of customers. It now has in its kitty Sony Pictures Entertainment and many start-ups, small businesses and enterprises across the world. *"We are adding 1,000 customers a month,"* says Mathrubootham. Our list of tech customers is growing rapidly. Brick and mortar companies are not catching on so fast as yet.

The growth has been exponential. It has almost 300 employees at the time of writing this. Freshdesk is now headquartered in San Francisco, and has a development centre (backend, product development, support) in Chennai.*"When you are headquartered in the US you win bigger deals. You get plugged into the ecosystem. It always helps when you meet your potential customer face to face."*

Freshdesk has recently developed a mobile app (mobihelp) for its customers. Mathrubhootham wants to develop a global SAS product from India. He doesn't rule out the possibility of becoming a billion dollar company in the near future.

THE EMERGING STARS

Suresh Sambandam and OrangeScape

OrangeScape is a successful start-up from Chennai promoted by Suresh Sambandam. It has been named the prime technology partner for 'Google App Engine' recently and it is the first and only company worldwide to be chosen by Google. Sambandam who discovered computers as a teenager in small town Cuddalore set up OrangeScape in 2004 with a vision of simplifying the entire programming paradigm. *"When cloud computing came, we took our chances with Google and it paid off,"* says Sambandam. The cloud has three layers; one is hardware, which is at the bottom. The software application is at the top. In the middle is the platform and OrangeScape is at the platform level. OrangeScape is today among the Global 10 companies featured by Forrester and Gartner (a leading US based independent technology and market research company) in the PaaS (Platform as a Service) category. This $5 million company hopes to grow into a billion dollar company in five years.

"Building an IT product company is very different from building an IT service company. You require a gestation period of at least three to five years to create a product. When there is a lot of buzz around an industry, as in services, it becomes a noise. People don't settle down.

In Bangalore people change jobs within 18 months. In services it may work, not in products." Chennai offers a reasonably stable workforce. Tamil Nadu is known for its engineering colleges. *"Graduates from Coimbatore, Erode or Salem just don't switch jobs"*, says Sambandam.

When Suresh was studying for a commerce degree in Cuddalore, he started dabbling in computers. Five of his friends pooled ₹25,000 each to start a computer centre. He started learning programming languages on his own. The centre made decent money but Cuddalore lacked connectivity. He made his way to Bangalore to find a job in the IT industry. Till the turn of the century, people went to Bombay or Bangalore to find IT jobs. He found a job in Hewlett-Packard in Bangalore as a JAVA programmer and before you knew it he became a software analyst. He developed a compression technique (though it was not his area of specialisation) to compress data that travelled between the client and server, thereby speeding up the communication between the two.

He was awarded a patent but to his dismay, he found the patent's inventor was HP, not him.

His boss, who was head of R&D at HP, left the company to start Selectica, based out of the Silicon Valley with an office in Chennai. Suresh joined Selectica as a software analyst and rose to the position of Director of Product Engineering in three years.

Selectica was acquired by Accenture and Suresh did not want to work in a large consulting company. That's when he started OrangeScape in 2004 along with his co-founder Mani Doraiswamy who also left Selectica to join him. OrangeScape consulted with Accenture for nine months as the product Suresh had developed for insurance in Selectica needed support and that earned them ₹2.5 crores. This was their seed capital for OrangeScape. His erstwhile boss also put in ₹2 crore.

The first product of OrangeScape was Dimension, which they sold to Numeric UPS, Rane Group, Unilever, and Citibank. The only handicap was that this product could be used by companies that had revenues of only ₹500 crore or more. Suresh and his team switched to 'cloud' technology when it was just getting popular as the cloud offered benefits of lower cost and some freedom. That was in 2008.

Being an early adopter of cloud brought recognition from market research firms such as Gartner and Forrester. Convincing customers to switch to cloud proved to be a challenge initially. OrangeScape reached $5 million in revenues in 2011.

Around this time, OrangeScape raised $1 million from angel investors to expand into the US market. Till that time, the company was bootstrapped. In 2012, OrangeScape developed another product named KiSSFLOW for Google App users. KiSSFLOW is a Workflow-as-a-Service platform that can be used by corporations to automate workflow in a division or across the organisation. The company now boasts of marquee enterprise customers that include Unilever, Citibank, Pfizer, AstraZeneca across the two software platforms it offers and its KiSSFLOW is the number one in its category and used by 9000+ companies across 108 countries. OrangeScape's products are in the business-to-business (B2B) category with innovative software platforms to compete with the best in the world.

Sambandam does not give up. He is gritty and tenacious and wants to carry the company he founded to success, despite a huge churn that saw some very senior people leaving OrangeScape in the last couple of years, including Mani Doraiswamy who has moved to Silicon Valley.

CARATLANE

CaratLane is India's largest online diamond and diamond jewellery portal (with a wide range of gold and platinum jewellery as well) which was launched by Mithun Sacheti in Chennai in 2008. Sacheti is from a family from Mumbai who have dealt in gems and particularly solitaires for generations. After finishing his undergraduate studies, he went straight to the USA, did a two year course to get certified as a gemmologist from the Gemmological Institute of America, California. As soon as he returned, he headed to Chennai in 2000 to set up Jaipur Gems, an upmarket jewellery store promoted by his family. His family wanted to set up a showroom in Chennai as the city is a large buyer of jewellery. "*I had to make a success out of this venture. You don't get any respect unless you work well in our family,*" he says.

"*I used to attend on every customer morning and evening. With the success of the Chennai shop I expanded to Coimbatore as well. All the while I was thinking of a different model for this business where the returns do not exceed 3 or 4 per cent. The financing cost is very high. So are the Inventory carrying costs. We as a family do not borrow any money. I knew I had to go online, do something disruptive to restructure the balance sheet of the jewellery business,*" says Sancheti about why he wanted to launch CaratLane.

One of his customers was Srinivasa Gopalan, a founding member of Sify who was running Lister Technologies which provides solutions to e-commerce businesses. Sacheti started persuading him to be his partner and help him set up CaratLane. "*He was finally convinced when a friend of his from the US bought a diamond ring online.*" CaratLane.com was officially launched in 2008.

Sacheti's business model works like this. "*Solitaire buying is traditionally a time consuming process. The jeweller gets in touch with various suppliers to get the diamond the customer wants which takes time. CaratLane is an aggregator and so we got the backend in place first. We started with solitaires and have the largest selection to choose from. They are all certified from the best labs in the world. We give the lowest prices in the market and help consumers save up to 25 per cent of retail prices. We work across six countries with several vendors and with over 100,000 stock keeping units for solitaires. Depending on the arbitrage of currency on that day, the demand and supply in that country, we locate the one with the lowest price. We sell this under the CaratLane brand name. We don't create inventory. When the customer buys the solitaire she can choose the pattern to mount it on the jewellery piece. The website provides a 3-D model of how the piece will look.*"

Sacheti says the early days of CaratLane were a nightmare. "*We had a series of press conferences. A national TV channel presented us almost as a joke. It took some time to catch on as jewellery online was not that big internationally that its shadow could be seen in India. The site was funded by Gopal and me and we were struggling. At this time the global meltdown happened. We told the suppliers that we will take the diamonds directly to the customer. We had 50000 diamonds in our kitty. It took one year of convincing and we began supplying to Titan. After experimenting with one shop Titan sourced from us for six more Tanishq showrooms. Ours is an omni channel model.*"

In the first half of 2011 Sacheti got a LinkedIn request from Tiger Global, a New York based international investment firm. "*I had been talking to a couple of venture capital firms for almost a year and nothing had worked out. At this point I hadn't heard of either Tiger Global or its famous partner, Lee Fixel. So I didn't respond. A week later a friend called me and told me to take Tiger Global seriously. I met Lee in Delhi. We had a meeting which lasted three hours. I left with a term sheet in my hand"*. A month later (in June 2011), nearly $6 million were transferred to CaratLane's bank account. The first investment by Tiger Global in CaratLane was in place and the company was on a roll. This year (2015), CaratLane raised $31 million from Tiger Global, the fourth capital infusion by the fund in four years.

Sacheti has opened up nine hi-tech stores in the major cities in the country which exhibit an array of solitaire, diamond jewellery and CaratLane's signature collections of precious jewellery. These stores have been designed to encourage 'browsing', similar to shopping on a website, and are equipped with several touch screens and tablets that showcase CaratLane's collections. They also have a lounge to create a feeling of seeing the products at home. *"I believe that these stores will cater to those who are still unsure about the online buying experience. These showrooms have far exceeded our expectation and they give us five times better ROI than any other jewellery store."*

Sancheti says he is not threatened by the mushrooming competition. *"We are four times larger than our nearest competitor and technology will keep us several steps ahead. Jewellery contributes to four per cent of India's GDP. There is room for everybody"*. At the pace with which he is growing and expanding (300 per cent per year since 2011) when will he break even? He is confident that his turnover will hit ₹650 crore in a couple of years and he will show profits.

Postscript

Titan has now acquired a majority stake in Caratlane. It will acquire shares from Caratlane's investor Tiger Global. Sancheti will continue to hold around 20 percent and run the company.

MAGZTER

Girish Ramdas is the co-founder and CEO of Magzter, which is headquartered in New York. The company's back-office work is done in Chennai, his home town. Magzter with 25 million users and more than 30,000 downloads per day is the world's largest digital magazine service app. Magzter's growth rate, since it was launched in 2011, has been nearly 300 per cent. Magzter offers thousands of magazines in international and Indian languages, including certain niche publications that would otherwise be very difficult to find online. It has recently added book titles to its offerings. Ramdas wants to make 1 million books downloadable from his platform and has made a beginning with the introduction of 10,000 book titles. Magzter wants to establish itself as a one-stop reading destination in the digital world. It is about to add news as well.

Ramdas has a hectic travel schedule. *"Last year (2014) I was in India for 100 days,"* he grins. *"What we want to be is the YouTube of this space. You think videos and you look up YouTube, and we want you to think reading and look up Magzter."* His friend and co-founder Vijayakumar Radhakrishnan (the President) started Magzter. Before launching Magzter, Radhakrishnan had a software engineering company, Network Technology Solutions, while Ramdas had set up a software company called Dot Com Infoway.

He had also launched a film magazine called Galatta. *"My company used to outsource projects to Radhakrishnan's company for web clients and soon we merged the two companies to create a single entity in 2005,"* Ramdas says. When the iPhone and iPad came to India, he and Radhakrishnan decided to turn the magazine into an app. Galatta was Asia's first magazine app for the iPad. Then came the Android and other new platforms.

It struck Ramdas and Radhakrishnan that theirs was the perfect app to serve magazine publishers who were eager for a user-friendly, one-stop solution to reach the digital readership. The content owner uploads pages, and the magazine is published on multiple platforms almost instantly. Built-in MIS reporting functionality allows publishers to monitor metrics in real time. When Ramdas approached a large publishing house in Delhi, he was given one of their magazines on a trial basis. The publishing house was trying to build its own platform, but within 45 days Magzter was given all the 17 publications of the group.

Magzter rapidly scaled up to become the world's largest creator of Apple Newsstand apps. Within a year, it attracted more than 3 million users and a growing list of top magazines. Kalaari Capital, a leading investor in early-stage businesses, spotted Magzter. What works for the company is that its technology is device-agnostic, unlike Apple or Google Play Newsstand which is restricted to a single technology and device. *"Google's Newsstand has 600 magazines. We have content from 60 countries,"* he says.

Magzter's application can be downloaded for free onto any device including smartphones. Its OREY (one-click real-time everywhere) publishing system allows publishers to upload content with a single click where the cloud software crunches the content to suit multi-device distribution. This is done in less than 60 minutes. *"You know, 'orey' means one time in Tamil. We are local as well as global."* Magzter acts as an 'aggregator for aggregators'. *"Nearly 25 per cent of the content on Apple's Newsstand is provided by us, so we really do not view them as direct competitors."* Samsung and other device manufacturers, who are keen on creating a device app, approach Magzter to partner them on content aggregation.

In December 2013, Magzter raised Series B funding to the tune of $10 million. The round was led by a wholly-owned subsidiary of Singapore Press Holdings with participation from its existing investor Kalaari Capital. A significant portion of this investment is being used for Magzter's global expansion. *"We had to have our headquarters in New York. It is the nerve centre for publishing industry. Many publications such as all Hearst Group's magazines, Newsweek, Bloomberg are on our platform and they all are around one kilometre from our office,"* Ramdas adds.

Magzter currently has eight offices across the world. *"We create local teams that will represent Magzter to publishers in the regions we don't know the language. In Spain they speak English and Catalan in addition to Spanish. There are 140 publications in Catalan. We have both English and Afrikaans publications on our platform in South Africa. All Indian language publications are with Magzter. We have been bringing vernacular publishers online. This is a huge hit with the Indian diaspora. Our multilingual focus has set us apart from other aggregators who tend to focus on single geographies. We plan to be in most geographies"*, he says.

Ramdas says the digital publishing platform is free to all publishers where there is a 50:50 revenue-sharing agreement on sales. *"We make all our money through subscriptions."* he says, In the next two years, subscription will only be 30 per cent of Magzter's revenue. *"The rest will be from digital and experiential advertising,"* says Ramdas. This will be a mix of video and interactive advertisement in the magazines. The template for Rolex advertisement in Forbes India magazine, for example, was developed by Magzter and given to Rolex. The user can see what the watch looks like and how it works, and can click and buy it. Forbes' tablet version was sponsored by Rolex.

Has Magzter started making money? Ramdas has started a monthly subscription model which was launched early in 2015. *"It is like the successful monthly subscription model adopted by Netflix for movies and TV shows. We are opening access to a library of about 2,000 magazines, for ₹499 a month under the Magzter Gold plan."* In another plan, Magzter Gold Lite, users can read five magazines of their choice at ₹249 a month. Both the plans are priced at $10 and $5 a month, respectively, for the global markets. *"Because of the plan, more than 100 new publishers signed up to Magzter across the globe. We have a larger library than our rivals."*

Ramdas says Magzter could have broken even if it was not spending on growth. *"We have to keep coming up with new ideas and introduce them to 100-year-old publishers. The $100-billion print industry is going digital. Can you imagine the potential?"*

TRIVITRON

Trivitron is the largest Medical Technology Company in India, offering 360 degree solutions in Laboratory Medicine, Imaging—Ultrasound Machine, Critical & Cardiac Care, Operating Room, and Ophthalmology along with providing expert consulting services. Its founder, a first generation entrepreneur, GSK Velu floated Trivitron in 1997, in a market dominated by American and European MNCs as a small medical equipment and instruments distribution company. A year later, he went into the diagnostics business, Metropolis Healthcare, with his partner Dr Sushil Shah, a pathologist. By 2006, Velu had consolidated Metropolis with private equity investment from ICICI Ventures. He then raised a separate round of PE funding for his med-tech venture.

In 2010, Warburg Pincus entered Metropolis with an $85 million investment. Velu then handed over the management to Shah's daughter. Today, Metropolis is the second largest diagnostics chain in the country with over 200 pathology labs located in India, Sri Lanka, UAE and South Africa. Metropolis has grown through the inorganic acquisition route.

Velu started seriously focussing on Trivitron. Since then, he has transformed it from a trading to a manufacturing unit. With ₹400 crore in funding from Fidelity Growth Partners, it already has a few acquisitions under its belt, notably the Finnish group Labsystems

Diagnostics. In the last three years, Velu has gone further and founded two health care services businesses—Apollo White, a dental and dialysis care hospital, and eye care chain Medfort/Maxivision.

Medfort has raised its own capital and private equity of over ₹100 crore and replicates Metropolis's business model of bringing individual doctors under one roof for better economies of scale, technology upgradation and wealth maximisation for the doctors. It runs around twenty eye care super speciality hospitals with a high technology focus in Hyderabad, Chennai, New Delhi, Vishakapatnam and Vijayawada.

Apollo White is a joint venture between Apollo Hospitals and Trivitron to run stand-alone dialysis centres and dental clinics that leverage Apollo's operational expertise and technology with the contact and network base of Trivitron. The alliance today has over 75 dental clinics in the name of Apollo White SPA and five dialysis clinics and is fast expanding to become a100 dental clinic and 20 dialysis clinic network soon.

According to Forbes India magazine, *"Velu is buoyed as well as blasé about the hospital business. For him, they can run on autopilot if the foundation is set right. For his group, they just form one of the growth engines. What keeps him ticking, perhaps even on his toes, is the scope and challenges in medical technology."*

At the core of Trivitron's business is its manufacturing of medical technology products, sales and after sales support. Having gained a reputation in the Indian market for its service Trivitron has gone on to build its brand in South Asia, the Middle-East and Africa. The company's management team with an average age of thirty-five—many of whom have been with the company since its inception—started focussing on innovation, manufacturing and international operations as the three pillars of its growth.

Today, Trivitron has eight manufacturing plants across Chennai, Mumbai, Pune and Helsinki (Finland). They manufacture products across In–Vitro Diagnostics (IVD), Imaging-Ultrasound Machine, Intensive Care and OT that are approved by US FDA and CE. According to Velu, Trivitron is probably the only company to have survived the MNC domination in the country with its multi-product focus, comprehensive solutions and after-market support which is equal to or better than MNCs. *"MNCs have no concern for costs. Trivitron wants to bring in innovations and new concepts in this space to improve access and affordability,"* Being an emerging market brand, Trivitron aims to achieve this by combining local innovation, frugal engineering, partnership with MNCs and local acquisition strategies.

Trivitron has opened up an Innovation Centre at IIT Madras in strategic partnerships with several academic institutions and scientists to look at innovative product concepts in the areas of in vitro diagnostics, cardiology, imaging sciences, critical care and ophthalmology. The company is in the process of acquiring a majority stake in some Indian/European medical technology companies with strong innovation and manufacturing skills. It has already forged many manufacturing joint ventures with leaders such as Hitachi Aloka Japan Ultrasound/ColorDopplers, Biosystems Spain Diagnostics Reagents, Johnson Medical Sweden Modular OTs and Diasorin Italy. The factories are in construction at Trivitron Medical Technology Park, Chennai.

"Though the government of India has refused to even recognise medical technology as a core industry within healthcare, we strongly believe India can be a viable alternative to China in medical technology innovation and manufacturing," asserts Velu. In the absence of clear direction and fiscal incentives for import substitution, MNCs have shown little or no interest in bringing substantial investments to India, preferring to sell China-made products.*"We do hope that at some point the government will understand the intricacies of this industry and make this import independent and export oriented like the pharmaceutical industry,"* he says. Trivitron wants to be the torch bearer in the medical technology space.

The group, with revenues currently in excess of ₹500 crore, aims to grow to over ₹1,000 crore by 2015, with more than two thirds of its revenue coming from manufacturing, services and international operations. Velu's ambition and achievement must be looked at in the context of an industry where imports still account for over 70 per cent of the estimated ₹30,000-crore med-tech sector. Much of what sells in India is not made in India.

Life would have been very difficult for him if he was operating only in India. Trivitron has a global outlook, with a limited view on India. There may be better opportunities in the country coming his way.

There are about 2,000 medical devices sold locally—from reading glasses and gloves to critical MRI machines and implants. Only 22 of them are presently under any direct regulatory supervision. The Drugs and Cosmetics Amendment Bill, 2015, is looking to change this, bringing all medical devices into its fold. The government has opened up the sector to 100 per cent foreign direct investment (FDI). While opening up FDI, the Government needs to introduce a caveat that 70 per cent of the products be made locally as this will bring down the price for consumers. Local manufacturers deal with an inverted duty structure, explains Velu. Import duty on finished products is less than on raw materials, which makes it easier to import a product than make it locally, he says, adding that it defeats the 'Make in India' sentiment. India has 750 local manufacturers and over 1,000 trading companies, according to industry data.

With a few policies in place, Velu believes the med-tech business could grow the way pharmaceuticals did in the previous decade.

Velu has exited from Metropolis selling out his share to the other founders at an estimated price of around ₹800 crore.

PERFINT HEALTHCARE

Another Chennai-based medical technology company which is attracting a lot of investor and industry interest is Perfint Healthcare. Nandakumarthe CEO and co-founder of the company, started his career in GE Healthcare. He and four ex-GE professionals came together in 2005 to start an R&D services company. Two years later, it was converted into a product company, Perfint Healthcare.

Perfint introduced robotic diagnostics in India for cancer treatment in 2009. With an image-guided system that helps practitioners place the needle on the tumour, Perfint provided, for the first time, options for a 3-dimensional look and treatment of cancerous body parts. Earlier, such tools were restricted to the brain.

Perfint's newest product MAXIO, allows clinicians to visually plan, execute, and validate ablation procedures on a single system, and all in 3D. MAXIO has been designed to make complex, multi-probe ablations simpler, which will help to make these life-saving procedures available to more cancer sufferers than ever before. In the fastest growing field of interventional oncology, it has the world's largest installed base of 100 targeting devices, 40 being in India. Perfint was recently in the news for Maxio getting the approval of the US Federal Drug Administration (FDA). This is a milestone for being able to sell the product globally, particularly since India lacks a strong and transparent mechanism for the testing and certification of medical devices.

Perfint is one of the early ones to focus both on procedure planning and placement. Cues came from practitioners, it says. Its comprehensive 'planning station' is co-developed with experts in over eight countries. In the coming months, Perfint will launch devices that will work with all imaging sources, MRI, CT, ultrasound, PET, etc. It already has a global footprint, with presence in Australia, Japan, Korea, Canada, West Asia, and Latin America among others.

At least 2 million such procedures are performed globally, whose market is estimated to be worth 'a few billions of dollars' and growing at over 50 per cent. In India, this technology holds much potential as it can be wheeled in a clinic and used for an outpatient procedure, enhancing access to a rapidly growing cancer patient population.

Says Rishikesha T Krishnan, Director, IIM, Indore, "*Several things about Perfint are noteworthy. First, the core team that set up Perfint came out of GE. This has always been one of the hopes of encouraging MNCs to invest in India—that these MNC subsidiaries will be incubators for Indian entrepreneurs. Second, the company has been able to raise a fair amount of capital—more than $30m in four rounds so far. This shows the faith of investors in the company, considering its revenues are reported to be only in the region of $6-7 m and raises some questions about our usual assumption that it's difficult to raise capital for high tech startups out of India. Third, the company has been granted three patents so far, with more applications pending. Fourth, the company already has a global footprint with more than 2,000 patient procedures being conducted on its equipment across the world last year.*

Perfint appears to be more in the advanced technology game than in the affordable healthcare arena. While it's safe to assume that Perfint's development costs would be lower than its foreign competitors since its R&D is predominantly based in India, clearly it is competing in the global healthcare market based on the quality of its solution. In fact, when I was reading recent accounts of its achievements, the company sounded more like a typical Israeli technology company than an Indian one!"

Perfint is now setting up a development centre in Seattle. Getting people with the right skills—clinical understanding coupled with product engineering—is one of the biggest challenges the company faces.

CONCLUSION

This book is an attempt at telling the story of a state which has chosen to hide its light under the bushel. One hears of the Gujarat model constantly. There is no such talk about the Tamil Nadu model. The state might catch a little more attention than earlier, and some for wrong reasons, but not as much as it deserves.

The seeds for Tamil Nadu becoming one of the top three states in the country had been sown as early as pre-independence days. It has always been teaming with entrepreneurs. Many who should have been celebrated have remained anonymous. They may have been conservative in their ambitions but enterprising they were.

When the country finally opened up its economy things began to change in the state. Expansion, growth and going global became the new mantra. New entrepreneurs emerged. The family groups started shedding many inhibitions. Everybody started talking export. From automobile, auto-component manufacturers to those who make condiments, spices and shampoo are looking at international markets. Some are possibly better known outside than they are in the country.

Some things remain the same in spite of visible growth and prosperity.

Generally the big groups have funded their expansion plans mainly through promoter infusions and internal generation.

Compared to groups in the West and North they still do not approach their shareholders with frequent rights or public offers. They generally are not worried too much about their stock price movements or even valuations. "We'll look after our business, let the markets recognise it if they please" has always been their attitude. They continue to maintain a very low profile. Only in recent years have groups such as Murugappa or TVS even engaged a PR agency unlike their counterparts elsewhere.

The promoters have believed in retaining significant control of their businesses. The equity culture in Tamil Nadu is very underdeveloped because retail investors too prefer deposits to shares which has also forced these companies to rely mainly on internal resources for their expansion. They know equity money is not easy to come by. Groups like Sanmar, Rane and Ramco are highly thought of, respected for their ethical standards and quality products. Yet they have not crossed ₹10000 crore turnover in spite of their longish histories.

Investors feel Tamil Nadu now has enough number of large sized units which can afford to dilute their share holding. The promoters no longer have anything to fear. The truth is, it is really not fear of risk taking which makes them hold on to control. They fiercely believe in their highly paternalistic management paradigm. Just like the GOI (which has always been reluctant to privatise) the Tamil Nadu business heads just do not like to let go.

These are some of the reasons why some notable big ticket projects have given the state a miss. Despite the kind of IT skills the state has there is not a single home grown soft ware billionaire. There is no Infosys or Wipro in the state although it is the second largest exporter of IT services in the country.

Infrastructure is another area Tamil businessmen have not even considered unlike Andhra.

The infrastructure firms in Andhra have gone into irrigation projects, roads, airports and power, having outbid established players and outpaced them in growth. In fact, India's four best airports—Hyderabad, Bangalore, Mumbai and Delhi—are all managed by AP entrepreneurs. Most of them come from agricultural backgrounds.

Andhra's politics gave a big push to the growth of infrastructure companies. Both during the time of Chandrababu Naidu, whose Telugu Desam Party was a key player in the United Front and later NDA Government at the centre, as also during YS Rajasekhara Reddy's Congress Government, this entrepreneurship flourished. Some politicians too turned entrepreneurs. The former editor-in-chief of *The Indian Express* Shekhar Gupta has coined the term Andhrapreneur for these promoters.

Tamil Nadu entrepreneurs are very uncomfortable in getting close to politicians.

In spite of a couple of pioneering ventures in telecom (Sanmar Group and Sivasankaran's Sterling ventures) no business house has either entered or made it big in this sector. Nobody has taken a risk and built up a telecom giant like Bharati Telecom, which was set up by Sunil Mittal in 1995. Many of the older family houses rue the fact they missed out on software and telecom. Getting into infrastructure however is not in their DNA.

It is also in their DNA to obsess over quality, productivity and efficiency. In this preoccupation they forget at look at what is happening outside, forget to look at what competition is doing and forget to recognise what customers want. There is a danger that some of them can go the Motorola way. Motorola one of the biggest tech giants of its time, the developer of six sigma quality process did not shift from analogue to digital technology with any sense of urgency and lost its market share to Nokia.

As things stand one cannot imagine an Ambani, Adani or Mittal emerging from Tamil Nadu. But in its favour there are widespread industries with turn overs between ₹200 and ₹500 crore in almost all the districts.

On the other hand some things have changed. The fear of outsiders, the earlier reluctance to accept them has gone. The local businessmen no longer resist either foreigners or those from outside the state setting up business here. The state government welcomes investors.

When Tamil Nadu hosted a Global Investor's Meet in September in September 2015, it was a first for the state. It had never had road shows or events to attract investment till then. Yet from the '90s the state has been an attractive investment destination. It finally decided to call attention to itself. Gujarat started investor meets and states such as Madhya Pradesh, Chhattisgarh and West Bengal have followed suit and have started staging their own investor summits. Chandrababu Naidu is wooing investment from all over. There is a lot of competition coming in the state's way and it has been receiving a lot of bad publicity from 2011.

In the last few years the state's reputation started taking a beating, especially after the Gujarat model became so popular. It has had to deal with all kinds of negative news. It has been hit on many sides with the closing down of the high-profile Nokia and Foxconn factories and the persisting infrastructure and power problems. There are whispers of corruption always blowing in the air. Many complain about how governance standards are falling and the bureaucracy not being as efficient and pro active as it once was. There has been widespread criticism of the freebie culture in Tamil Nadu.

Politicians point out that the freebies provide socio-economic benefit to the society at large, as has been the case with many of the schemes introduced over the years by successive governments. They are really providing a social security net. The distribution of televisions mixer grinders, cows, and goats are sneered at. The political class claims that these schemes should be seen as asset building for the poor.

There is a movement building up against the state's liquor policy which brings it an income of ₹20000 crore a year. Liquor flows freely all over the place and its marketing and distribution tightly controlled by the state. If the state listens to the protests and imposes some sort of prohibition, can the freebie reign continue?

In spite of the negative publicity the state can continue to spring surprises.

Tamil Nadu's Global Investors Meet, an event that was postponed twice and at one point even seemed a doubtful starter was a huge success. Investors have pledged ₹2.4 lakh crore, more than double of what the initial target seemed to be. One of the important implications of investment is in job-creation. Tamil Nadu, with its huge talent pool of engineers and students with technical skills, needs those jobs.

There are many issues waiting to be resolved and questions to be answered. The health of the economy, both global and domestic will also matter to Tamil Nadu.

But then people always tend to underestimate the state. There are many things going for it, skilled manpower, peaceful industrial relations and a strong manufacturing ecosystem. Something else that could attract investors is its amended Land Acquisition Act.

One has to wait and see if Tamil Nadu will be able to maintain its growth momentum in the coming years as well.

ACKNOWLEDGEMENTS

My sincere thanks to :

Ashok Advani who with great generosity gave me complete access to *Business India* magazine and photographs.

The kindness of the Directors of Kasturi & Sons who let me use their library and photo archives.

Madhu Vasanthy, Director, Confederation of Indian Industry Southern Region.

TiE Chennai Secretariat.

Prem Sivakumaran, the publisher of *Smart CEO* who let me refer to the stories on the new entrepreneurs of Tamil Nadu.

S Gurumurthy who gave me insights into the entrepreneurs from Western Tamil Nadu and the importance of community and family support in these regions.

Chandu Nair who was my go-to person to resolve and clarify issues.

R Ramaraj, Co-Founder and former Chief Executive Officer, Sify who told me about the success stories outside Chennai.

V Sriram, G Kameshwar, Raja Vaidyanathan, Padma Chandrasekaran, Baradwaj Rangan all of whom helped me in more ways than they realise.

R (Naru) Narayanan, early serial entrepreneur, angel invester, member TiE, Chennai , for allowing me to discuss ideas whenever I needed to.

Malvika Singh, former associate publisher, *Business India* and publisher, *Seminar Magazine*, for opening the byzantine doors of Delhi and always being there.

All my former colleagues in *Business India*, particularly those in Chennai office. What would I have done without Kannan, Natarajan, Kanakaraj, Damodaran, Suresh and Balu.

T S Ramesh for the photos and Kombai S Anvar for the little known rags to riches stories.

Aarati Krishnan, *Business Line* who explained Tamil Nadu businessmen's reluctance to go public.

L N Revathy, *Business Line*, Coimbatore who answered all my questions about Coimbatore industry.

S Muthiah who unfailingly asked me for many years when I was going to write my book and his many acts of kindnesses.

Gautam Padmanabhan who read the synopsis and agreed there was a book somewhere there.

Karthik Venkatesh for showing me the path to take.

and

Raksha Patel, colleague and friend without whose patience and help this book would not have been possible.

REFERENCES

1. *An Uncertain Glory* – Amartya Sen & Jean Drèze (Allen Lane)
2. *Championing Enterprise* – V Sriram (Madras Chamber of Commerce Publication)
3. *Tamil Nadu Economy: Performance and Issues* – Madras Institute of Development Studies (Oxford and IBH)
4. *Looking back from "Moulmein": A biography of A.M.M. Arunachalam* – S Muthiah (EastWest books)
5. *The TCS Story* – S Ramadorai (Penguin)
6. *Indian Models of Economy, Business and Management* – Professor P Kanagasabapathi (PHI Learning Private Limited-New Delhi)
7. *Othaiyadi Padaiyil* – Gnanavel
8. *India's New Capitalists* – Harish Damodaran (Permanent Black in Association with the New India Foundation)
9. *Young Turks* – launched by Yi (Young Indians) Coimbatore in association with TOI (Times of India) and CIBI (Coimbatore Innovation and Business Incubator)